CRITICAL ACCLAIM FOR
FIRST KILL THE LAWYERS

"In Edgar winner Housewright's gripping fifth Holland Taylor mystery...savvy, empathetic Taylor and some of his attorney clients grapple with questions about the conflict between professional requirements and personal ethics. Housewright draws the Twin Cities with lovingly detailed strokes. Gripping...This tightly plotted installment with its many twists will satisfy both series fans and newcomers."

—Publishers Weekly

"Minneapolis private eye Holland Taylor is called on to bail out the only people in the Twin Cities more morally compromised than he is: members of the bar...readers are advised just to hang on for the ride and not to sweat the small stuff, like who killed whom and how come. An irresistible premise and a fast-moving plot carry Housewright's latest along for a miraculously extended flight..."

—Kirkus Reviews

"*First Kill the Lawyers* is a complex, beautifully plotted mystery. It is an often dark, frequently funny roller coaster ride of a read that you won't soon forget."

—Open Letters Review

"Clearly David Housewright, a former President of the Private Eye Writers of America, knows his stuff. Just open the pages of this noggin-spinning page-turner, and you're sure to catch a strong whiff of private eyes past: a nod to the swirling plot complexities (and dysfunctional familial Strum und Drang) of Ross Macdonald, goosed by the cold-blooded pragmatism of Hammett (or is it the brutal expediency of Spillane?), and tempered by the battered romanticism and world-weary cynicism of Chandler...This is real detective work, an honest-to-goodness PI procedural...If the plotting were any tighter it would squeak...(Taylor is) the decent Everyman wading through a rising tide of sewage, clinging to his ideals, but practical as spit..."

—*Mystery Scene Magazine*

"Housewright's best: fast-paced with funny dialogue and interesting characters combined with thoughtful discussions of grey areas in the law, lawyers' responsibilities and how individuals cross—or do not cross—ethical lines...Holland Taylor is an interesting character. He likes women and doesn't hesitate to enjoy consensual relationships. He walks ethical lines but just barely, and he has a French lop-eared rabbit named Ogilvy. All the secondary characters in this crime thriller are believable and fleshed-out..."

—*St. Paul Pioneer Press*

FIRST KILL
THE LAWYERS

ALSO BY DAVID HOUSEWRIGHT

Featuring Rushmore McKenzie
A Hard Ticket Home
Tin City
Pretty Girl Gone
Dead Boyfriends
Madman on a Drum
Jelly's Gold
The Taking of Libbie, SD
Highway 61
Curse of the Jade Lily
The Last Kind Word
The Devil May Care
Unidentified Woman #15
Stealing the Countess
What the Dead Leave Behind
Like to Die
Dead Man's Mistress
From the Grave
What Doesn't Kill Us
Something Wicked
In a Hard Wind

Featuring Holland Taylor
Penance
Practice to Deceive
Dearly Departed
Darkness, Sing Me A Song
First Kill the Lawyers

Other Novels
The Devil and the Diva (with Renée Valois)
Finders Keepers
Full House (Short Stories)

DAVID HOUSEWRIGHT

FIRST KILL
THE LAWYERS
A HOLLAND TAYLOR MYSTERY

Cover design by JT Lindroos

ISBN-13: 978-1-970861-23-5

Big surprise! This too is for my wife,
Renée Marie Valois

CHAPTER ONE

We were surrounded by lawyers in a smoke-filled room found deep in the bowels of an intensely exclusive club located on the edge of downtown Minneapolis; one of those prestigious joints accessible only to the select few that possessed the money, personal connections, and social capital to claim membership. If it had a name, no one bothered to tell me what it was. I wouldn't have even known it existed except David Helin asked my partner and me to meet him there after business hours. He had thrown a lot of work our way, so, of course, Freddie and I arrived on time and sober. I wasn't told about the other attorneys until we arrived, yet I recognized them all. Each of their law firms had retained Fredericks & Taylor Private Investigations at one time or another.

Greetings were exchanged, and we were led to a bar. Helin served as bartender. I asked for bourbon, and two inches were poured into a squat glass. Freddie was content with water. That didn't tell the lawyers anything, but it told me plenty. Freddie was nervous. I didn't blame him. Forget that he was a black man in a room filled with rich and powerful white men. No one ever calls a secret meeting at night unless they want to discuss something that if not straight-up illegal is at least of questionable ethics.

Once we had our drinks, we were led to the leather chairs set around a large table made of shiny dark-colored wood.

"Cigar?" Helin asked. "They're from Havana."

The lawyers were all puffing away. I hadn't seen any of them smoke before, and I wondered if it was an affectation, if they were doing it simply because they could. The club didn't have employees per se, and it wasn't open to the public, so it wasn't subject to Minnesota's smoking restrictions. I suspected that a lot of laws went unheeded in that room.

Freddie and I declined the cigars and sat next to each other at the far end of the table. Most of the lawyers sat on the other end. Helin settled midway between us.

"Forgive the intrigue," he said. "We burned through God knows how many emails deciding where to meet until we agreed on this place. In fact, the only other thing we seem to agree on is that you're the guys for us."

It was meant as a compliment, and we were supposed to respond accordingly. "Thanks, fellas. You know we'd do anything for you"—something like that. Only I was as nervous as Freddie.

"Okay," I said.

"We've always been impressed by your professionalism, your resourcefulness, and most particularly by your discretion," Doug Jernigan said. He was the oldest of us and the only one in the room who seemed comfortable. Instead of a cigar, he was smoking a long-stem pipe. The tobacco smelled like cherry. Not too long ago, we had helped him successfully sue a sports bar that had overserved an underage drinker who rolled her vehicle shortly after last call by identifying eleven other kids it had sold alcohol to without first verifying their age. I think he won $258,000 in actual and punitive damages.

"Okay," I said again.

Some mutual staring took place after that, us at the lawyers and the lawyers at us and each other. Freddie sipped his bottled water, and I slowly rotated my glass on the table in front of me one quarter turn at a time. The cloud of blue-gray smoke above the table grew ominous. It seemed as if none of the lawyers wanted to be the one to explain why we had been summoned.

"Oh for God's sake," Scott Mickelson said. "Taylor, Fredericks, what do you know about an organization that calls itself NIMN?" He pronounced the acronym "Nim."

"Not in Minnesota," Freddie said. "Name of a website for whistle-blowers. Brands itself as a local version of WikiLeaks."

"Freddie is the smart one in the organization," I said.

"That's only because I use my computer for more than looking up porn."

"You can do that?"

"Everyone here has seen your Key and Peele routine," Mickelson said. "This is serious."

"How serious?" I asked.

Jernigan pointed his pipe at me.

"We're the ones they're blowing the whistle on," he said.

"I don't understand."

Cormac Puchner sighed heavily and looked up at the ceiling, the gesture suggesting that I should already be familiar with his problem. Puchner was a Harvard man. I had learned that within the first ten minutes of meeting him. Everybody learns that within the first ten minutes of meeting him.

"Taylor, Freddie," Helin said. "The computers in each of our law firms have been hacked. Information was stolen."

"What kind of information?" I asked.

"Do we need to draw you a fucking picture?" Puchner asked.

"If it wouldn't be too much trouble."

He glared at me.

I glared back.

Puchner didn't care for that, and I thought, usually he's pleasant company. What gives?

"Law firms hoard secrets," Helin said. "For corporate clients, we hold intellectual property and merger and acquisition data, secrets that can be used for insider trading. For individual clients, well, it can be pretty personal."

3

"Sadly, this is not all that unusual," Mickelson said. "There is no such thing as one hundred percent effective security anywhere. Insurance companies, banks, hospitals, even the federal government—they've all been hacked. It's not surprising that law firms would be hacked as well. What happens—it's like a smash-and-grab. Hackers steal whatever information they can get their hands on and analyze it later to see how valuable it is. Willie Sutton said that he robbed banks because that's where the money was. Breaching law firms is a great way to make money."

"What concerns us most, though…" John Kaushal glanced at his fellow attorneys as if he hoped he was speaking for all of them but wasn't sure that he was. "We have an ethical obligation to safeguard our clients' information. Especially those secrets protected by attorney-client privilege."

Kaushal was the smartest man in the room as far as I was concerned, and if he was worried then I was worried. The last time Freddie and I worked for him was over a year ago, but only for a couple of days. He was defending a man accused of murdering his wife for her considerable fortune even though the woman's body was never found. He hired Freddie and me to basically shadow the investigators working for the Ramsey County attorney and interview every witness they interviewed to learn what they learned or didn't learn. Kaushal hated surprises. Four days in, though, he called off the investigation. I never did learn why. Now I was wondering—what secrets protected by attorney-client privilege?

"Why you?" Freddie asked. "Why were your law firms targeted?"

"Small and medium-sized firms typically operate with a minimal IT staff," Jernigan said. "That makes us more vulnerable. An easier hack."

"Speak for yourself," Mickelson said. He had a smug expression that, I suppose, came from working for a firm that had a worldwide presence. Puchner looked like he wanted to wipe it off his face, but then he was always ultracompetitive.

"In any case," Jernigan said, "it's not the size of the firm that matters but the sensitivity and value of the data that we maintain that makes us targets."

"Or not," Puchner said.

"What does that mean?" I asked.

"All lawyers have enemies."

"Look, we discussed this," Mickelson said.

"So now we're discussing it again," Puchner said.

"We don't know if we were singled out for a reason. We don't know that it's personal."

"Hackers are only interested in money or revenge or both."

"Then pay the man," Freddie said.

"Excuse me?" Puchner said.

"Pay 'im. You're not the first business that's been black-mailed by hackers, whose confidential information was held hostage. What was the name of that hospital in LA had to pay a ransom to get its computer system back?"

"Christ, Freddie. You don't think we haven't thought of that? I love making deals."

"How many bitcoins are they asking?"

"None."

"None?"

"The hacker isn't looking for payment," Helin said.

"He's looking for payback," Puchner said.

"We don't know that."

"What do we know?" I asked.

"Think Panama Papers."

I connected the dots quickly.

"NIMN," I said.

"You see it now, don't you," Jernigan said.

"I'm beginning to."

"A couple of years ago, over eleven and a half million documents were leaked to a German newspaper," Helin said. "Financial and attorney-client information stolen from a law firm in Panama that demonstrated how wealthy individuals and politicians were using offshore banks to commit fraud, evade taxes, launder stolen funds, what else?"

"Hundreds of people were exposed," Mickelson said. "Presidents, prime ministers, top cops, government wonks, businesspeople, sports figures, actors—some very important and famous people. Governments fell; people went to jail; lives were ruined. The hacker was never identified. He said he leaked the information because he wanted to expose the injustices that the documents described."

"Do you think that's what's going to happen to your clients, that their privileged information will be revealed?" I asked.

"That's what we're afraid of, yes. You see, someone from NIMN contacted us each in turn. He sent emails to our personal addresses on Saturday."

It's Tuesday evening, I told myself. They waited this long before making a move?

Helin seemed to read my mind. "It took us this long to determine that the hack wasn't widespread, that it was just us," he said. "It took us this long to decide what to do about it."

"Of course," Mickelson added. "The hacker used an anonymous server, so the emails can't be traced back to the domain that sent them. The sender said he had received a cache of documents from an unidentified source."

"Fuckers probably hacked us themselves," Puchner said.

"He claimed that the documents demonstrate beyond a reasonable doubt that the legal system in Minnesota is corrupt," Mickelson said.

"Who knew?" Jernigan said. "Am I right?"

"That we—meaning the men in the room—were suppressing the truth. NIMN said it was going to post the information over the next couple of days as soon as it was verified to their satisfaction."

"Why?" I asked.

"To make us look bad, why do you think?" Puchner said.

"No, I mean why did they contact you? From what you're telling us, you might not have even known you were hacked if they hadn't called."

"They just want to see us twisting in the wind."

"Or drive up the price," Freddie said.

"I hope so," Kaushal said. "We're attempting to take legal action to prevent disclosure. Unfortunately, there's no name attached to the website. The way NIMN is structured, Freddie, it has no registered address or property in Minnesota. We don't even know where to send the cease-and-desist order. In any case, not even the Feds have had much luck dealing with WikiLeaks. I doubt we'll do better with these people."

"Your hacker might not even be in Minnesota. Could be some guy with a laptop in the Ukraine."

"We're convinced he's local," Helin said. "Using a local whistle-blower site. Local law firms being hacked. Local cases being singled out. We hired a team that specializes in cyber investigations. What they're telling us so far isn't very encouraging."

"I know some people, hackers themselves, that I could recommend," Freddie said. "People who are expert at combating hacktivism."

"Hacktivism?" Puchner said. "Do you think this is some activist promoting free speech, human rights? This isn't civil disobedience. It's cybercrime. He's not an activist. He's a thief."

"I stand corrected."

"If you think differently, then we're talking to the wrong people."

"Local cases?" I said. "You mentioned local cases."

Helin slid a USB flash drive across the table. Freddie caught it.

"Very specific cases," Helin said.

"How specific?"

"Each case NIMN referenced is on the flash drive," Mickelson said. "We don't need to lecture either of you about confidentiality, do we?"

"Is all the information that was stolen on this drive?"

"Only what you need to know," Helin said. "Taylor, Freddie, we need you to find the hacker or whoever is running NIMN. Maybe Cormac is right. Maybe he's one and the same. I don't know. Whatever, we need you to stop the disclosure of this information any way you can. It's not just about us. Yes, we'll lose business if clients fear we can't protect their confidential data. But repeating what John said earlier, it's about our clients. Imagine the embarrassment and worse that they'll suffer if this information gets out."

"You once told me that you can find anybody," Kaushal said. "Remember?"

"I remember."

"Something else," Puchner said. "We need to keep this off the books. A law firm's reputation is built around confidentiality as much as anything else. If word got out that we've been compromised..."

I honestly didn't see who slid them across the table, yet two bundles of one-hundred-dollar bills appeared in front of me.

"Twenty thousand to start," Jernigan said. "If you need more, call David."

They're paying cash, no signed contracts, and I bet they can all prove they were somewhere else tonight instead of in their secret clubhouse. The thought sent an electric charge up and down my spine.

Stop the disclosure any way you can, they said.

Off the books, they said.

Did they mean it or were they merely being theatrical?

I stared at the money. The money said they meant it. I could be wrong, though.

I reached out and covered one bundle with my hand and slid it toward me. I waited—one beat, two beats, three, four, five, six—and watched as Freddie did the same.

"We'll be in touch," I said.

* * *

The club was located in the shadow of Target Field in the Warehouse District, about a mile from our downtown offices. Yet with the way the streets were laid out and a stretch of Interstate 394 slicing through the neighborhood, it took us a while to walk back. Not that we were in any hurry. I, for one, could have used more bourbon.

I eyed the strip joint on Second Avenue. It had been one of Freddie's favorite hangouts right up until he married a Chinese American woman called Echo. I didn't think he'd been in the place since. He glanced at its bright neon signs as we passed, though, the way some men look at the parks where they used to play ball as kids.

"How much of our combined income was sitting in that room, do you think?" Freddie asked. "A third?"

"I was thinking closer to half. Maybe more."

"Which means if we don't come through, we're screwed."

"I got that impression, too."

"You know what they want us to do, don't you?"

"Not necessarily."

"C'mon. 'Stop him any way you can,' they said."

"I heard what they said."

"We find this guy—"

"I'll bet you a nickel there's more than one."

"*These* guys, then. What would they be guilty of? Computer theft? Unauthorized computer access? That's not even a felony in Minnesota 'less there's a risk t' public safety, which in this case, there ain't. Lousy misdemeanor. Thousand-dollar fine."

"Hacking is a federal rap."

"Not if it don't involve interstate commerce. Not if it don't involve identity theft or fraud, some criminal activity."

"We'll need to look into it."

"My point being, if they don't actually go the blackmail route, if they really do plan t' just throw this shit up on the World Wide Web, there ain't a whole helluva lot we can say or do that's gonna scare 'em into stopping, is there? I mean legally."

"Probably not."

"Well, then?"

"Freddie—"

"Twenty stacks they gave us, Taylor. These days only criminals deal in cash. You know who told me that? Douglas Jernigan, the lawyer who slid the money across the table at us."

"We took the money."

"Yes, we did."

"Okay."

"So are we gonna do it?"

"Do what?"

"You know fucking what."

I stopped in the middle of the sidewalk and stared at him because, honestly, in all the time we've known each other first as rivals and later as partners, that was the dumbest question Freddie's ever asked me.

"Just checkin'," he said.

"Okay."

"So what *are* we gonna do?"

"First thing first, hire a hacker of our own."

"Who?"

"Someone really good. I don't know who the lawyers are working with, but I'd like someone I trust on the job."

"Who?"

"You know who."

"No. No, Taylor. Hell no."

"Who do we know better than Sara?"

"Steve?"

I laughed because I thought it was funny. Freddie didn't laugh, but then he was the one who tried to seduce Sara into bed back in the day, not me.

"For all we know she—he—whatever—they're the ones behind it all," Freddie said.

"Nah, they would have taken the bitcoins."

"Yeah, that's prob'ly true. But I'm gonna make the call, okay?

Set something up for tomorrow A.M. And I'm callin' Steve."

"Whatever makes you comfortable."

"There ain't no reason Echo has t' know anything about it, either."

"Keeping secrets from your wife—how sad."

CHAPTER TWO

Freddie hung on to the flash drive. I told him we should review its contents first thing since we were on the clock. He said, speaking of clocks, Echo was holding dinner for him. Mu shu pork. I asked if it was an old Chinese recipe. He thought Echo got it from Rachael Ray.

Neither of us returned to the office. Instead, we found our respective cars and drove home. Mine was on the second floor of a four-story brown-brick apartment building in St. Paul in a neighborhood known for Victorian manors, carriage houses, and converted mansions that harkened back to the days of F. Scott Fitzgerald and bootleg booze.

I was in 2A. I crossed the landing, though, and rapped three times on 2B before returning to unlock my door and step inside. I left the door open. A few minutes later Amanda Wedemeyer entered, still wearing her private school uniform.

"Hi, Mandy," I said.

"Ogilvy," she called.

My gray-and-white French lop-eared rabbit bounded into the room. He stopped and glanced from me to Amanda as if wondering whom he should greet first. Amanda sat on the hardwood floor and made a nest out of her skirt. She waved a leaf of romaine lettuce at him. Ogilvy hopped into her lap without giving me a second's thought.

"How's school?" I asked.

"Junior high is hard." Junior high starts in the seventh grade where we live. "I have to take life science."

"I don't know what that is."

Amanda closed her eyes. "Life science comprises the fields of science that involve the scientific study of living organisms such as microorganisms, plants, animals, and human beings." She opened her eyes. "That's all I know so far."

"Every journey begins with a single step."

"Is that a science thing?"

"Something I read in a fortune cookie."

"I've got so much homework to do. It's wrong."

"So do I—have homework, I mean, so I'm going to have to shoo you out of here."

"Okay," Amanda said. She kept sitting on the floor, though, and Ogilvy kept sitting in her lap eating lettuce out of her hand.

"Where's his brush?" she asked.

"On top of his cage."

From the way Amanda looked at me, clearly it wasn't the answer she was hoping for.

Ogilvy had a large wire cage with a permanently open door that he hopped into only when he needed to use the litter box or eat the alfalfa I fed him. Otherwise, he roamed the apartment like a cat and, also like a cat, slept anywhere he damn well pleased. I found his brush and gave it to Amanda. She used it to gently stroke Ogilvy's fur while he nibbled the lettuce.

"Since you're staying, can I get you something to drink?" I asked. "Root beer?"

"Mom says I drink too much pop; it'll rot my teeth."

"Water? I have some orange juice."

"It's unfair, Taylor."

"That pop is bad for you?"

"That I have so much homework. Mom used to work so hard for us I hardly ever saw her and then she got promoted and I see her more than I ever did except now I'm the one who's busy all the time with school and band and if I want to play soccer…I don't even get to see Ogilvy hardly anymore."

I came close to saying, "Get used to it, kid," but the way Amanda hugged the rabbit, who didn't seem to mind at all, I found myself agreeing—life isn't fair.

I sat at the computer and checked my emails. There wasn't much there to hold my interest. Next, I typed "Not in Minnesota" into my search engine and hit ENTER. Eleven results were posted on the first page. Before I could access any of them, I heard a voice coming from the open doorway.

"There you are, Mandy," Claire Wedemeyer said. "I knew you'd be here."

Claire was holding a stack of plastic storage containers that she kept stable with her chin. Like Amanda, she was still dressed in uniform—black suit coat and skirt, white silk blouse, black pumps. She smiled at me as best she could.

"Help," she said.

"What's this?" I asked.

"Leftovers. I would have brought them over sooner, but you're never around."

Which was Claire's way of asking where I've been lately. I had no intention of telling her about Alex Campbell.

I took half of the storage containers and led her into the kitchen area.

"You're so good to me," I said.

Claire stacked the containers on the counter that separated the kitchen from the living room.

"I have pasta sauce, but you'll need to make your own pasta. It's a sweet sauce. Not sweet like sugar, what I mean—sweet Italian sausage, sweet bell peppers, carrots, plenty of basil, tomatoes, red wine—"

"I really like it," Amanda said.

We could see her on the other side of the counter.

"This is kung pao chicken," Claire said.

"It's spicy," Amanda said.

"I might've used one Thai pepper too many. There's white

rice in the blue container. This is tortellini in a porcini mushroom sauce."

"I don't like mushrooms," Amanda announced. "The rest of it is okay, though."

"Don't you kids ever eat, I don't know, hot dogs and hamburgers?"

Both women smiled at me. Mother and daughter were opposites in appearance. Claire had a dark, brooding vibe, while Amanda was all sunshine and wheat fields. Except for their brilliant smiles. Their smiles were identical.

"If you insist on something unhealthy there's a piece of red velvet cake with chopped walnuts," Claire said.

"What do you mean, unhealthy? There's milk in cake, isn't there? Eggs? What's healthier than milk and eggs?"

Amanda giggled.

"Honestly, Taylor," Claire said. "Which reminds me, I need my other containers back."

I fetched her used plastic containers—yes, I had washed them—and slipped them into a plastic bag and handed it to her.

"You guys are so good to me," I repeated.

"That's because you're so good to us," Claire said.

She hugged me then. The hug was just this side of something else, and I was anxious to keep it that way. She and Amanda were among the few unblemished fragments in my otherwise disjointed life, and I didn't want to screw it up. Literally. Claire had already made it clear that she was willing. Friends with benefits. Relationships like that never last, though, and I wanted Amanda to come over and play with my rabbit whenever she felt like it. I wanted Claire to bring me leftovers. I wanted to help them out whenever I could. Without any awkwardness. So no, no, no, I refused to hug her too close.

"Time to go, Mandy," Claire said. "Homework."

Amanda sighed dramatically. "All right," she said.

She gave the rabbit a gentle squeeze and slid him off her lap. He looked as if watching her walk out the door were the saddest moment in his life.

"See ya later, kid," I said.

Amanda handed me Ogilvy's brush.

"Bye, Taylor," she said.

"Don't be a stranger," Claire said.

She gave me another quick hug, and then she was gone, too.

I closed the door. Ogilvy rammed my foot with his head, something he did when he wanted to be petted.

"Yeah," I said. "I know how you feel."

Not in Minnesota impressed me.

At first glance, it seemed to pattern itself on WikiLeaks, claiming it was a "state-wide media organization and library specializing in the analysis and publication of censored or otherwise restricted documents." It proudly announced that it "has and will continue to resist all censorship attempts." There was even a highlighted link that explained how it was able to thwart government interference.

Apparently NIMN was hosted by an internet service provider based in Sweden. The Swedish constitution forbids all administrative authorities including foreign entities from messing with any type of newspaper. Through some computer magic that Freddie probably would understand that I didn't, it also employed an encrypted network that made it virtually impossible to intercept internet communications, guaranteeing that whistle-blowers would remain anonymous, even from NIMN.

The reason I was impressed, though, is that as I looked closer, I discovered the site wasn't as irresponsible or partisan as WikiLeaks. It didn't seem to have an axe to grind or an agenda to promote. It didn't provide a single "disclosure" without also providing context the way any decent newspaper would.

The Police Are Recording Our Every Movement
Here is an interactive map showing the exact location of nearly 390 video cameras that the Minneapolis and St. Paul Police Departments are using to record the actions of private citizens. There are potentially hundreds more that they won't talk about.

The Dirty War over Sulfite Mining in the BWCAW
1,287 documents showing how the Chisholm Mining Corporation is manipulating data to downplay the threat of pollution caused by sulfite mining operations on the southern edge of the Boundary Waters Canoe Area Wilderness to state and federal government agencies.

Dunbar Emails
A collection of documents from Minnesota Department of Public Safety Director Monica Dunbar's nongovernment email account. Dunbar occasionally used the account to discuss security-related projects, including keeping protestors away from the Minnesota Republican Party convention site.

Secret Reports from the State Senate
347 reports comprising over 2,500 pages of material concerning some of the most contentious issues in the state, from the expansion of Indian casinos to the taconite industry.

State Supreme Court Policies
More than 100 private or otherwise restricted documents and emails from the Minnesota Supreme Court covering the rules and policies con-

cerning how justices decide which court cases to review.

Sexual Abuse Correspondence
Dozens of unredacted legal documents that passed between the office of the Ramsey County attorney and the Archdiocese of St. Paul and Minneapolis dealing with charges of sexual abuse in the church.

What's more, the stories were presented as if they had been written by actual journalists instead of activists attempting to advance a cause or discredit an adversary. Given the decline of print journalism—the St. Paul Pioneer Press had become a mere sliver of its former size—I wondered if sites like NIMN weren't becoming essential. Who was going to report the local news if they didn't? Who was going to read the documents? Who was going to attend the city council meetings? Who was going to ask the county commissioner why his brother-in-law was awarded the trash-hauling contract over a less expensive competitor? The local TV stations? Puhleez.

Unlike WikiLeaks, though, NIMN didn't list the name of a spokesperson or editor or provide any means to contact the organization. But it did claim that all documents were vetted before release; with investigators scrutinizing both the material and the source of the material if it was known to avoid printing misleading or fraudulent information.

"Investigators," I said aloud. "Like me?"

My landline rang. Originally I kept it because I wanted a number that family, friends, and charities could use, leaving my cell strictly for business. The last thing I needed was to interrupt the close surveillance of some miscreant because my mom wanted to know why I never call. Except so many of those people have acquired my cell phone number over the years that I now keep it more out of habit than anything else.

The caller ID read DR. ALEXANDRA CAMPBELL.

I said, "Hello."

She said, "Do you think college cheerleaders are hot?"

"Excuse me?"

"I have acquired a uniform. It's very becoming, if I do say so myself."

"Is that a fact?"

"Ski-U-Mah," she said, a slogan used by sports teams at the University of Minnesota.

"I'll be there in ten minutes."

CHAPTER THREE

The aroma of fresh coffee greeted me the moment I stepped through the office door, Cinnamon Sugar Cookie from Cameron's Coffee. It came as a surprise. Not the coffee—it was one of Freddie's favorites. The fact that he was in the office before me. The man was never early.

"Morning," I said.

He replied without looking away from his computer screen. "Holland." It was my first name. Freddie rarely used my first name. Hardly anyone did.

We had one of those expensive, high-tech machines that brewed one cup of coffee at a time. I popped in a canister and waited while it poured a mug of Chocolate Caramel Brownie. I sat behind my desk, swiveled the chair, and watched downtown Minneapolis come alive outside the window. Freddie and I had talked on and off for months now of reducing overhead, of finding less expensive digs outside downtown, except we both would miss the hustle and bustle of the city—and the view—so we hadn't pulled the trigger yet.

Eventually Freddie ejected a flash drive from his computer and crossed the office with it, stopping at my desk.

"Sidney Poitier," I said. I never used his given names, either, unless I wanted to tease him. He wasn't in the mood.

Freddie dropped the flash drive in front of me.

"I started reading this last night," he said. "Couldn't sleep afterward. That's why I came in early."

"Does it have a happy ending?"

"Some fucked-up shit in there, man."

I slipped the drive into a USB port, brought its contents up on the screen, and began reading. I could understand why the attorneys didn't want this information falling into the wrong hands, especially the public's.

Meanwhile, Freddie moved to the center of the room, his back to the windows. We had a combination dry board and cork bulletin board on the wall where we kept track of our open cases. There was a white curtain that we could close to hide our work from visitors.

Freddie moved to the bulletin board side and started pinning up index cards labeled MURDER, DIVORCE, CLASS ACTION, BRIBE, and RAPE using thumbtacks. He put up a sixth card labeled HACKER and ran a thin strand of red yarn from that card to each of the first five. Afterward, he pinned up a seventh card—NIMN—and used more yarn to connect it to HACKER.

"I spent some time on the site last night and again this morning," I said. "I don't think we can connect the hacker and NIMN yet."

"NIMN contacted the attorneys."

"Someone claiming they were from NIMN contacted the attorneys. Could be a bluff. Could be that you were right the first time, that it's a shakedown and the blackmailer wants our clients good and frightened before he names his price."

"Point."

Freddie disconnected the yarn that linked HACKER to NIMN and let it just hang there.

I gestured at my computer screen.

"I haven't had the time to study it like you did, just skimmed, but—some of it really is fucked up. I know I wouldn't want it to get out, either. Would you?"

"How much of it is illegal, do you think?"

"What the lawyers did? That's the thing. I'm not sure any of it is illegal, just—"

"Fucked up?"

"Yeah."

"Read it more carefully," Freddie said. "Afterward, I'll tell you my theory."

"Tell me now. That way I can poke holes in it as I go along."

"Asshole."

Freddie gestured at the bulletin board.

"Remember what Mickelson told us last night about this being a smash-and-grab?" he said. "About how hackers steal what they can and figure out later what's valuable?"

"I do."

"Here you got two famous cases, cases that were covered big-time in the local media." Freddie tapped the index cards labeled MURDER and BRIBE. "This case—" He tapped RAPE. "This case had some attention, but nothing compared to the others. These—" He tapped DIVORCE and CLASS ACTION. "No media coverage at all."

"Okay."

"Two of the law firms deal mostly with local clients, one is regional, but both Stanislav Kennedy and Hannum, Hillsman, and Byers, they're multinational. Are you telling me that of all the clients they have and all the business they do all around the world that this is the best the hacker could come up with? One specific case per law firm? Nothing else interested them? C'mon, man."

"Maybe it is. Who were the lawyers? David Helin…"

Freddie wrote a name on each card: Kaushal MURDER, Helin DIVORCE, Puchner CLASS ACTION, Mickelson BRIBE, and Jernigan RAPE.

"I don't think these cases were chosen based on whatchacall notoriety is what I'm sayin'," Freddie said. "Or how fucked up they were or how damaging they might be t' the law firms."

"What's your theory?"

"I'm thinkin' Puchner mighta been right last night when he said that it was personal. Somehow these five cases are all connected directly to the hacker, or vice versa. He wasn't phishing. The hacker went after our clients *because* of these cases."

I gave it a couple of beats and turned to my phone. I punched in a number. A moment later a woman answered. "Stanislav, Kennedy, Helin, and DuBois. How may I direct your call?"

I asked for David Helin.

"Just a moment, please."

A few seconds later another woman spoke to me. "Stanislav, Kennedy, Helin, and DuBois. David Helin's office."

"Hi, Judy. It's Holland Taylor."

"You handsome devil, how have you been?"

"Pretty fair, Judy. Pretty fair. Say, is the boss in?"

"Just a sec, hon."

Helin was on the phone before I could take a sip of coffee.

"Don't tell me you already need more cash," he said.

"What you already gave us should last until lunch. Listen, I have a question. The answer is important."

"All right."

"We know that the five law firms we met with last night were hacked. Do you know if there were any others?"

"No."

"You don't know if—"

"I spent the weekend making calls," Helin said. "You need to be discreet because no one wants to publicly admit they've been compromised. Mickelson and Doug Jernigan made calls as well. As far as we can determine, it was only the five of us. At least, we were the only ones who were contacted by NIMN. Or, I should say, we were the only ones willing to admit it."

"You're sure?"

"Pretty sure. Why?"

"Just wondering if we need more index cards. I'll talk to you soon, David."

I hung up the phone.

Freddie and I have a thing—whenever we come across a piece of evidence that might or might not be significant to a case we're working, we make a production out of resting our index finger against our cheek and saying "Hmm." I was doing it now.

"Where do we start?" Freddie asked.

"Where do we always start? With the victims."

"The law firms?"

"No, no. The clients of the law firms. They're the ones who are gonna be most compromised by the hacks, the ones who're going to be hurt. The question we need to answer—why them? Why their cases? There must be a common denominator. We should examine all of the media accounts of each case. I know you did some of that already. We want to take note of what a casual observer of the proceedings could learn about each case, the defendants, victims, lawyers, etcetera. We'll also interview the victims individually, assuming the lawyers let us, to see if there's anything that connects them. Try to find out what's this guy's motive."

"Fuck motive."

"When I was with the cops, motive was a big thing with us."

"When I was a member of the United States Air Force Security Force…"

"Say three times fast."

"We never worried about it. You try to figure out what motivates some asshole, you'll go nuts."

"Motive, means, and opportunity—didn't you read the detective handbook? They're the backbone of any investigation."

"I'm just sayin', you need to be a shrink to figure out the reason most people do the shitty things they do, and half the time you'll get it wrong. Get the facts and prove some asshole did a certain thing at a certain time in a certain place. Leave the ultimate truth, the why, to someone gets paid a helluva lot more than we do."

"Still, if we knew why—"

"The hacker could be like us. Did you ever think of that?"

"What do you mean?"

"A free agent selling his services, happy to do a client's dirty work for a price."

"He'd probably make more blackmailing the law firms for bitcoins."

"Unless he thinks he's an honest man."

"Like us?"

"Man doin' what he's doin' cuz someone's payin', motive ain't gonna find him, is what I'm sayin'."

I rested my index finger against my cheek again. At the same time, we heard a soft knock on our office door and Sara Vandertop entered.

"Darlings," she said.

I rounded my desk and moved toward her. She held her arms open and we hugged.

"Always good to see you, Holland," she said.

"You, too."

Sara turned toward Freddie. She opened her arms again.

"Give me some love, sugar," she said.

"I thought our appointment was with Steve," Freddie said.

"Steve is having a bad hair day." She tousled her own golden locks.

"Dammit." Freddie walked into her arms and they embraced tentatively. "You know you make me nervous."

"Are you afraid you'll lose control again?"

"I never did hear what really happened after Freddie took you back to your loft that one time," I said.

"A girl never tells," Sara said.

"You two are messed up." Freddie pointed at me. "You especially."

"Me?"

"My, my, my." Sara fanned herself with the flat of her hand. "Did I come at a bad time?"

"Best time," I said. "We have need of your particular skill set."

"Should I sit down?"

"I would."

Our office is one long rectangle with six large windows in one wall facing downtown Minneapolis and a single door in the middle of the wall across from the windows. Freddie's desk, chairs, and file cabinets were on the right. I was set up on the left. In the middle were the coffeemaker resting on top of our safe, a small refrigerator, a low round table, and four stuffed chairs arranged around it. Sara sat in one of the chairs and crossed her exquisite legs. Her skirt hiked up to there to reveal plenty of deliciously smooth thigh kissed with gold.

The American Psychiatric Association used to list transvestitism as a paraphilia or fetish. It claimed people derived abhorrent sexual pleasure from cross-dressing. Hell, maybe it still did. Steve Vandertop—yes, he was one of *the* Vandertops—once told me that he simply enjoyed dressing like a woman.

"Is that wrong?" he asked.

It didn't bother me, I told him.

It did bother Freddie, though. At least it used to.

I think that might have been because he met Sara first and Steve later. I knew Steve long before meeting Sara. He was a hacker. Excuse me—"an intelligence research professional." I asked him once, what was the difference? He said about $150 an hour. Back then—was it really seven years ago?—he was living cheap in a loft in the Warehouse District, before it became gentrified, and rebelling against his old man's obscene wealth. Personally, if my father had been rich I would have embraced it like crazy, but that's just me.

Anyway, I hired him to help with a case that I was working, hired Steve. We had our ups and downs. Turned out he wasn't above skimming a few bucks off the top if he had the opportunity. Yet I liked him. Besides, it wasn't my money. Afterward, he introduced me to Sara and actually gave me a step-by-step demonstration of the process he went through to become her. It was fascinating if a little disconcerting.

Steve told me that he began cross-dressing when he was about twelve, Amanda Wedemeyer's age, quit when he started high school, and picked it up again after college. He wasn't gay, bi, or transsexual. He didn't think of himself as a woman trapped in a man's body or even for a moment contemplate gender reassignment. He just liked to dress as a woman, and he became so skilled at it that women seldom realized he was a man, and the vast majority of men never did.

Like Freddie.

I had introduced him to Sara over drinks. He actually kissed the back of her hand and complimented her on her figure—Freddie was a smooth operator in those days. 'Course, Sara was flirting back, so I just sat there and watched, waiting for the train wreck that never occurred. At least not in front of me. Instead, Sara said she had to return to her loft, and Freddie volunteered to walk her there. What happened next had never been fully revealed by either party, although Freddie did call me several obscene names the next time we met for not giving him a heads-up.

"How's the family?" I asked.

"They've seemed to mellow considerably over the years," Sara said. "Steve's invited to all of the Vandertop family gatherings now. 'Course, I never get to go."

"Bastards," Freddie said.

Sara's head snapped toward him. "Freddie," she said.

"I'm just sayin'."

"My, my, my." She began fanning herself again.

"If you two are done flirting," I said.

"Dammit, Taylor," Freddie said.

"Let's get down to business."

27

"Is this a straight-up security job?" Sara asked. "Or are we going rogue again?"

"This time we're on the side of the angels."

"Where's the fun in that?"

I gave her the basics.

"What do you want from me?" Sara asked.

"Is it possible to trace the hacker?" I asked.

"Track the hack?" Sara smiled. "Depends."

"On what?"

"On how it was done. Lawyers are no different than anyone else. They put themselves at risk because they do stupid things. Emails. Attorneys may be wary when they receive generic-looking emails from businesses. But what about an email from the hacked address of a professional organization? The bar association or the Minnesota Association of Criminal Defense Lawyers, for example? Or even an email that comes to them from an attorney within the same law firm? I have legitimate clients, believe it or not—"

"Are you sayin' we ain't legitimate?" Freddie asked.

"One of the things we do is send test emails to employees with attachments that they're not supposed to open. Half the time the attachments are opened anyway. The employees are chewed out big-time and told never to do it again. Six weeks later, we send them more test emails and the attachments are still opened. Unbelievable. My experience, lawyers aren't much brighter than anyone else when it comes to this stuff.

"Also, you have Wi-Fi networks. Attorneys travel a lot. They need to use their smartphones and laptops, so what do they do? They use public Wi-Fi networks. Which means they could be logging into a hacker's network. They look just like a legitimate connection offered by a business. An untrained user can't spot the difference. The result—all the data they send is intercepted.

"Or thumb drives. A hacker litters the place with USB devices branded with the logo of an attorney's client or the logo of a convention the lawyer might be attending, something like that.

Only it's loaded with all kinds of malicious software that hackers can use to siphon off intel once they're plugged in.

"What else? Passwords. People use the same damn passwords for everything. LinkedIn. Your bank account. Your company's server. It's like making a hundred copies of your house key and leaving them scattered around. Hacker finds one and now he has access to everything.

"Lawyers, like everyone else, also have a tendency to live online, posting about their family, their friends, their pets, their vacation to Wisconsin Dells. This helps hackers guess both passwords and the answers to security questions. 'What's the name of your pet? Where were you born?' Give me access to your Facebook account and I'll probably be able to figure it out.

"I'll tell you this, though—it's much harder for us to catch a hacker than it is for them to hack a system or network."

"But you can do it," I said.

"Well..."

"C'mon, Sara," Freddie said. "It's a simple question."

"It's not a simple answer, though. Tell me this—is the information we gather going to be turned over to the authorities for prosecution?"

"What difference does it make?"

"The cops are required by law to obtain warrants issued by a judge to compel a service provider to give up its records, to tell the cops exactly who was using a specific IP address at the time the illegal activity was taking place. Most hackers, though, hide behind a digital smoke screen of multiple service providers. By the time the cops work their way through them all, poof, they're gone. This also assumes the service provider actually keeps records. In the United States, they're supposed to for a minimum of a year. Not all countries are as diligent. That's why it shouldn't come as a big surprise that most hackers attack targets outside their own countries. If it takes time to get a warrant for a provider in the US, imagine getting a warrant for a provider in Belarus. And if the hacker is using a proxy server—"

"Proxy server?" I asked.

"I won't bother you with the details."

"Please don't," Freddie said. "My eyes are already glazing over."

"I'll just tell you that proxy services are free and widely available. It allows anyone using a computer to bounce their activity off a system that is either in a distant country or keeps no records of where the activity originated. They were set up to help people in hostile regimes like China, say, get their information out anonymously."

"Whistle-blowers?" I asked.

"Absolutely. But, of course, hackers quickly saw their potential. Then there's onion routing—"

"Stop," Freddie said.

"I'm just trying to make you understand, there's finding the hacker and then there's building a case against the hacker. Only about one percent will actually do time because it's so hard to gather evidence legally."

"Find 'im first," Freddie said. "We'll worry what's legal later."

"What it comes down to, then, is the hacker's skill set," Sara said. "Everyone makes mistakes. Did he? Plus his ego. Hackers tend to be boastful. They like to show off to their peers. They like to brag about their technical prowess. Some will even taunt their victims, the companies they hack. 'Catch me if you can,' they'll say. That might help, too."

I stood and walked to the bulletin board and stared at the index cards pinned there.

"The hacker sent emails to each of the law firms," I said. "He wanted the attorneys to know what he did."

"Ego," Sara said.

"Or part of a revenge fantasy."

"Which brings us back to my theory," Freddie said.

"Why is he so pissed off at these five law firms and no

others?"

"Yeah."

"We're going to have to do this the hard way. With good old-fashioned police work."

"Except we ain't the police anymore."

"That's why it's fun to work with you guys," Sara said.

"We also have more than one client," Freddie said. "There are subpoenas we need to serve the sooner the better, skip traces for Henderson, some employee background checks for Sackett, and one of the few lawyers we work with who wasn't hacked— she needs us to finish vetting some jurors."

"I know."

"I'm just sayin'."

"I know. Most of it is computer work, though, so why don't you do all that, and I'll get started on the legwork for the lawyers."

"'Kay."

"In the meantime, Sara, I'll contact the law firms and tell them to give you access to their computers. Anything you can do to track this guy…"

"I'll do what I can."

"I just had a thought," Freddie said.

I might have made a joke about it—something like *Is it lonely in there?*—only it didn't seem the proper time.

"Maybe we should *reveal* ourselves," Freddie said.

"What do you mean?" I asked.

"Maybe we should make just as much noise as we can goin' after this guy."

"The clients want it done quietly."

"Yeah, but if this guy's got crazy skills and an ego to boot like Sara says, and he learns that we, meaning you and me, are after 'im, what's gonna stop him from comin' after us? Even if it's just to laugh at us. You follow me?"

"Set a trap? I like it. Sara?"

Sara spread her arms wide, stretching the material of her thin bodice over what I would have thought was an ample bosom if I hadn't known better.

"Boys," she said. "It's me."

CHAPTER FOUR

Seven in the evening, forty-two hours before her wedding was scheduled to take place, Brooke St. Vincent heard a knock on her apartment door. She was naked except for her matching bra and panties, so she threw on a thin robe, knotted the belt, and peered through the spy hole. Kurt Guernsey stood on the other side. Brooke opened the door.

"Hey, you," she said.

Guernsey stepped across the threshold and the two embraced. Brooke closed the door. Guernsey reached for her, his fingers working the knot of her belt.

"I like your outfit," he said.

Brooke slapped his hands and backed away.

"Stop it," she said. "Melissa and the others will be here in thirty minutes. I still need to get dressed, put on some makeup."

"You don't need any makeup, and it won't take thirty minutes."

"Oh, really? That's what I have to look forward to? A lifetime of quickies?"

"We'll take as much time as you like."

They embraced again. This time they kissed as if nothing gave them greater pleasure. Eventually Brooke put her hands on Guernsey's chest and backed him up.

"I told you I'm having dinner with your sister and my bridesmaids," she said.

"I know."

"What are you doing here, anyway?"

Guernsey turned his head so she couldn't see his face.

"Brooke, we need to talk," he said.

"About what?"

"Let's sit down."

"Kurt, you're scaring me."

They found chairs at Brooke's kitchen table.

"I'm so sorry," Guernsey said.

"What? What, Kurtis?"

"My family. I'm sorry Brooke, but my family…"

Guernsey pulled several sheets of paper from his inside pocket, unfolded them, and smoothed them out in front of Brooke. He held a pen in his hand.

"My family insists that you sign this before the wedding," he said.

"What is it?"

"A prenuptial agreement."

"A what?"

"A prenup. My family—"

"You bring this up now? We're getting married on Saturday."

"I know, I know. But my family—"

"You mean your father."

"My father, then—"

"How old do you need to be before you stop taking orders from that man?"

"Brooke."

"You told me that you didn't want a prenup. You stood right there." She pointed at a spot in her living room. "You said that you didn't want to negotiate your divorce before we were even married. You said it was bad luck."

"I know what I said. Brooke, I'm sorry, I really am. You know how my father is."

"He thinks I'm a gold digger. He thinks that I'm only marrying you for your money because that's what your stepmother did."

"It's just that you're so very beautiful. You could have any guy you want and you chose me. I'm not a handsome man, Brooke."

"Who says? Your father?"

"I'm also eleven years older."

"He's forty years older than—"

"Brooke, please."

"What if I don't sign?"

"The wedding—Father said that when the minister asks if anyone here can show just cause why this couple..."

"Are you kidding me?"

"Brooke, I promise—I promise that one year from now, we'll do it on our first wedding anniversary, we'll burn the damn prenup in front of him. We'll throw a party at Axis Mundi. Invite everyone we know. For now, though..."

"Do I even get a chance to read it?"

"Of course, of course, take your time."

Guernsey sat there, pen in hand, and waited.

"Not now," Brooke said. She spun in her seat until she could read the clock on her microwave oven. "Melissa will be here in fifteen minutes."

"Tomorrow, then? I need to get my father off my back."

"Tomorrow."

"I'm sorry, Brooke, springing it on you like this. I promise it's only temporary. Give it a year and we'll burn it."

"All right."

Brooke walked Guernsey to her door. They embraced, and Guernsey kissed her cheek.

"Have fun tonight," he said.

"I'll try."

"You are so beautiful."

She was, too. A beautiful bride. My experience, most aren't. We say they are when we watch them walking down the aisle; we actually speak the words "What a beautiful bride." Mostly, though, we're just being polite. After all, if we're at the ceremony in the first place it's because we're family or a friend. But Brooke *was* beautiful. She looked like she should be modeling gowns for one of those bridal magazines. She seemed happy, too. She was smiling in every pic David Helin showed me. He had downloaded a bunch of them into the personal file on his computer. Guernsey seemed happy as well, especially when his arm was draped around his wife's shoulder or her arm was wrapped around his waist, or they just stood there holding hands. It occurred to me the actual wedding was probably the high-water mark of their relationship, as blissful as the couple would ever be, because they divorced only three and a half years later.

"They never did burn the prenup," Helin said. "It was always going to be done next year. Finally, Brooke had enough. Enough of the insults, enough of the abuse—"

"Guernsey abused her?"

"It's a long story. The bottom line—they divorced. Kurtis asked the court to enforce the agreement, which incidentally left Brooke with absolutely nothing. She told the court that he had reneged on his oral promise to tear up the prenuptial. Unfortunately, that promise was not referenced in the parties' written agreement. Moreover, the parties had disclaimed reliance upon oral statements by either party, a relatively standard provision in most prenups."

"In other words, Guernsey's promise wasn't worth the paper it was written on," I said.

"Exactly. The court enforced the prenup, which it nearly always does."

"What happened next?"

"Brooke came to me. We appealed the court's decision claiming coercion. We argued that the premarital agreement was unenforceable because Brooke's consent to the agreement came as the result of duress and that, because of the timing, she didn't have access to independent legal representation. The fact that the prenup had left her with nothing proved that there had been no bargained-for benefit. The appellate court agreed. It ruled—well, here, read it for yourself."

I did, starting where his finger pointed. "'Under these circumstances we find it would be unfair, unjust, and inequitable to enforce this prenuptial agreement. The timing of the agreement negated any inclination Mrs. Guernsey may have had to secure independent advice. The first meeting to review the agreement took place two days before the wedding; the signing of the agreement was done the evening before the wedding. Mr. Guernsey admitted that any hesitation by his future wife would have resulted in at least a delay of the wedding. Obviously, the night before her wedding a bride has concerns that seem more important and immediate than the potential dissolution of her marriage and waiver of her interest in future community property.'"

"What happened next?" I asked.

"We went back to square one," Helin said. "Negotiated the divorce as if there had been no prenup. Eventually we settled for a onetime payment of three-point-seven million and no spousal support."

"Nice."

"Yeah."

"Now tell me about the hacked email."

Brooke had stared at the door after her fiancé left. Truth be told, she actually did care for him. He was funny, he was smart, and he treated her like a princess. The fact that he was a member of the Guernsey family that owned Minnesota River State Bank, among other things, only added to his appeal. She didn't want to lose him. On the other hand—did her future father-in-law really think that Brooke was foolish enough to sign a contract without reading it first, without having her own lawyers read it?

Her cell rang. Melissa. Did she know what her brother was up to? Brooke wondered.

"Lissa," she said, "I'm running way behind. Give me twenty minutes."

"Okay, but hurry. The driver's anxious to see some male strippers. Aren't you, Fisk?"

"Whatever you say, miss."

Brooke hung up. Instead of donning her red silk, though, she took the prenup to her computer setup and scanned in the pages one at a time. Afterward, she prepared an email, attached the prenup, and sent it off to the older brother of the man who had taken her virginity a decade earlier with the note "Tell me what to do?"

"She and my brother were deeply in love," Helin said. "I was a little in love with her myself, to tell you the truth, even though I was ten years older. Unfortunately, their devotion to each other lasted only until they went off to college on different sides of the country. They kept in touch, though, had many friends in common, and I would run into her from time to time.

"Anyway, Brooke sent me the prenup, and I read it. I called her immediately. I begged her not to sign it. I told her that it was ridiculously one-sided. She was in a limo with her brides-maids at the time and heading to a club. She said she couldn't talk. She said to send an email explaining what she should do and she'd read it when she got home. I did, picking the document apart in gruesome detail. I was shocked when Brooke signed it. She told me later that she was afraid that if she put up a fuss the marriage would have been postponed if not canceled altogether. She also said she believed Guernsey's promise that he would destroy the prenup once she proved she was going to be a good wife to him. Girl in love, what are you going to do?"

"So," I said. "Your argument before the appeals court that Brooke was unfairly coerced into signing the prenup..."

"That part was valid."

"Not the part about having access to legal representation, though."

"Technically—we never actually spoke about this matter

except for the brief phone conversation when she was in the car, never met in person. Moreover, Brooke hadn't formally hired me. She wasn't a paying client, and no money changed hands."

"Technically."

"That's right."

"What would happen if Guernsey learned about the email?"

"He'd probably move to have the appeals court's decision reversed, ask that the provisions of the original prenuptial agreement be enforced, and demand that Brooke return his three-point-seven million bucks."

"Would he win?"

"He'd have a strong argument."

"What about you? Would you be in trouble?"

"It could be argued that I had failed to fulfill my candor obligations to the court."

"Meaning?"

"If Guernsey made an issue of it, I could receive an admonishment by the ABA's disciplinary council. I might even get a reprimand by the court or the Lawyers Professional Responsibility Board."

"Suspension of license?"

Helin shrugged.

"These are not good things," I said.

"No, they're not."

"Why did you do it, David? I've never known you to skirt the rules before."

"When you meet the woman you'll understand."

"Who knew about the email?"

"What do you mean?"

"Who knew that the email existed?"

"Me. Brooke."

"Who else?"

"I never told anyone. I didn't have a reason. When I sent it—it was well over four years ago now. I can't speak for Brooke, though."

"We have a theory, Freddie and I. We don't believe the attack was random. We believe the hacker knew about this email, that he hacked your computer specifically to get at it."

Helin thought about it for a few beats. "And the others?" he asked.

"The same. He knew what you all did and searched your computers to find evidence that would prove it."

"Five separate law firms. We never work together. We don't spend time with each other. Why us?"

"There must be a common denominator of some sort. Something that ties all the cases together."

"I can't imagine what."

"Neither can I. That's why I want your permission to interview Brooke and anyone else involved with the case. I'm going to ask the same thing of the others as well. Something connects the five of you. If we can find out what it is…"

"This could take time."

"That's why I got up early this morning."

"I'll call Brooke and tell her you're coming over. I already told her about the hack. I don't know what the others might have told their clients, though, if anything."

"I'll deal with them later. I picked you first because you're my favorite attorney."

"Is that true, Taylor, or are you saying it because I bill more hours?"

"Both."

She moved with a peculiar grace, a kind of gliding motion that gave the impression that she was walking an inch above the floor. Her golden tresses required no hairdresser's magic, and her clear blue eyes spoke for themselves. I understood instantly why Dave Helin would lie and cheat for her. Given the proper motivation, I would probably do the same.

Despite her millions, Brooke St. Vincent worked for a living.

She was a loan servicing specialist for an investment firm concentrating on funding energy companies. I was lucky she agreed to meet me in a coffeehouse located in the lobby of the building where she was employed.

Mostly my job is asking questions. Personal, business, social, thousands of questions of hundreds of people over—how long had I been doing this now? Ten years? I ask the questions during business hours or just as often in the evening and on weekends because I need to talk to people when they're available, not when I am. Often, it involves role-playing, transforming myself into someone people would readily confide in because many of them hate to talk to *private investigators* just as much as they hate to talk to cops. Sometimes it requires me to become Sam Spade or Philip Marlowe or Jim Rockford—remember Rockford?—or even Sherlock Holmes because many of them love to talk to *private eyes*.

Brooke didn't seem to care one way or the other. To her I was just a guy interrupting her day. She bought a cup of coffee, light cream, and made her way to the table where I was sitting. I stood for her.

"David Helin said I should speak to you," she told me.

"Thank you for your time."

We sat across from each other.

"I knew Kurt would never let bygones be bygones," Brooke said. "I knew that he'd come after me. Being forced to pay a hundred thousand dollars for every month we were together, it must have felt like losing to him, and the Guernseys, they don't like to lose. Even Melissa. She claimed that she was my friend and always would be right up until the judge ruled the prenup was invalid. We haven't spoken since."

"I'm sorry to hear that."

"It's what comes from being a girl from the wrong side of the tracks."

"Where are you from?"

"Edina."

"That's one of the wealthiest suburbs in the Twin Cities."

"It's not Lake Minnetonka, though. Or North Oaks. Or Sunfish Lake. You need to understand. These are people who never attend the Minnesota State Fair for fear of rubbing up against the wrong kind of people."

"You should be glad to be out of the family, then."

"I loved him, Taylor. Kurtis. I would have done anything for him. Sexual things that I found appalling because...You don't want to hear about that. It was never good enough anyway. I was never good enough. No one could possibly be good enough. It's what Kurt was taught every day of his life, him and his siblings. There's the Guernseys and then there's everyone else. They live above the rest of us."

"Yet he married you. From the photos I've seen, I would guess you were both in love."

"I was in love. Kurt was making a protest against his family. No, that's not fair. Kurtis did love me, and if we had lived somewhere else besides Axis Mundi we might have made a go of it. Only there's something about that place that drains the soul out of these people. If you meet them anywhere else—Kurt, Robert Jr., and Melissa, too—you'll believe they're good people, smart, funny, considerate, brave. At Axis Mundi, though—"

"What is Axis Mundi?"

"That's the name the old man—Robert Paul—that's the name he gave to his estate. It means 'center of the world.' All of the Guernseys live there. The old man insists. He rules over the place like a feudal baron, controlling everybody's lives. He has a personal assistant named Fisk following him around, doing his bidding. Once early in my marriage, Robert Paul didn't approve of something I said at dinner about the Federal Reserve Board. He waved his hand and said, 'You're dismissed.' His flunky, minion, servant, aide—I don't know what to call him—Fisk walked over, picked up my plate, utensils, and wineglass, and carried them from the room. That's Axis Mundi.

"Don't get me wrong, Taylor. I have no one to blame but

myself for what happened. I saw it coming. I knew the moment Kurtis dropped the prenup on my kitchen table the marriage would end with a bang instead of a whimper. He promised to destroy the prenup. I didn't believe him. Yet I thought at the time—I could make it work. I could rescue the love of my life from Axis Mundi. Arrogance on my part, I suppose. Or naïveté. Or maybe I read too many young adult fantasy novels when I was a kid. Take your pick."

"When he left you—"

"Kurt didn't leave me. I left him. He was shocked when I walked out the door. He didn't think I would do it. He thought his money would bind me to him. I stayed with my sister and her family while I was sorting out my life. He had Fisk hand-deliver a note reminding me, first, that I wouldn't get a dime if I divorced him and, second, that he was still willing to take me back. I found out later it was the old man who actually composed the note. Fisk was supposed to wait while I packed my bags. I sent him away. Melissa told me later—we were still talking back then—she told me that Kurt had a fit when I didn't return. It went against everything he was taught about being a Guernsey, that money was always the deciding factor. As far as the old man was concerned, Kurt was a weakling, not a man at all, because he couldn't hold a wife. Eventually they had to call the family doctor to give Kurt a sedative. Again, it doesn't surprise me that he just won't let it go."

"It's possible that Kurtis isn't involved in the hack," I said.

"We'll see."

"In any case, you did go after his money."

Brooke's appearance didn't change, yet I could see that the remark had distressed her. She expressed her concern with her hands, which began picking at invisible fibers on her clothes.

"That was David's idea," she said. "He told me it offended his sense of justice that I had so little to show for the time I spent being Kurt's plaything. He told me he could have the prenup dismissed, that he would do all the work and all I would need to do was nod my head. I nodded. I was in a vulnerable place back then. If David had told me to dive off the Lake Street Bridge, I probably would have."

"How did you meet?"

"I used to date David's brother."

"No. I meant you and Kurtis."

"Oh. Grad school. I had a bachelor's degree in economics from the University of Minnesota and was working for an investment bank. It became apparent that I wouldn't be able to move into a management position unless I also had a master's or better. I decided to go back to school. My employers encouraged me. They even paid part of my tuition. I began taking courses at Hamline University's Minneapolis campus. I was twenty-seven and wondering where my career was headed. I was also wondering if I would ever meet Mr. Right. The first day of class, Kurtis was the guest speaker. Mr. Wrong, as it turned out, yet at the time…He scored a lot of points with me when he insisted that I get my master's before we set a wedding date. He said he didn't want his friends to think he was marrying a dumb blonde. I thought he was being cute. I discovered later that he had meant it. In his circle, you see a lot of trophy wives. It was a matter of pride with him that his people didn't think I was one of them. Yet that's what they thought anyway, probably more so now because of the settlement."

"What did you do with it?"

"I invested it. All three-point-seven million. I may be a lousy judge of men, Taylor, but I know money. If this all goes back to court and a judge orders me to return the money with interest, I'll pay it back with interest. It won't break my heart at all. I understand David might be in trouble with the ABA, and I'll be sorry for that. That's all I'll be sorry for, though."

"Let's hope it doesn't come to that."

"Why would you care?"

"I like you."

"That's kind of you to say. Tell me, what happens next?"

Dinner and a movie, I thought, before dismissing the suggestion. I tell myself all the time to never get involved with a subject of an investigation, that it never works out and sometimes can be downright unethical. Mostly, I listen. On the other hand, after all this was settled...

"Have you ever told anyone about the email Helin sent you?" I asked.

"The one telling me not to sign the prenup? No. I read it the day before the wedding. I remember I had a hangover at the time. Afterward, I deleted it. I've thought about it a few times over the years, about David's advice, yet I never spoke of it. I never said, 'I should have listened to my attorney.' 'Course, he wasn't really my lawyer at the time. He was my friend. We didn't become lovers until...it must have been two, three weeks after my divorce was final. The second time, I mean. After we beat the prenup."

Probably more information than I needed to hear. On the other hand, if Brooke and Helin were the only two who knew about the email, then maybe Freddie and I were wrong about this. Maybe it was a smash-and-grab after all.

"Did you speak of it while you were going through the divorce?" I asked.

"No."

"Not even among yourselves?"

"No."

"At a restaurant, a bar, someplace where you might have been overheard?"

"I don't think so. I can't remember...No. I have to say, no."

"Okay."

"I'm sorry I can't be more helpful."

"Don't worry about it."

"Oh, I won't. I have family, good friends, a good job, money in the bank, more than enough money to pay Kurtis if it comes to that, and won't that piss him off. And his father, too. So I'm not worrying at all. It's like a man once said, living well is the best revenge."

Unfortunately, I thought, it's not the only revenge.

CHAPTER FIVE

I made a mental note to ask Sara if the Vandertops and the Guernseys hung out together at wherever it was that the one percent hung out while I walked the four blocks from Brooke's building to the skyscraper that accommodated the law firm where Cormac Puchner worked. It was another reason why Freddie and I hesitated to leave downtown Minneapolis. So many of our clients were within walking distance of our office.

Puchner agreed to meet me without an appointment, yet he made it sound like he was not only doing me a great favor, it was the last one he was allowed to perform until next month. He softened somewhat when I told him Freddie and I agreed with his assessment of the situation, that he and the other attorneys had been targeted for a specific reason.

He puffed himself up and said, "Money. It's always about money."

"Unless he really does consider himself to be a hactivist who thinks fucking you over is for the greater good."

"Bullshit."

"We won't know until the shoe drops. So far, NIMN has been silent."

"What are you doing about it?"

I told him.

Puchner didn't think it was enough. Yet, in the same breath, he forbade me from contacting anyone working for Standout

Investments Worldwide LLC.

"There's no requirement that we inform the public that our firm has been a victim of intrusion," he said.

"It's your client. Not the public."

"Mr. Taylor, do you presume to read the law to me?"

"I wouldn't dream of it."

"I'm a graduate of Harvard Law School."

"So I've been told. Cormac, if we're going to find a connection between the cases—"

"I'll give you everything I have. However, we will not inform Standout that its most private data has been violated unless and until it becomes absolutely necessary. Taylor, do you know how close I am to making partner?"

Puchner moved to the huge window and gazed out. The view he already had looked pretty spectacular to me, but what did I know? Freddie and I bill only sixty dollars an hour.

"I read the information you put on the USB drive," I said. "It was pretty thin. Especially from you. You're usually much more forthcoming."

"It's a sensitive matter."

"Exactly what is the lawsuit about?"

Puchner's answer was to direct me to his computer. He pulled up a website and stepped away while I read from the screen.

WELCOME TO
THE HEATHERTON V. STANDOUT INVESTMENTS
WORLDWIDE LLC SETTLEMENT WEBSITE

Consumers who received unauthorized text messages from Standout Investments Worldwide LLC advertising goods or services may be eligible for a share of the $7.3 million settlement over allegations of violations of the Telephone Consumer Protection Act.

A Settlement has been reached in a class action lawsuit

against Standout Investments Worldwide LLC ("Defendant" or "Standout"). The suit concerns whether Standout violated a federal law called the Telephone Consumer Protection Act by sending unsolicited text messages to the cell phones of consumers advertising its goods and services ("Advertising Text Messages"). Standout denies any wrongdoing and maintains that the Advertising Text Messages were made with consumers' consent and were authorized by law. The Settlement does not establish who is correct, but rather is a compromise to end the lawsuit.

You are included in the Settlement if you received an Advertising Text Message on your cell phone from Standout between August 6, 2016, and April 14, 2018. You may be entitled to a cash payment if you affirm that you received such an Advertising Text Message without providing your consent.

Those who submit valid claims will be eligible to receive an equal, or pro rata, share of a $7.3 million settlement fund that Standout has agreed to establish. Each individual who submits a valid claim will receive a portion of this fund, after all notice and administration costs, the incentive award, and attorneys' fees have been paid. Standout has also agreed to implement procedures to ensure that it has the appropriate consent to send Advertising Text Messages in the future.

YOUR LEGAL RIGHTS AND OPTIONS IN THIS SETTLEMENT

Submit a Claim Form:
This is the only way to receive a payment.

Exclude Yourself:
You will not receive any benefits, but you will retain any rights you may currently have to sue the Defendant about Advertising Text Messages sent to you.

Object:
Write to the Court explaining why you don't like the Settlement.

Do Nothing:
You won't get a share of the Settlement benefits and will give up your rights to sue the Defendant about the claims in this case.

"It's a perfect example of what's wrong with our tort system," Puchner said. "No different than the suit filed against Subway by the customer who claimed that after buying a footlong sub, he discovered that the sandwich was only eleven and three-quarter inches in length. Bottom-feeding trial attorneys do nothing all day but troll for petty offenses that they can turn into a huge payday by filing abusive lawsuits designed to force a company into an exorbitant settlement to avoid bad publicity or a protracted legal battle. Do you have any idea how much Standout's customers, the ones who received the text messages—do you know what they'll make from this frivolous lawsuit? About fifty bucks each. The lawyers, though, they're going to line their pockets."

"What about the hacker?"

"The hacker? What he stole…As far as we can tell, what he stole were copies of a couple of memos that were circulated among upper management before the advertising campaign was launched."

"What did they say?"

"What did they say? They said…The original memo was composed by a team leader in the firm's marketing department who said…Ahh, fuck. It said that in his opinion the advertising campaign was in violation of the Telephone Consumer Protection Act. The other memos was management putting in writing its opinion that the law was ridiculous and that they should just ignore it."

"You're kidding."

"You know, Taylor, I never swore when I was at Harvard. I started...It wasn't until I moved to the Midwest and began working with people who think New York is Sodom and LA is Gomorrah and in between is the real fucking America."

"What little I know about the law, wouldn't the memos have been revealed during discovery anyway?"

"I'll give you a quick tutorial. A class action lawsuit is done in steps. First is the drafting of the complaint. The complaint is filed in court and served on the defendants. You've done your share of that for us, working as a process server. Second, the defendant will file an answer denying the allegations and/or file certain motions challenging the lawsuit. If a judge rules the suit may proceed, then the plaintiffs take the next step by formally demanding documents, asking for answers to written questions, scheduling depositions—it's a fucking fishing expedition is what it is. Except, in this case, it's the reason why we agreed to settle. We didn't want the plaintiffs to discover the memos, which might have boosted the settlement, what? Three times? Four times? It would have at least doubled it. The court doesn't like it when you purposely decide to ignore the law. It's kinda prickly that way."

"Isn't the case already settled? Isn't there a double jeopardy clause?"

"Not in civil cases. The court holds that civil and administrative proceedings are more remedial in nature. They seek to compensate injured persons for losses they've suffered and serve various functions unrelated to deterrence or retribution. Besides, we never actually went to court. The point of the settlement was to avoid going to court."

"So..."

"So if these memos are exposed, the plaintiffs will reopen the suit, Standout will get creamed, and I'll lose my corner office."

"Can I at least speak to the junior exec who wrote the original memo? I promise to be discreet."

"Oh fuck, they fired him right away. The minute the lawsuit was filed."

"What's his name?"

"Taylor..."

"Cormac, the man has motive to hurt Standout."

"That he does. I'm surprised he didn't file a lawsuit himself. You know, it just occurred to me, for these memos to be admitted in court, they'd first need to be authenticated. He could do that. All right, give me a minute."

Puchner went to his computer and started moving and clicking his mouse. I said, "I never heard of Standout Investments."

"It's relatively new. A division of Minnesota River State Bank."

Something about the way my body reacted to the news caused Puchner's head to come up.

"What?" he said.

"It couldn't possibly be that easy," I told him.

Clinton Siegle had his own website. It read:

HOW WILL YOUR COMPANY RISE
TO ITS NEXT MARKETING CHALLENGE?

SIEGLE MARKETING INC.

Over 15 years experience providing strategy and marketing consulting to both B2B and B2C clients across a wide range of sectors

I am a freelance marketing professional providing flexible and affordable services and support to help small and medium-sized businesses achieve your goals through strategic, targeted marketing planning and implementation. I offer help with all aspects of marketing including planning, communications and

PR, social media, SEO, digital marketing, copywriting, and event management. I can also provide in-house services whereby I can act as your company's very own marketing manager for as long as you require.

His office was a converted bedroom located in his house in Richfield. He met me on the front porch. We were standing beneath a flight path leading to the Minneapolis–St. Paul International Airport and had to pause several times during our conversation while jets passed overhead.

"I'm sorry," Siegle said. "It didn't occur to me until after we spoke on the phone, but I can't talk to you about Standout after all."

"Why not?"

"When I was terminated I signed a nondisclosure agreement in exchange for a severance package. I'm not allowed to talk about Standout in any way to any one for a period of two years. The agreement still has seventeen months to run."

"This agreement, it refers to outside parties, am I right? I'm not an outside party. I work for the attorney who represents Standout."

"I'm not sure about that."

"You could call the attorney. His name is Cormac Puchner."

"What will he say?"

"He'll say that talking to me is like talking to Standout. We're all on the same side."

"I'm not sure about that, either. What I mean—I'm sure the lawyer and Standout are on the same side. Maybe you are, too. I'm not."

"Why's that?"

"I sent upper management a memo stating that they might be breaking the law, and then when they got caught breaking the law, I'm the one who got fired. How are we on the same side?"

"What happened exactly?"

Siegle paused while a two-engine passenger jet passed overhead.

"I'm taking a chance that you're telling the truth," he said.

"Why wouldn't I be?"

"You're not the first to ask about this."

"I'm not?"

"Taylor, right? A couple of years ago, Taylor, my team was tasked with creating and implementing an integrated marketing campaign designed to introduce Standout's investment products to the greatest possible number of people in our target audience. This included customers who were already doing business with Minnesota River State Bank. We put together a package of print and broadcast ads, public relations, direct marketing, email, and digital and in-store promotions that would run in multiple stages throughout the fiscal year. It was suggested that this package should also include text advertising to the cell phones of Minnesota River's existing customers.

"I sent a memo to my director pointing out that the text messages would be in violation of the Telephone Consumer Protection Act and we should drop that part of the campaign. A couple of days later I was told the higher-ups said it was okay, it was fine, and I should proceed. I didn't believe it, but what am I going to do? Argue? It's the Golden Rule. The man with the gold makes the rules. Right?

"About eighteen, nineteen months later, the campaign was still going strong, our numbers were very good, and I was called into the boss's office. I honestly thought I was going to get promoted. Instead, there were a couple of security guys standing there ready to escort me off the premises."

"Were you told why?"

"I know why. It was because of the memo. Standout didn't want anyone to know about it."

"Is that what they told you?"

"It's what the severance package told me. Two years' salary? Plus healthcare? Who gets a deal like that? The company wanted me to keep my mouth shut. I almost didn't. I thought about it, though, and decided—you know what? I could have sued Standout myself for unlawful termination, but I figured I wouldn't get much more than what they were already paying me. Not to mention a lawsuit would have derailed my career."

"Did you ever tell anyone about the memo?"

"Before today? No."

"Not even your wife?"

"Well, Linda knew. I had to tell her why I was fired, didn't I?"

"Did she tell anyone?"

"No."

"Are you sure?"

"I am, because of what happened."

"What happened?"

"It must have been, oh, I want to say two months ago? Three? This was right before Standout agreed to the settlement. I didn't know about that, though. Not at the time. What happened, Linda and I were at the Twin Cities Jazz Festival when this woman, girl really, she came up to us and started acting like she knew me, like we had worked together at Standout. There was no way I could have forgotten her, what with the tattoos and piercings. She was so young, too. I was polite, trying to remember who she was, and then she said, 'You're the guy who wrote the memo,' and I said, 'What memo?' and she said, 'You know, the memo,' and I told her I didn't know what she was talking about and walked away.

"My first thought was that this was some sort of test, that Standout was trying to figure out if I was keeping my end of the bargain. Or perhaps the company was looking for grounds to terminate the severance agreement. You know, I wouldn't put it past them. I kind of cross-examined my wife about it, asking her, 'Did you ever tell anyone about the memo?' and she said she hadn't. A week later, I heard that Standout had agreed to the settlement. That's when I started wondering if the girl had been among the plaintiffs, that somehow she heard about the memo and approached me for confirmation."

"Authentication."

"What?"

"Something the lawyer told me. No one else asked you about it, though, the memo?"

"No."

"No one from Standout?"

"I haven't spoken to anyone over there since I was fired. Seven-point-three million they had to cough up because they wouldn't listen to me. Clowns."

"What about Minnesota River State Bank?"

"I've never had any dealings with the people over there."

"Have you ever met anyone from the Guernsey family?"

"No. Why would I? It's not like we travel—no, wait. I did meet...What was her name? The daughter?"

I took a chance.

"Melissa?" I said.

"Yes. At the Xcel Energy Center last...I want to say February, a full month before I was fired. I have a friend who has season tickets to watch the Minnesota Wild play hockey. He took me to a game. We were wandering the concourse in between periods, and we met a friend of his who was dating Melissa, at least she was at the game with him, and I was introduced. But the conversation, we didn't talk about Standout or the bank or anything like that. It was all about whether or not the Wild had a chance to make the playoffs this year, and it only lasted five minutes."

"She wasn't the girl at the jazz festival?"

"Oh, no. Melissa was older and not very pretty. The girl, though, was young and pretty but trying hard not to be pretty, you know?"

Siegle didn't have much more to say that was interesting after that, so I gave him my card and asked him to contact me should anyone else come knocking on his door to ask about the memo.

"Is someone going to knock on my door?" Siegle asked.

"You never know."

* * *

My Camry was parked on the street. I climbed into it and wrote a few notes in fractured shorthand in a hardcover notebook I always carried that I would later transcribe onto my computer. Clients love detailed reports. Especially lawyers. Freddie keeps telling me to use a smartphone or tablet and save myself the extra work, yet I continue to resist. Not because I'm some kind of Luddite afraid of computers, but rather because I never learned to type with my thumbs.

After I finished, I drove off. I covered at least four miles before I realized I was being followed. It caused me to do something I disliked immensely. I used my cell phone while I was driving.

Freddie answered with the words "My man."

"Where are you?" I asked.

'The office. I just served a couple of subpoenas, why?"

"I'm being tailed."

"That a fact? You need some backup?"

"I don't think so, but listen." I recited the license plate number of the car behind me. "Think you can get an ID in the next couple of minutes?"

"Whatshisname, Franklin in the MPD's gang unit, he's always up for a quick twenty. I'll get back t' ya."

I didn't want to lead the tail to my next appointment. Yet neither did I want him to know he had been made, so I deliberately steered him into the traffic slowdown that always occurred around the I-94–Highway 280 interchange at about that time of day. It bought enough time for Freddie to call back.

"You're not going to believe it," he said.

"I believe everything you tell me."

"Walter O'Neill."

"No way."

"I knew you wouldn't believe it. Sure you don't need backup? Man's an ex-cop."

"Most of us are."

"Most of us don't get retired because we're loose with our hands."

"That's true. I'm guessing O'Neill picked me up when I was interviewing Clinton Siegle."

"Who's Clinton Siegle?"

"I'll tell you all about it later. In the meantime, where's Sara?"

"Probably in her man cave. Why?"

"Ask her to come in first chance she gets and sweep the place for bugs."

"Our place?" Freddie said.

"Just in case someone's listening in. We've been on the case for less than a day and all of a sudden we're being followed? Also, when I say we, it wouldn't hurt for you to watch your back, either."

"Who do you think hired O'Neill? The hacker? Agents of NIMN?"

"A little closer to home, I think."

"Our clients? Man, you'd think they didn't trust us."

"Just a guess."

"I have a thought," Freddie said.

"Oh? Is it lonely in there?"

"You've been carrying that line with you all day, haven't you?"

"What thought?" I said.

"Ask O'Neill."

There was an empty space directly in front of my apartment building, a rare occurrence. I parked there, exited the Camry, and walked up the concrete steps to the front door. O'Neill drove past me. I knew without looking that he would flip a U-turn at the corner and come back up the other side of the street.

I entered the apartment building, negotiated the first-floor corridor, and went out the back into the small parking lot that opened onto an asphalt alley. I followed the alley to its end. Along the way, my hand moved to the spot where I would have been carrying my gun if I had thought to bring it. Most private investigators rarely carry, if ever, the idea being that you shouldn't arm yourself unless, one, you're sure you might need a gun and, two, that you're completely and absolutely sure you're willing to use it. Freddie and I have both squeezed the trigger. So has O'Neill. It did not make us virtuous. It did not make us superior to our colleagues. On the contrary.

I circled the block. O'Neill had parked on the far side of the street about eight car lengths down, with a clear view of both my Camry and the front door of the apartment building. I came up on his blind side, moving carefully. The worst cops are the ones who choose anger as the first response to a bad situation, and Walter had been their poster child. I doubted that getting bounced from the Minneapolis Police Department a few years ago improved his disposition.

Among the things I carried was a tactical penlight with a pointed end. I pressed the point hard against O'Neill's passenger-side window, and the safety glass shattered into a thousand shards. Most of them fell inside the car. O'Neill was startled. His head actually hit the roof.

"Hi, Walter," I said.

"Sonuvabitch." He massaged the top of his skull. "Trying to be fucking dramatic, are you?"

"I wanted to announce my presence with authority."

"You gonna pay to replace my window?"

"I think you could pass it off as a legitimate business expense. Why don't you call your client and ask him?"

"Client? What client?"

"Let me guess. You weren't following me."

"I was just in the neighborhood and decided to stop by and say hello. I haven't been invited here for a long time."

"You've never been invited here."

I noticed O'Neill was careful with his hands, letting them rest on top of his steering wheel while we spoke. He was trying hard not to escalate the situation, which seemed unlike him.

"Who are you working for, Walter?" I asked.

"I can't say."

"Can't or won't."

"You know the rules, Taylor. *No license holder shall divulge to anyone other than the employer, or as the employer may direct, except as required by law, any information—*"

"Really, Walter? You're quoting the statutes to me?" I waved the penlight at him. "Why don't you step outside the car?"

"You want to go, Taylor? With me? Whaddya think that's gonna get you? Besides your ass kicked? Even if you got lucky, you and I both know you won't do much more than make me uncomfortable for a few days. You certainly won't kill me, so I have no incentive to talk."

"I won't, but Freddie has a volatile personality."

"Frederick's not here."

"I called him. He's on his way."

"Gonna have your boy do your dirty work? That sounds like you."

I tried to open his car door to get at him, only it was locked.

"I don't have time for this shit," O'Neill said. He started his car.

"Don't let me catch you again, Walter," I said.

"You won't."

The way he smirked, though, gave me the impression that instead of quitting the job, he intended to be more careful in the future.

CHAPTER SIX

I didn't go inside my apartment. The only reason I had stopped there in the first place was because I knew O'Neill already had the address. Instead, I drove to a sandwich shop on Grand Avenue and had a quick bite. Afterward, I carefully maneuvered the Camry into downtown St. Paul. John Kaushal had agreed to meet with me when I called earlier, but only after hours. To guarantee I wasn't being followed, I parked at a meter near Mears Park and walked down streets and through buildings for six blocks until I reached his offices near the Ramsey County Courthouse.

The sign read ASSOCIATES & KAUSHAL, ATTORNEYS AT LAW. The door next to it was unlocked, but there was no receptionist at the desk. I paused for a few beats and listened. I heard no noise whatsoever. I called Kaushal's name. A moment later he appeared. His coat and tie had been removed, and his sleeves were rolled up. He was carrying a glass filed with a dusky-colored liquid.

"Taylor," he said. "Good of you to come."

Kaushal slipped past me and locked the door. He pointed his glass more or less at the corridor behind the receptionist's desk.

"Shall we?" he said.

I followed him to his office at the far end of the corridor. All the offices we passed were empty, the lights off.

"My people don't usually keep such punctual hours,"

61

Kaushal said, "but I told them it was a beautiful day and they should go out and enjoy what was left of it. I wanted us to be alone. None of them know what I did."

We stepped inside his office. He didn't guide me to his desk but pointed toward a small sofa facing a low glass table in the corner. There was a bottle of Knob Creek Smoked Maple Bourbon and an empty glass on top of the table. I sat.

"Have a drink with me?" Kaushal said.

"I'm good."

"No, Taylor, you're going to want to have a drink. Trust me."

He poured an inch and a half into the glass and slid it toward me. He added more liquor to his own glass and sat in the chair across from me. He took a long sip while I watched.

"I'm going to tell you a story," Kaushal said. "A true story. Most attorneys in the country probably know it, or at least they know one like it. I was told this story when I was in law school. It was presented as a central example in our development and understanding of what it means to be a lawyer. When I finish, I'll tell you why it's important. All right?"

"Of course."

Kaushal drank more bourbon.

"To begin at the beginning," he said, "a man named Robert Garrow assaulted a group of campers in the Adirondack Mountains in upstate New York and tied them all to trees. Three of the campers escaped, but the fourth, an eighteen-year-old boy named Philip Domblewski, was killed. This was in the summer of 1973. Garrow was finally arrested after a massive eleven-day manhunt and charged with murder. The court appointed a lawyer named Frank Armani to defend him. Armani turned to a second attorney, Francis Belge, for help.

"Garrow was clearly guilty; the evidence was unassailable. It was also clear that he was one deeply disturbed individual. Together, Armani and Belge sought to defend him according to the insanity statutes, with the hope that he'd be sentenced to a mental institution instead of prison. Unfortunately, in the course of debriefing by his lawyers, Garrow not only confessed that he killed Domblewski, he also admitted to murdering a second camper, abducting, raping, and murdering the camper's female companion, and then abducting, raping, and murdering a sixteen-year-old girl. Garrow even told the lawyers where he dumped the bodies of his female victims. The lawyers went to the locations Garrow had identified and confirmed that he was telling the truth.

"Armani and Belge told nobody about their client's confession, although the lawyers did approach the prosecutor in secret and said that if a deal could be made that would put Garrow in a mental institution for life, they might be able to help him with a couple of high-profile missing persons cases. The prosecutor rejected the deal out of hand. Eventually the bodies of the women were discovered. Even then the lawyers kept Garrow's secret.

"It was during his trial about a year later that Garrow admitted on the witness stand to everything—killing Domblewski, the other male camper, and the two women who had been missing, as well as, God, I don't know how many other abductions and rapes throughout upstate New York. It became apparent then that Armani and Belge had known all along about the other murders and the locations of the bodies. They publicly acknowledged that they had kept the information secret, withheld it even from the grieving families, because of their sworn duty to maintain client confidentiality.

"You need to understand something, Taylor. In the legal profession, these men are widely regarded as heroes, lawyers who made the tough choices to protect a client. Frank Armani in particular has been compared to Atticus Finch, the noble small-town attorney who defended an unpopular client in *To Kill a Mockingbird*."

"Except," I said, "the defendant in *To Kill a Mockingbird* was innocent."

"That's pretty much the way the public looked at it, too. Armani and Belge were branded as the worst kind of immoral bastards. A grand jury investigated both men. Belge was indicted because he had moved one of the bodies. Parents of the victims filed an ethics complaint against them with the state bar association. Eventually the charges and ethics complaints were dismissed, but their law practices withered. They received hate mail and death threats. Colleagues abandoned them. Longtime friends refused to speak to them. They were forced to move out of their homes for their own protection. Belge eventually gave up practicing law altogether. Armani's own mother told him he was insane for protecting confidences told to him by a serial killer.

"You've been in this business a long time, Taylor, as a cop with the St. Paul Police Department and as a private investigator. You know how it works. Most people believe the criminal justice system is designed to favor the guilty. Defense lawyers are routinely blamed for helping bad and dangerous people go free."

"Sometimes you do help bad and dangerous people go free," I said.

"It's the system that we live by," Kaushal said. "When you become an attorney, you're making a commitment to the values found in the Bill of Rights, the process the government must go through before it can punish any one of us—the right to counsel, the privilege against self-incrimination, the right to confront witnesses and to call witnesses. These are values that protect the dignity and the freedom of the individual. As a lawyer, you serve the public and you act as an officer of the court by upholding those values with all of your resources. It's the only way that we can maintain a free society."

"The first thing we do, let's kill all the lawyers," I said.

"Most people think that means the world would be better off if we didn't have lawyers. But when Shakespeare wrote that line in *Henry VI*, he was really saying that it was attorneys and judges who instill justice in society, and if you want to become a dictator the first thing you have to do is get rid of them."

The way he attacked his glass of bourbon, though, I wasn't entirely sure he believed what he was telling me.

"John, you're leading up to something," I said. "What is it?"

"The Peterson murder case. Because Dawn Peterson was a wealthy woman, it became a media sensation. The supposition that a husband killed his wife for her money when she threatened to divorce him made for some lurid headlines and sound bites. Yet despite the overwhelming negative publicity, I managed to get the man acquitted. Mostly that was because the Ramsey County Attorney was unable to produce a body or any physical evidence to prove that a crime had actually taken place, much less that Clark Peterson had committed it. Marianne Haukass, you know her?"

"We've had our moments."

"I don't know what it is with some prosecutors. They stop being lawyers and become...They all think they're going to become governor. Marianne had no case. It should never have gone to trial. She paraded witness after witness in front of the jury, each one claiming that the marriage was on the rocks and that Dawn had made an appointment with an attorney to discuss a possible divorce. She put Dawn's mother on the stand. The woman testifying that Dawn had called her the evening before she disappeared to tell her that she knew Clark was sleeping with one of her friends. Only the mother couldn't provide a name or any other specifics."

"Was Peterson sleeping with one of Dawn's friends?" I asked.

"Probably. The point is, though, Marianne couldn't offer an iota of tangible evidence to prove that Peterson murdered his wife and disposed of her body. Which, of course, is exactly what he did."

I took a deep breath, leaned back against the sofa, and closed my eyes. When I opened them again, Kaushal was staring at his empty glass.

"He told me," he said. "Peterson told me that he murdered Dawn. He told me exactly where he hid her body. As far as I know, it's still there. That's what was in the notes that the hacker stole."

"Shit."

Kaushal had been correct. I suddenly wanted to drink the bourbon very much. I took a long pull of it. He refilled both of our glasses.

"When I first spoke to Peterson, he was very evasive," Kaushal said. "He refused to answer my questions directly. I explained that I was like a priest. Nothing he said to me would ever leave the confessional. A few days later, after he became more comfortable, he told me what he had done and where he had hidden the body."

"How did he manage it without leaving any physical evidence?" I asked.

"I didn't ask. I didn't want to know. It wouldn't have…Knowing the details wouldn't have helped me defend him."

"Is this why you took Freddie and me off the case?"

"I didn't want you to find the body."

"Would I have?"

"I couldn't take the chance. You're pretty resourceful. Taylor, my brain just started screaming at me to tell someone, anyone. Tell the police. Tell the prosecutor. Tell Dawn's family and help relieve their suffering. If you were a normal person, that's what you would do. Simple morality would demand it. It would be your duty as a human being. But a lawyer…

"As a society, we want clients who are accused of crimes to communicate fully and openly with their counsel. So we set up rules by which the lawyer is obligated to keep everything the client says confidential. Otherwise, if a lawyer were to go running off to the authorities every time a client admitted to a crime, then all of a sudden the lawyer would become an agent of the state, a member of the police department and the prosecutor's office. He would essentially be helping to convict the client. You need to ask, what is the higher moral good? I'm content that I did the right thing, Taylor. I would do the same thing again. Only if it gets out, if NIMN uploads my notes..."

He drank some more bourbon while I finished his thought.

"What happened to Frank Armani and Francis Belge will happen to you," I said. "Only worse. With today's social media and the twenty-four-hour news cycle, it will be much, much worse."

"I'm no hero, Taylor. I'm not looking to martyr myself for the Fifth and Sixth Amendments. It's taken me a long time to get where I am today."

"Where are you today?"

"I'm recognized as one of the best attorneys in Minnesota. I have a highly successful practice. I employ five lawyers."

"Certainly sounds successful."

"I don't want to lose it."

"I don't blame you."

"What would you have done, Taylor? Tell me. If it was you?"

"I'm not as honorable as you are, John. I'm not as law-abiding. I probably would have made an anonymous phone call."

Kaushal shook his head sadly. "No. You can't. If you're not willing to go all in, you shouldn't be sitting at the table."

We drank some more.

"What about Peterson?" I asked. "If the notes get out—"

"The court will still consider it privileged information. As such, it's inadmissible. Even if it becomes common knowledge, it can't be used against him. In any case, he's protected by the double jeopardy clause. I refused to allow him to take the witness stand and tell the jury he was innocent when I knew he wasn't, so he can't be tried for perjury, either."

"He wins anyway?"

Kaushal's cell phone rang. He answered, listened, and said, "I'll be right there." As he rose from his chair, he added, "You can ask him yourself."

Kaushal left the office. I stood and waited. A minute later, he returned. Behind him was a tall, good-looking middle-aged man with sunglasses perched on top of his head and a smile that suggested he knew exactly which Scotch to order in a high-class saloon.

"Clark Peterson," Kaushal said, "this is Taylor."

Peterson offered his hand, and I shook it even as my own brain screamed, Are you fucking kidding me?

"Taylor," he said. "John-Boy told me about you. You're trying to help us with our little problem. I hope you can. There's a possibility I could lose a lot of money because of this."

"In what way?"

"Dawn's family filed a wrongful death suit against me in civil court. The estate has been frozen until this matter is dealt with. If the jury finds against me, I'll lose all the money I inherited when she died. A tidy sum, if I do say so myself."

I pivoted toward Kaushal.

"Are you defending him?" I asked.

He shook his head.

"He can't," Peterson said. "Isn't that right, John? See, they couldn't make me take the stand in my criminal case. In the civil case, though, I'll be deposed and called to testify whether I like it or not. When I swear that I didn't have anything to do with the disappearance of my wife, I'll be lying. As an attorney sworn to uphold the law, John-Boy can't be part of that. He'd be suborning perjury. Isn't that right? So I had to hire a different attorney to rep me, one that doesn't know that I—"

"Clark," Kaushal said.

"I thought you said that anything I tell Taylor in your office is protected by attorney-client privilege."

"He doesn't need to know everything."

68

You got that right, I told myself.

"Anyway," Peterson said, "even though my confession can't be used against me in civil court, a sneaky lawyer might find a way to use it to impeach my testimony."

"Unlikely," Kaushal said.

"Yeah, well, I'd just as soon not take the chance. Besides, if everyone knows what really happened, and they will with the media the way it is, c'mon. You know it's going to be tough for me to get a fair trial."

Peterson smiled some more. Actually, he hadn't stopped smiling since he entered the office. For a moment, he made me feel the way that Kaushal said he felt when Peterson had confessed his crimes to him. I wanted to call the cops, call the prosecutor, call his wife's family—I wanted to burn the sonuvabitch to the ground. Yet I was trapped. Just like Kaushal.

"Is that bourbon?" Peterson asked.

Kaushal got him a glass.

"Ice?"

Kaushal left his office. I presumed the suite had an employee break room with a freezer, because he returned a few minutes later with a bowl full of cubes.

"What do you say, Taylor?" Peterson asked. "Ice or no ice?"

"It depends on how fast you want to get drunk," I told him.

Peterson dropped three cubes in his glass and filled it an inch high with alcohol. I kept drinking mine straight.

"I've been drinking only in moderation ever since Dawn disappeared," he said. "Cheers."

He sat on the sofa next to me. Kaushal resumed his perch on the chair opposite.

"John tells me that his wasn't the only law firm that's been hacked," Peterson said.

"There have been others," I said. "Right now we're trying to determine if there's a connection."

"Anything so far?"

"Let's talk about your enemies."

Peterson thought that was awfully funny.

"All five and a half million of them? The Minnesota media had me convicted of killing Dawn long before my trial even took place. When I was declared not guilty, all that meant to people was that I got away with murder. Should I tell you how shitty my marriage was, Taylor?"

"No."

"I didn't think so. No one wants to hear about my problems. I can't even get a librarian to talk to me, much less the kid at the coffeehouse down the street. Once my legal problems are behind me, I'll probably move. What do you think of New Orleans?"

"I've never been there."

"I hear it has a pretty wide-open lifestyle."

We talked some more. I was shocked at how forthcoming Peterson was. Kaushal would glower with warning whenever the conversation veered toward his wife, yet beyond that he was happy to answer my questions. I thought it must be a social media thing. Average people have become so accustomed to answering any number of personal inquiries on Facebook and Twitter and God knows where else that now we're nearly incapable of telling people to mind their own damned business. It seems these days virtually anyone will reveal virtually anything about themselves once they're convinced that the questions and answers are purposeless. Which is one reason why identity thieves have it so easy.

Eventually I asked, "What do you know about the Guernsey family?"

The question seemed to surprise Peterson.

"Nothing," he said. "The Guernseys? Nothing at all. We didn't associate even during the best of times. I mean, here's us." Peterson held his hand palm down in front of his face. "Here's them." He moved his hand far above his head. "I think Dawn might have known the younger brother and sister, though. In school, I think. She was in the same class as—was it him or her? I don't remember."

"Kurtis and Melissa?"

"One of them. Like I said, though, I never met either. Does it matter?"

"Hell if I know."

It went on like that until the ice melted in Peterson's glass. He behaved very pleasantly. If he hadn't been a stone-cold killer, I probably would have liked him.

After a while the conversation ground to a halt. Everyone stood up. Kaushal thanked Peterson for dropping by. They shook hands. I gave Peterson a business card and the same spiel as everyone else—*if you should think of something...*He shook my hand, too.

"I hope you can help us out," he said. "It'll save us a lot of trouble all around."

"I'll do what I can," I told him.

"Good man."

With a smile and a wave, he was gone. I finished my drink and set the empty glass on the table.

"What do you think?" Kaushal asked.

"I think he's going to do well in his civil case."

"Probably. Goddammit, Taylor. I want so much to—is it possible for a knot to get any tighter than this?"

"I'm reminded of a line from *The Godfather,* the second one—*It's the life we've chosen.*"

"It is kind of exciting, isn't it?"

The remark surprised me. The alarm must have shown on my face.

"Like you said," Kaushal told me. "We could've done something else for a living."

"If a man can't enjoy himself he might as well go out and get a real job," I said. But I didn't mean it. At least, I didn't think I did.

I shook Kaushal's hand.

"I'll be in touch," I said.

71

I headed for the door but stopped before I reached it.

"Just out of curiosity, whatever happened to Robert Garrow?" I asked.

"He was convicted and sent to prison for twenty-five years to life. Four years later, he escaped, leaving behind a hit list that included the names of Armani and Belge. Something else. During Garrow's trial, Armani's teenage daughter came to the courthouse to see her father. Garrow said to her, 'Nice to see you again, Dorina.' Since Dorina had never met the man and Armani never spoke of her, it became apparent to Armani that Garrow must have been stalking her before he was arrested. Because of that, Armani disclosed to the police information that Garrow had given him in confidence that led them to a field where Garrow was hiding. He was shot and killed when he refused to surrender."

"So Armani maintained his client's confidentiality until his own family was threatened," I said.

Kaushal raised his glass to me.

"Nothing is ever completely black and white, Taylor," he said. "Not even the letter of the law."

Dr. Alexandra Campbell didn't look like a tenured professor in the Department of Horticultural Science at the University of Minnesota with a PhD in agronomy and plant genetics. When she opened her front door, appearing before me in a tight Golden Gophers T-shirt and shorts, her auburn hair tied back, she reminded me of a phys-ed teacher who did her own gardening.

"Hey," she said. "I didn't expect to see you tonight." Alex opened the door wide to let me pass inside. "I'm glad you're here, though."

The way she hugged and kissed me, I believed her.

Alex went to the sofa and sat, curling her bare legs beneath her. She took the tie from her hair and shook her head so that

that it fell loose. She looked up at me with soft little-girl eyes and spoke in a soft little-girl voice. "I'm sorry, Mr. Man. I don't have the money to pay my rent this month."

I smiled at her; of course I did. The simple truth was she pleased me. Hell, she delighted me. I never grew tired of watching her, of playing with her. Yet I didn't love her, and I don't think she loved me. I wasn't even sure the word appeared in either of our vocabularies. I had believed in it once, believed in love everlasting. Only a drunk driver put an end to that when he ran a red light and killed my wife and daughter. I didn't become a cynic about it, though, until an attorney named Cynthia Grey stomped on my heart with remarkable thoroughness. As for Alex, sex to her seemed to be a purely natural urge that demanded satisfaction. She felt the urge quite often. This didn't make her a bad person in my eyes. Far from it. I just didn't think love was part of the equation.

"Alex, can we pretend to be ourselves tonight?" I asked.

The smile left her mouth, but not her brown eyes.

"What's the fun in that?" she asked.

"It's been one of those days," I told her.

She unfolded her legs and tapped the cushion next to her. I sat.

"What happened?" she asked.

"Sadly, I'm not allowed to tell you. I wish I could. Then you'd be as appalled by humanity as I am."

"That bad, huh?"

"It isn't that people do crazy things, it's just that sometimes they do them for reasons that seem so sane that instead of being outraged you come away feeling, I don't know. Confused, I guess. I'm a little confused. Nearly every person I spoke with today is a rat. Most of them are my clients. Some are my friends."

"*There isn't anyone you couldn't learn to love once you've heard their story.* Fred Rogers said that. You know, *Mr. Rogers' Neighborhood?*"

"Should you love them, though? That's the question. I make no claims to virtue, God knows, yet these guys have offended even my tenuous sense of right and wrong. Alex, all defendants lie in court. They're criminals, after all. All lawyers are taught, are trained, to take advantage of loopholes, to pat and prod and squeeze and manipulate the system to benefit their clients. I know that. Everybody knows that, understands that. How many years has *Law and Order* been on TV, for God's sake? But to actually see it up close and personal—it's just so depressing."

"*I love mankind. It's people I can't stand.* Charles Schulz wrote that."

"You're quite the quote machine tonight, aren't you?"

"I don't know what you want me to tell you, Holland. You can't give me specifics about your case, I appreciate that. But it means I can't really advise you. I'm not sure you're looking for advice, anyway. Are you?"

"Not really. I just wanted to vent. Usually you call me Taylor, like everyone else except my mom."

"Right now you seem more like a Holland."

She rested her hand on my thigh and began to stroke me ever so gently through the material of my Dockers. The air suddenly felt alive.

"You're welcome to jump up and down and wave your arms," Alex told me. "I can take it. You'd be astonished by the hue and cry around Alderman Hall when midterm grades come out."

"What do you tell your irate students when they go off on you?"

"I tell them you get what you deserve."

"If only that were true."

"Oh, it's true. Sooner or later we all get what's coming to us. It's spelled K-A-R-M-A. But it's pronounced 'Screw you.'"

"I like that philosophy."

"Well, then…"

I stood abruptly, placed my hands on my hips, and looked down at her.

"What's this about you not being able to pay your rent?" I asked.

CHAPTER SEVEN

For the second consecutive day, Freddie beat me into the office. I said, "Are you going for a personal record?" He didn't know what I was talking about, and I didn't feel like explaining. I went to the coffeemaker instead and brewed a cup.

"You look like shit," he said.

"Between John Kaushal's bourbon and Alex Campbell's imagination, with any luck I'll be dead by noon."

Freddie smiled at the mention of Alexandra's name.

"The professor teachin' the old dog new tricks, is she?" he asked.

"Shut up, Freddie."

"Touchy."

I sat behind my desk. Freddie sat behind his, his fingers locked behind his head.

"Where are we?" I asked.

"The Fredericks part of Fredericks and Taylor is doin' good. I'm not so sure about the Taylor part."

"Are we all caught up with our other clients?"

"Close. What about the lawyers?"

I told him.

"Man." He made the word sound like it had multiple syllables.

"I've only spoken to three of them so far," I said. "God knows what the others have to say."

Freddie placed an index finger against his cheek.

"The fact that all three cases somehow involve the Guernsey family makes me go 'Hmm,'" he said.

"I don't know. The hacker works for them in Helin's divorce case, but he works against them in Puchner's class action suit. As for Kaushal's murder, all it proves is that rich people sometimes are acquainted with other rich people."

"At least it gives us a place to start."

"I suppose."

I sipped my coffee without appreciating it. Freddie watched me do it.

"What's your story t'day, Taylor?" he asked. "Feelin' sorry for yourself or somethin'?"

"There's a guy out there who killed his wife and stashed her body, and he not only got away with it, he's gonna profit big-time."

"You sound like this is somethin' new, guys gettin' away with shit. It happens every day. You and me know that. Man, what we do for a living, sometimes we help."

"I know, I know. It's just that when I woke up this morning my first thought was—do we really want to catch this guy? The hacker, I mean. Do we really want to stop him?"

"The way I look at it—we've talked about this before. The way I look at it, we're workin' for the lawyers, not their clients, you know? I don't care all that much for Puchner. Man's kind of a dick. But the others—Helin, Scott Mickelson, Doug Jernigan, Kaushal. If the hacker's shit hits the fan, they're the ones gonna get fucked up. I like those guys. They're good customers. So, yeah, let's get this asshole. What? We gotta talk about it?"

"You're the one who said we shouldn't have taken the money."

"I never said that. I just asked what we were willin' to do t' earn it."

"It's still a good question."

"Yeah, well, while you're ponderin', Mickelson said he can

meet with you at ten this mornin'.'"

Freddie held up a pink slip of paper taken from the pad we use to jot down phone messages, $9.49 for two dozen at OfficeMax. I crossed the office and snatched it from his fingers.

"Have you talked to Sara?" I asked.

"She said she'll bop in later this mornin'. Or maybe Steve. You never know with them. Do you really think our clients are surveilling us?"

"Someone is."

"O'Neill wouldn't give 'em up?"

"He's not afraid of me."

"I shoulda talked to 'im."

"Yeah, you're a bad man."

"Naw, I'm not. I got the rep, though, and sometimes that's enough. What's the plan?"

"I'll keep on the lawyers. Once you're caught up with our other clients, why don't you go ahead and cross-index the five cases, where were they tried, who were the prosecutors, the judges, the bailiffs, I don't know what else. Might be the hacker is someone in the legal system that's witnessed so much bullshit he finally snapped. It could happen, right?"

"I'm surprised it doesn't happen all the time. My thing, though—I still think it's about blackmail. If not, why hasn't NIMN uploaded all those documents by now?"

"Authentication. They're trying to verify that the documents are legit."

"In that case, time's a-wastin'."

Associates and Kaushal consisted of six attorneys with a single office in downtown St. Paul, and yet if it wasn't the best-known law firm in Minnesota, it was in the top three. Hannum, Hillsman, and Byers employed over 250 attorneys with offices in eleven locations in the United States, Canada, Great Britain, and China, but I doubted one person in a hundred had ever heard of it. It made me wonder if that was on purpose.

Its Minneapolis headquarters was actually located in Plymouth, about thirteen miles west of the city. I arrived ten minutes early and waited twenty-five minutes before Mickelson would see me.

A young woman who wore her dress the way tomatoes wear their skin led me to his office. She noticed my eyes occasionally drifting to her backside as we walked, yet she didn't seem to mind. She announced my name when we entered the office, but not the names of the three people who were waiting for me. That was left to Mickelson. Introductions were made and hands were shaken. The four of us sat in a circle around a low glass coffee table not unlike the one in John Kaushal's office, and I wondered if lawyers all shopped at the same furniture store.

Mickelson was on my right, Mary Feeney, the mayor of the City of Minneapolis, was on my left, and across from me was Bryan Daggett. All I was told about him was that he represented Ryan-Reed Inc.

The woman found a chair outside the circle, crossed her slender legs, and began recording every word that was spoken in a green steno book. I kept glancing at her. There was nothing sexual about it, though. The woman wasn't *that* pretty. It was because she gave me an idea that made me go "Hmm."

"We are greatly distressed by the events that have transpired," Feeney said.

"I don't blame you, Madam Mayor, Ms. Mayor—how should I address you?"

"Mary is fine. As I was saying, if certain documents were made public, the consequences would be quite embarrassing."

"Yes," Daggett said. "Very much so."

He was looking directly at Mickelson when he spoke, and it occurred to me that Ryan-Reed would not hesitate for a moment to sue its own law firm in retaliation for failing to secure the firm's private data. Mickelson, though, didn't seem to mind the stare or the veiled threat.

"Have you made any progress?" he asked me.

"We've identified a number of possibilities that seem promising."

"I know poli-speak when I hear it," Feeney said. "Are you telling us the truth or just blowing smoke?"

"I'm telling you the truth, Madam—Mary. We do have a few ideas that we're pursuing. The problem is time. If my partner is right and this is all part of an elaborate extortion scheme, good. We can deal with that one way or another. If, however, the hacker keeps his promise to upload the material on NIMN...I've been checking the website every couple of hours."

"I've been doing it every ten minutes."

"Tell us what you know," Daggett said.

"I will," I said. "First, though, tell me what you know."

"You have the facts."

"I want to hear the story. In your own words. My experience, how you say something is almost as important as what you say."

The way they squirmed in their chairs, neither the mayor nor Daggett seemed comfortable with that idea. Mickelson, on the other hand, spoke right up.

"Are you familiar with the Supreme Court decision that vacated the conviction of former Virginia governor Bob McDonnell?" he asked.

"No."

"McDonnell was originally convicted of federal corruption charges. It was proved that he accepted a hundred and seventy-five thousand dollars' worth of goods, including a Rolex watch, and over twenty thousand dollars' worth of designer clothes for his wife from a supporter who ran a company that manufactured nutritional supplements. In exchange, he texted an aide and told him to make sure that the supporter got the meetings he wanted with certain state officials.

"The court ruled, however, that the Virginia jury was wrong to think that McDonnell's actions counted as official corruption.

Instead, it said, to prove bribery there must be an official act that involved the formal exercise of governmental power. Setting up a meeting with regulators, telling a government worker to listen to the supporter, issuing a directive that says the supporter should be assisted in every way, none of these things are official acts. According to the court, it's merely access. That's why the charges against Mayor Feeney were dropped."

"Okay," I said.

"Taylor, should I explain to you the nature of politics in America?" Feeney asked.

"If you like."

"Everyone wants access. Everyone wants to be heard. Conscientious public officials arrange meetings for constituents all the time so that they can be heard. We contact other officials on their behalf. We include them in events. That's part of our job. Should I ignore even the most commonplace requests for assistance, should I blow off citizens with legitimate concerns, simply because they might have donated money to my campaign? Of course not.

"I personally believe that business is overregulated. I believe if we want to grow the economy, we must get government off the backs of business owners. That's the platform I ran on. Ryan-Reed agreed with me and donated two hundred and fifty thousand dollars to my election. I won, by a seven-point margin, I might add. Afterward, Ryan-Reed contacted my office and asked to discuss the possibility of building a new plant on the North Side. Should I have refused to take the meeting?

"It's routine political courtesy, Taylor. It's part of the everyday functioning of elected officials. What I'm doing is allowing citizens to participate in the democratic process. So what if Ryan-Reed helped pay for my daughter's wedding reception or gave me the use of a Lexus convertible? So what if they provided me with a fifty-thousand-dollar no-interest loan?"

"If you want government to listen to you, you have to pay

up," Daggett said. "That's what the Supreme Court ruled."

"Are you sure that's really what it had in mind?" I asked.

"The federal prosecutor claimed my actions were improperly influenced by Ryan-Reed," Feeney said. "But she couldn't prove there was a direct exchange of an official act for money. That's why the charges were dropped. From the outset, I strongly asserted my innocence before God. I swore that I did not betray the sacred trust bestowed on me by the citizens of Minneapolis. I was right to do so."

"Why, then, is everyone worried about our hacker?" I asked.

Mickelson eventually ended the long pause that followed my question.

"The mayor likes to make to-do lists," he said. "She writes down items of importance, tracks their progress, and checks them off when completed."

"So does my mother."

"Did your mother ever begin proceedings to evict sixty-two at-risk families from their low-income housing so that Ryan-Reed could build a plant at a location with easy access to the freeway? Did she do it on the same morning that fifty thousand dollars was deposited in her private account?"

"The plant would bring much-needed jobs and tax revenue to the city," the mayor said.

"Whose side are you on, anyway?" Daggett asked.

"Don't mind me," Mickelson said. "I'm just playing devil's advocate."

I was shocked, not by the idea that the mayor of the City of Minneapolis would take a bribe. C'mon. It's politics in America. I was surprised that she put it in writing. I said so.

"I like to keep track of things," Feeney said.

"How many deals like this are you involved in, that you need written notes to keep track?"

"That's an insulting question," Daggett said. "I demand that you apologize to the mayor. Apologize, I say."

"What are you going to do?" I asked. "Challenge me to a

duel?"

"Taylor," Mickelson said. "Cut it out."

"How many people knew about this?" I asked.

"The plans for Ryan-Reed to expand to the North Side or my notes?" the mayor asked.

"Both?"

"The plans were common knowledge in my office. Certainly once we began evictions from public housing and eminent domain proceedings they became well known. The media covered it extensively. As for my practice of note keeping, it was never something I talked about, just did. People who knew me might have been aware I kept them, but they weren't available to anyone else. No one read them but me. The federal prosecutor was unaware that they even existed, and once we learned she was snooping around, I destroyed them."

Meaning it wasn't one of her people who ratted her out, I told myself. If so, they wouldn't have waited until now. They would have done it when the prosecutor first began asking questions.

"What about your people?" I asked Daggett.

"Expanding our operation was not a secret by any means," Daggett said. "It was discussed at our shareholders meeting. As for the details, I expect that most of the people in our corporate offices knew at least bits and pieces of what we were attempting to accomplish. Plus there were architects and construction firms involved, and lenders."

"Was Minnesota River State Bank one of them?"

"I believe so, yes. Is that significant?"

"I couldn't say. It's a name that keeps popping up."

"We weren't trying to be secretive," Daggett said. "We weren't deceiving anyone. Why would we? We did nothing wrong. This is simply how business works."

"Apparently the federal prosecutor disagreed."

"She's incapable of seeing the big picture," Feeney said. "Making sure that Ryan-Reed remains in Minneapolis is for the common good of our citizens. Does she think that having them move to St. Paul—or Wisconsin, for God's sake—is a more desirable outcome?"

"None of this is important," Mickelson said. "What's important, Taylor, is that the mayor's notes might prove to a jury that the quid pro quo relationship that the Supreme Court believes is essential to proving official corruption existed between her and Ryan-Reed."

"Nonsense," Feeney said.

"Even if it doesn't, this affair will not survive the smell test. The mayor's deal with Ryan-Reed will probably collapse. The possibility of her remaining in office past her current term is problematic at best. That's assuming she's not impeached."

"Scott," Feeney said. She was clearly shocked by Mickelson's assessment of her situation.

"These notes must not, cannot be revealed," he added. "Do you understand, Taylor?"

"Perfectly," I said. "But if they were destroyed…"

"The content of the notes—and thus the fact they were kept in the first place—was on the server the hacker hacked."

"How did that happen?"

Mickelson's eyes flickered onto the young woman sitting outside of the circle and flicked back.

Daggett was staring at Mickelson again when he said, "There is much at stake."

"For me, too," Mickelson said.

"On advice of counsel, we have not intervened. That might change."

Mickelson didn't respond to Daggett's warning.

"Personally, I think this is all much ado about nothing," Feeney said. "I'm innocent."

"That's the spirit," I said.

CHAPTER EIGHT

Neither Daggett nor Mickelson appreciated my cavalier attitude, but that was okay. The idea of getting fired from the case didn't bother me a bit.

I told everyone I'd be in touch and left Mickelson's office. The young woman in the tight dress escorted me to the lobby. The idea that had formed when she first opened her steno book came back to me.

I asked, "Do you make the record at all of Mickelson's meetings?"

She smiled slightly. I think she was impressed that I knew the technical term for what court reporters and legal stenographers do.

"It depends," she said. "Sometimes Mr. Mickelson wants a record but not a recording."

"No stenograph machine?"

She smiled at that, too.

"Again, it depends on the meeting. If we're taking a deposition we'll use a stenograph as well as digital recording equipment. I can type three hundred and ten words a minute with a ninety-eight percent accuracy rate."

"Were you making the record at the meeting when the mayor first told Mickelson about her notes?"

"Uh-huh. I remember because it was after the federal prosecutor filed charges, and Mr. Mickelson was angry that she didn't tell him about the notes way before that." Her voice dropped three octaves. "It was my record that was stolen."

"Who did you tell about it?"

The woman stopped in her tracks and turned to face me.

"What?"

"Who did—?"

"No one. Never. Mr. Taylor, maintaining a client's confidentiality and security is everything. That's why we're all so upset that we were hacked. I used to be a court reporter, and I was taught that I'm not just making the record, I'm the guardian of the record. What happens in a deposition room stays in the deposition room. Always and forever."

"You never tell stories? You never tell friends about some of the funny things you've seen and heard?"

"No."

"I'm not saying you identify specific cases, or even use real names, just say things like, I don't know, 'This silly woman charged with bribery, she put it in writing, do you believe that?'"

The woman hesitated before answering. Her eyes looked away and then found mine again.

"No," she said.

"Miss—I don't even know your name."

"It's April Herron."

"See, I didn't need to know your name. I don't want to know your name. I'm certainly not going to talk to your boss about any of this. I just want to know who you told."

"No one."

"Okay. I just hope you remember that I gave you a chance to cooperate when everything starts going south."

"Wait. Are you saying I'm in trouble?"

It was a trick that I learned on the job and tried to perfect after I went private. Give suspects something to worry about and then wait for them to come to you.

"Forget I said anything."

86

I started moving down the corridor. April skipped in front of me and said, "This way." She kept looking back at me, though, and I could see the muscles in her face working as we walked. She stopped again and pivoted toward me.

"Wait," April said. "You work for Mr. Mickelson, too."

"Yes, I do."

"So the same rules of confidentiality apply to you that apply to me."

"Of course."

She hesitated for a moment and said, "Mr. Mickelson doesn't need to know this, does he?"

"I promise."

"I told a joke, just like you said, during happy hour with my friends, people I used to work with when I was a court reporter."

"Other court reporters?"

"Uh-huh. I said almost what you said, that this woman kept a detailed record of her crimes, including times and dates, and one of my friends who knew the people I work with, she said, 'Do you mean the mayor?' And I said, 'I'm not naming any names.' My friends and I, we never name names."

"Who were you talking to?"

"I don't want to get anyone in trouble."

"Neither do I."

April looked up and down the corridor to make sure no one was watching, then recited two names.

I thanked her.

She walked me to the lobby. At the door she leaned in close.

"Please," April said.

"I promise," I said again. "This will never come back on you."

From the look on her face, I don't think she believed me.

There was a three-story parking ramp adjacent to the building that housed the Hannum, Hillsman, and Byers law offices. My car was parked on the first floor in a slot reserved for visitors. My cell phone rang as I climbed in. The caller ID recognized Clinton Siegle.

"Mr. Siegle," I said.

"Taylor, Mr. Taylor, you said to call."

"What is it?"

"I'm being watched."

"By whom?"

"I don't know, but I saw a man sitting in his car a few houses down from mine this morning when I was walking my dog. Later, I noticed he was still there. And now it's past noon. He's been there for at least five hours. Maybe I'm being paranoid, but after talking to you yesterday..."

"Mr. Siegle, can you describe the man?"

He did better than that. He gave me the make and model of the car and its license plate number.

"Mr. Siegle," I said, "I assure you that you're in no danger. I'll be there in a few minutes. Just relax, okay?"

"If you say so."

I ended the conversation and called Freddie.

"My man," he said.

"Busy?" I asked.

"I can spare a few minutes."

I found Walter O'Neill's car exactly where Clinton Siegle said it would be. It was a pleasant September afternoon, and the driver's-side window had been rolled down. O'Neill was leaning against it, his elbow propped on the frame. The passenger-side window, however, was rolled up. It had that new-glass sparkle. I was almost sorry when I used the sharp end of my penlight to shatter it all to hell the same way I did the day before. Once again, O'Neill was startled enough to hit his head on the roof of the car.

"Goddammit, Taylor," he said. "What the fuck's your story?"

Because he was preoccupied with me, O'Neill didn't see Freddie until he placed both hands against the driver's door and leaned in.

"Hey, Walter," he said. "Long time no see."

Once again, O'Neill was flustered.

"Shit, Freddie," he said.

"Shit, Freddie? What kinda greeting is that? Taylor, see how the man says hello? I haven't seen the fucker in six months. Longer even."

"Possibly he's ill at ease."

"Can't figure why, racist piece of garbage like 'im usin' his badge to whoop on the brothers and sisters. 'Course, he ain't got a badge no more. Do you?"

"C'mon, you two," O'Neill said. "What gives?"

"You wouldn't answer my man Taylor's questions yesterday. I thought you might answer mine."

"We're all professionals here. You know I'm not going to give up my client."

"Is that right?"

O'Neill smiled, an odd thing to do, I thought, considering the circumstances.

"Word is you've mellowed since you married that Japanese girl and had a son," he said.

"She's fucking Chinese, asshole."

O'Neill stopped smiling.

"No disrespect," he said.

"No disrespect? What the fuck, you insult my woman—"

Freddie tried to yank the car door open. O'Neill grabbed the handle and pulled back to keep it closed. At the same time, he reached under his jacket with his free hand. Freddie and I saw it at the same time, both of us tensing up and trying to hide it from the other. We've both been threatened, beat up, and shot at and pretended it was just part of the job, like rush hour traffic, even made jokes about it from time to time. That didn't mean we liked it. At least I didn't. I was never sure about Freddie.

"Don't do it, Walter," I said. "Don't even think about it."

"Go 'head," Freddie said. "Give me a reason to cave your fuckin' head in."

Walter's hand came out from under his jacket. It was empty. Freddie stopped trying to open the door, but Walter didn't stop trying to keep it closed. He looked at me over his shoulder.

"I don't know what you two hope to accomplish," he said.

Clinton Siegle must have seen us from his window. He stepped out of his house and stood on the sidewalk watching us. I waved him over.

"Mr. Siegle," I said, "do you know this man?"

Siegle bent down to look at Walter through the driver's-side window. "Never in my life," he said.

"His name is Walter O'Neill, disgraced ex-cop trying to make it as a private investigator."

"Fuck you," O'Neill said.

"He's been conducting surveillance on you for at least two days. He followed me yesterday because he was surprised to see you speaking to another PI. Tell us, Walter"—I liked using his first name—"did you tap Mr. Siegle's phone, too? Are you monitoring his email?"

"Like you two would never do anything like that."

"We'd never get caught at it," Freddie said.

"Are you working for Standout?" Siegle asked. "Are you? Tell them I never violated the severance agreement. I've never told anyone about the memo I sent."

O'Neill grinned. "You just told me," he said.

Siegle stepped back from the car. He looked first at me, then Freddie, as if he wanted us to explain to him if he was in trouble or not.

"Do you have your cell phone?" I asked.

Siegle nodded.

"Call 911," I said.

"Goddammit, Taylor," O'Neill said.

"Call 911."

Siegle retrieved his cell from his pocket, connected the proper dots to give him access, and inputted the correct digits. I made a gimme gesture with my fingers, and he handed me the phone just as the operator identified herself.

"My name is Clinton Siegle," I said, adding his address. "I don't know if this is an emergency or not, but there's this man who's been sitting in a car near my house for the past two days watching the kids in the neighborhood."

"You bastard," O'Neill said.

I told the operator the make and model of O'Neill's car along with his license plate number. The operator said they would send a patrol car to investigate. By then O'Neill had flipped us the bird, started his car, and drove off. I ended the call and handed the cell back to Siegle.

"What just happened?" he wanted to know.

"The cops will come by," I said. "Tell them exactly what I just told the 911 operator. Okay?"

"All right."

"One of three things is going to happen. Either your enemies are going to end their surveillance of you, or they're going to send someone else, or O'Neill will be back with a different vehicle and resume his surveillance from a less aggressive location. In any case, keep a sharp eye out. If he or anyone else should come knocking on your door, call us immediately."

"But why?" he asked. "Why is Standout doing this?"

"Remember the girl with the tats who asked you about the memo?"

"Yes."

"You thought at first she was with Standout Investments trying to determine if you were keeping quiet about it, and then later you decided she was with the plaintiffs that sued the company—that she approached you to confirm the existence of the memo."

"That's right."

"We think that might happen again, that someone will ask you to authenticate the memo, confirm that it exists and that you wrote it. Standout wants to know who. That's my guess."

"Why? The lawsuit was settled."

"There's a chance it might be reopened."

"Am I in danger because of this?"

"No, I don't think so," I said. But then I tell people a lot of things that aren't necessarily true.

Freddie and I walked to our cars.

"So," Freddie said. "We're not being followed."

"That doesn't mean we shouldn't pretend that we are. What did Sara say?"

"She'll be in later this afternoon. Said she was having her hair done."

"That gir..." I was about to say "girl." Freddie smiled at my confusion.

"I know what you mean," he said.

"Have you been cross-indexing the five cases?"

"I was just starting when you called."

I gave him the names of April Herron and her two friends.

"Watch for 'em while you're doing your thing," I said.

"What do you know, an honest-to-God clue."

"Treat it gently. It's the only one we have so far."

"How did you make the leap from O'Neill to Standout Investments?"

"Who else would be interested in Siegle?"

"I'm asking because you told me that Cormac Puchner hasn't informed them about the hack yet. Said the man hoping the problem will go away so he won't have to."

"Apparently he has his eye on a corner office."

"Sounds like him," Freddie said. "Only if he didn't tell 'em, how does Standout know there's a problem? How'd they know to hire O'Neill?"

"Someone must have told them."

"But who?"

"I don't know."

"What about the Guernseys?"

"What about them?"

"Are they involved in Scott Mickelson's bribery case?"

"You tell me. You're the one with all the computer skills."

We both stopped and stared at the empty space where Walter O'Neill's car had been parked. There was a thin pile of broken safety glass along the curb.

"Do you get the feeling there's somethin' they're not telling us?" Freddie asked.

"Always."

CHAPTER NINE

Jernigan sucked on the stem of his dormant pipe. Apparently he didn't smoke it, even in his own office. I settled into a comfortable chair in front of his desk. He pointed the pipe at me and said, "I have never lost an acquaintance rape trial."

"You must be very proud."

"Are you giving me attitude, Taylor?"

"Sorry. It's starting to be a long day."

"Most rape cases, like this one, never even go to trial," Jernigan said. "Do you know why? Skeptical jurors. For a long time I would challenge women thirty-five and older during voir dire. I would try to keep them off the jury because research claimed they're the toughest demographic when it comes to rape cases. That was until I learned that they're also the toughest judges of victims. They'll tell themselves that if the victim was drunk or even had just a little bit to drink, she was putting herself out there. They'll tell themselves that she was at least partially responsible for what happened to her. Now I just load up the jury with older white women."

"There's nothing that justifies a rape," I said. "Ever."

"Did I say there was? I'm just trying to tell you that rape cases are notoriously difficult to try because the burden of proof is on the victim. If there's a lot of physical evidence, if she was beaten, if there are rope burns on her wrists, if the assailant gained entry through a broken window, that makes it easier. If there isn't any evidence of coercion..."

"Coercion?"

"For lack of a better word. If there's no physical evidence, then the defendant can argue that the sex was consensual, which is what we do most of the time. We make it an issue of he said, she said."

"From my own experience as a cop, the vast majority of women who report a rape are telling the truth," I said. "Something like ninety-eight percent."

"There's that two percent, though, isn't there? It's called reasonable doubt, Taylor. Now, that percentage might shrink a bit if there's an outcry witness. Someone who saw the victim soon after the incident who can testify that the victim was hysterical, shaking, trembling, and afraid. Someone who can not only tell a jury what the victim told her but can testify to the victim's demeanor, how she was behaving."

"Did you have that here?"

"Yes. The victim's sister. But the fact that she was related to the victim actually worked against her credibility, and having to testify that she had been drinking, too—she wasn't doing her sister any favors. Juries are judgmental as hell, Taylor. Besides, I was perfectly willing to have a forensic evaluator take the stand and testify that, from a clinical perspective, if a woman perceives that she was victimized she may develop symptoms similar to those that occur when someone is actually victimized."

"What?"

"If a woman perceives that she was powerless to stop a sexual encounter, then she may develop symptoms that mirror those exhibited by women who were actually raped, such as feelings of betrayal, fear, embarrassment, guilt, or depression and even symptoms of post-traumatic stress disorder. We argue that she might mistakenly believe she was raped even though the sexual encounter was consensual."

"How do you get away with this bullshit?"

"I told you, Taylor—juries. Lawyers are blamed for every little thing people believe is wrong with the judicial system, but really it's the juries. They're the ones who make the decisions, not us."

"What happened in this case?"

"Rachel Rozanski and Todd Kendrick were students at the same college. They met at a party just before Valentine's Day. They had a few drinks. They danced. Todd walked Rachel to her off-campus apartment, which she shared with her younger sister. They kissed at the door. Rachel said Todd forced her inside. Todd said Rachel invited him inside. Rachel insisted that she was an unwilling participant. Todd referred to Rachel's alleged resistance as mild protestations that he interpreted as a sign that Rachel was excited about the sexual contact. He claimed that they actually kissed good-bye before he left.

"Something else. Rachel also said that when Todd forced her facedown on the living room sofa, she heard the metallic sound that a camera makes when it's taking photos. She said Todd took selfies as he raped her. She said she saw a cell phone. Later, she said that she didn't actually see the phone, only heard it. The police confiscated Todd's cell phone. No photos. Nor did it make a clicking sound when taking pics.

"Taylor, you know how this works as well as I do. The victim will meet with uniformed police officers; she'll undergo a forensic sexual-violence exam in a hospital; she'll talk to detectives, county prosecutors, a judge, the defense attorney, and eventually a jury. By the time her case is heard, usually eight to fourteen months after reporting the incident, she'll have told her story from beginning to end a dozen times or more. If there's any discrepancy at all in any of the accounts, an attorney like me will clobber her on the witness stand.

"Now add that to the fact that Todd was squeaky clean. No convictions, no arrests, not even a parking ticket. A good student from a moneyed family who's never had a whiff of scandal attached to his name. Even his ex-girlfriends liked him.

All said, if you were the Ramsey County attorney, would you have prosecuted?"

"How moneyed?" I asked.

"Enough to afford me."

"Any relationship to the Guernsey family?"

"None that I'm aware of. Why do you ask?"

"Just a thought. Going back to the camera. There was one, wasn't there?"

"How did you know?"

"The hacker stole something that was incriminating."

"Pics that were sent to me," Jernigan said.

"Sent to you?"

"Todd didn't use his cell phone. He used a camera that belonged to a friend of his. Tiny sucker. Fits in the palm of your hand. He returned the camera to his friend as soon as he realized that not taking no for an answer might get him into trouble."

"He gave incriminating evidence to his friend?"

"Dumb, right? The so-called friend emailed sample pics to me after he learned that I had been retained by the family."

"Why?"

"Why d'you think?"

"How much did you pay?"

"I didn't pay anything." Jernigan pointed his pipe at me for emphasis. "No. Hell no. I didn't even think about it. Accepting evidence of a crime, and then what? No, no, Taylor. I would have been aiding and abetting an offender after the fact. I would have been guilty of a criminal offense. That wasn't going to happen."

"What did you do?"

"I replied to the email. I told Todd's friend to go to the police. I told him to take the camera, the SD card, and anything else he might have to the Ramsey County Attorney's Office. I told him not to contact me again. Afterward, I deleted his email and the attachment. Unfortunately, it's been explained to me that deleting something from your computer doesn't actually delete it. It was those pics that the hacker recovered."

"Deleting the pics, isn't that the same as destroying evidence?"

"I didn't actually see what was in the attachment. I never opened it. Only an idiot opens attachments sent by unknown sources. So I didn't actually *know* if it was evidence or not. At least, that's my story. Prove it isn't true."

"At the same time, though, you never told the prosecutor that Rachel was telling the truth, that her rapist did take selfies while he assaulted her?"

"Now we're in that gray area of an attorney's obligation to the court and his obligation to his client."

"Did Todd's friend try to blackmail the family after you turned him down?"

"I don't know. We never discussed the matter."

"The pics never surfaced, though."

"No."

"How convenient."

"Wasn't it?"

"Charges against Todd were dropped."

"Insufficient evidence."

"If the pics surface now—"

"He'd be recharged."

"Wouldn't anything stolen from your office still be considered privileged information and inadmissible in court?"

"It wasn't privileged. Todd didn't tell me about the pics or email them to me, a second party did."

"Do Todd and his family know that you've been hacked?"

"I told them immediately."

"What about the friend?"

"What about him?"

"Do you want to tell me who he is?"

"He can't be our hacker, Taylor. If NIMN uploads the pics, he'll lose his leverage. There'd be no reason to pay him."

"Is the family still paying him?"

"I don't know."

"He might have bragged it up some," I said. "Might have told a friend what a clever SOB he is. Someone might have overheard him."

"His name is James Cowgill."

Like most people his age, James Cowgill had Facebook, Instagram, Twitter, Snapchat, and Pinterest accounts. I knew what he looked like in about 10 seconds and where he lived in about 130 more. I knocked on the door to his apartment located just off Snelling Avenue in the Hamline-Midway neighborhood of St. Paul, so-called because it included Hamline University and was halfway between the downtowns of St. Paul and Minneapolis. No one answered, so I retreated to my Camry. I drove to a side street and settled in an unobtrusive spot that provided clean sight lines to both the building's front door and rear parking lot.

I waited.

I turned on my radio and hit the SCAN button. The receiver searched through God knows how many stations playing every kind of music you can imagine plus news and a lot of talk. Twice. I lingered on a jazz station for a song and then a golden oldies station. I used to like that kind of music, but somewhere along the line I lost interest. I don't know why. I turned off the radio.

And waited some more.

Traffic was very heavy on Snelling Avenue. There were a lot of pedestrians and bicyclists on the street and sidewalks, too, mostly college-age kids, mostly coming and going from the coffeehouse on the corner. A couple of times I thought I had my man only to discover that I was mistaken.

About an hour passed before I saw him. Cowgill had actually ridden his ten-speed Raleigh within inches of my parked car, slowed at the intersection of the four-lane street, and started riding through it toward the apartment building.

He managed to get halfway across before the car hit him.

It was a blue car, bigger than most, and caught him square.

There was no squeal of brakes and no lurch right or left to indicate that the driver was trying to miss his mark.

Rider and bicycle flew up and out of one lane of traffic and into the next.

A Ford F-150 hit its brakes, but not fast enough, crushing first the bike and then the rider under the front tires.

The blue car kept going.

That's when I screwed up.

I jumped out of my own vehicle and ran toward the accident scene.

I stopped before I reached it.

You should be chasing the blue car, I told myself.

Only by then it was too late.

I closed my eyes and tried to conjure the vehicle in my mind's eye.

It was hopeless.

I had been so startled by the hit-and-run that I didn't take note of the vehicle's make or model. I hadn't seen the license plate number and for the life of me couldn't picture the driver.

At least a dozen people had gathered around the pickup and the bicycle and Cowgill's body. The way it was twisted, I couldn't imagine that he had survived.

The sound of multiple sirens grew louder.

I told myself that I should hang around and tell the police that I saw everything, which amounted to nothing. I would also have to explain what I was doing there, though, which would have put my clients at risk.

I returned to my Camry and pounded the steering wheel.

An ambulance and two police cruisers arrived.

I hammered the steering wheel some more.

"Goddammit," I shouted.

I started up the car and drove off.

I was back in my apartment, puttering in the kitchen, when my cell rang. By then the local evening news had been on for twenty minutes.

"This is Taylor," I said.

"It's on TV." Jernigan was shouting so loud I decided he didn't need a phone. He could have just opened a window in his house and I would have heard him plain. "Did you see it? It's on TV."

"What?"

"Are you being coy with me, Taylor?"

My response was to sigh heavily into the phone transmitter.

"Please tell me that you didn't do it," Jernigan said.

"Are you asking me that?"

Jernigan took a deep breath and exhaled slowly as if he were attempting to calm himself. "I'm sorry," he said. "Of course you didn't. But Jesus Christ."

"I saw it, though." I explained, adding, "I couldn't identify the driver or his vehicle. I missed the opportunity."

"Cowgill was murdered."

"Not necessarily. Hitting a guy with a car, that's amateur night. You're sure to hurt the guy, but there's no guarantee that you'll kill him. It could have been a real hit-and-run accident."

"That's what the TV is calling it, but what do you think? I mean, what do you think the chances are?"

"All things considered? About three percent."

"Cowgill was murdered," Jernigan repeated.

"Do you know anyone who might have had a motive?"

"This is terrible."

"I'm sure Cowgill thinks so."

"I don't know what to do about this, Taylor. If I go to the police with what I know, I'd be compromising my client. If I...Actually, I do know what to do. Nothing. I'm not going to do anything."

"The police will investigate the crime as a hit-and-run."

"I know."

"There's a lot they can do. Interview witnesses at the scene to see if anyone can ID the make, model, color of the vehicle. They'll examine the footage taken from traffic cameras if there are any in the area, plus cameras in businesses that face the street. They'll gather forensic evidence, glass from headlights or the windshield, paint, metal parts, brush marks and impressions left on clothing—anything that'll help them get a profile of the car. They'll check with local auto body shops, too. Honestly, though, the last year I worked as an investigator for the St. Paul Police Department, we had three hundred and thirty-something hit-and-runs. I think we solved six, and that was always because someone came forward."

"I know what you're thinking."

"The detectives won't even think to check Cowgill's bank account or ask who his friends were. Unless somebody—"

"No, Taylor. The answer is no. You're a licensed private investigator in the state of Minnesota. You have legal obligations to keep quiet as well."

"Are you sure about that, Doug?"

"I'm sure. Listen, I don't like this any more than you do, but we have to think about the higher moral good."

John Kaushal used the same phrase yesterday, I told myself. *The higher moral good.* He was protecting a murderer. Jernigan was protecting a rapist. What's the greater good in that?

"Is that your professional advice?" I asked.

"It is."

"Maybe I'll call a lawyer and get a second opinion."

"Taylor, please. Don't do anything we'll both regret."

Someone knocked on my door, so I opened it. Amanda Wedemeyer walked in. She was wearing blue shorts and a red jersey with blue piping and her name stitched across the back. She made a big production out of crumbling to the floor and lying flat, her arms and legs outstretched as if she were making snow angels. She sighed like a martyr giving up her last breath.

"Hi, Mandy," I said.

I left the door open and walked back to the kitchen area. Ogilvy bounded into the room, paused when he saw the girl, sniffed around her as if looking for food, and nudged her arm when he didn't find any.

"Tough day?" I asked.

"First game of the season. We got—what's the word Coach used? Oh yeah. Crushed. Hear that, Ogilvy? Crushed."

The rabbit kept ramming Amanda's hand until she started to stroke his fur. The gesture made her smile. Apparently some rabbits know just what to do.

"Crushed happens," I said. "Although not always in the first game."

"Did you play soccer when you were a kid?"

"No."

"It's hard."

"A lot of running around, anyway."

"You played baseball, though," she reminded me.

"A little."

"Do you still play?"

"Just the game of life."

A voice came from the hallway.

"How's that going?" Claire asked.

"Sometimes I get crushed."

Claire stepped into my apartment and looked down at Mandy. She was also wearing blue shorts and a red jersey with blue piping and her name stitched on the back. A soccer mom, although I had to admit the uniform looked damn good on her. I wondered if Alex Campbell had a soccer uniform.

Claire poked her daughter with the toe of her sneaker.

"Are we going to go through this every time you lose?" she

asked.

"I hate getting beat," Amanda said.

"Why do we play the game?"

"We play to win," I said.

Both mother and daughter looked at me.

"I wasn't supposed to answer that question, was I?"

"We play the game for the fun of it," Claire said.

"Yeah, that too."

Amanda didn't remind me of my daughter; she was at least seven years older than Jenny when she died. Claire didn't remind me of Laura, either. They were very different people, different ages, different looks, with different perspectives on life. So it wasn't like I saw them as replacements for the family that I had loved and lost. Yet having them around often made me ponder what my life would have been like if John Brown hadn't run that damned red light. Would I be happy? Probably happier than I was, anyway, I told myself.

Brown was murdered shortly after he was released from prison, and the cops, including some very old friends, were convinced that I did it right up until the true killer was revealed. Make no mistake. It didn't break my heart to see the sonuva-bitch in the ground, and I felt no animosity toward his killer. His death didn't make me feel any better, though. Now I wondered what was going to happen when Claire's ex-husband was released from prison. He was doing time for embezzling to support a gambling addiction. Would it change the dynamic between the girls and me? Claire had divorced him, true. He was still Amanda's old man, though, and would probably be allowed visitation and at least some parental rights.

"You okay?" Claire asked.

"Hmm? Sure. I just have a lot of things on my mind."

Claire nudged her daughter again.

"Homework," she said.

"Haven't I suffered enough?"

"Go."

Amanda crawled off the floor and retreated to the apartment across the landing as if she were marching off to meet a firing squad, and not too bravely. Claire stayed behind.

"Are you okay?" she asked again.

"I'm fine."

"You don't look it."

"I'm okay, Claire. Trust me."

"You know, when I was going through all that upheaval with my ex-husband, I never spoke to anyone about it. Not when he bankrupted us, not even after our home was foreclosed on. Who could I tell? It felt so much like—like losing. I realize now that not having someone to talk to only made it worse."

"I understand."

"Do you understand that you can always talk to me?"

I don't know why I did it, but I wrapped my arms around her and hugged so tightly that I heard her groan. I didn't let her go, though, and she didn't push me away.

Eventually I released her and stepped back.

"I'm sorry," I said.

"No. It was nice."

"Good night, Claire."

"I should come back later."

"You shouldn't. You should leave. Go away, Claire, before I forget how much I like you, how much I like you both."

She did, but as she was closing my door she said, "You and I are going to have a long, long conversation, and soon."

The door closed, and I said, "Why? So you can learn for yourself how much of a soulless jerk I am?"

CHAPTER TEN

I was sitting behind my desk with my feet up and staring at the bulletin board. Freddie had put up a dozen more index cards and joined them to the appropriate cases with red yarn: O'NEILL to SIEGLE to CLASS ACTION, APRIL HERRON to BRIBE, and her friends ANDROMEDA WOHLWORTH to MURDER and LISA KING to RAPE. Also linked to RAPE was a card labeled KENDRICK. A second card tagged COWGILL was attached to RAPE, and another card marked HIT-RUN/MURDER? was attached to that. The stretch of yarn meant to join HACKER to NIMN was still left undone.

"It's starting to get complicated," I said.

"You think? You're gonna love this, then."

Freddie put up another, much larger card labeled GUERN-SEY FINANCIAL INC. Under GUERNSEY, he had written RPG HOLDING CO. Under that he wrote MINNESOTA RIVER STATE BANK, RYAN-REED INC., and STANDOUT WORLDWIDE INVESTMENTS. Under that he wrote the names ROBERT PAUL, ROBERT JR., KURTIS and MELISSA GUERNSEY. He then proceeded to run yarn from that card to DIVORCE, BRIBE, CLASS ACTION, and MURDER.

"I hit the computer last night like you said," Freddie said. "What I discovered, Ryan-Reed, according to the *Minneapolis/St. Paul Business Journal,* was purchased two years ago by an investment group called Pretty Good Pie Investments."

"Pretty Good Pie?"

"I have no idea where the name came from," Freddie said. "All I know, the *Kansas City Business Journal* wrote that Pretty Good Pie is a wholly-owned subsidiary of MNPride Inc. *Inc.* magazine had a piece that claimed MNPride was owned by RPG Holding Company. Wikipedia claims that, wait a sec..."

Freddie retreated to his desk and found a sheet of paper. He brought it to me.

"Read it for yourself."

I obliged.

RPG Holding Company ("RPG" or Robert Paul Guernsey) is a Minnesota-based company owned by Guernsey Financial Inc. and headquartered in Golden Valley, Minnesota. RPG is the largest family-owned financial and bank holding company in Minnesota, with assets over $1.4 billion. It operates 11 businesses including Minnesota River State Bank, Ryan-Reed Inc., Standout Investments Worldwide LLC, Oak Tree Stores, and Minneapolis-Butler. RPG is 86% owned by Robert Paul Guernsey Sr., Robert Guernsey Jr., Kurtis Guernsey, and Melissa Guernsey.

"Good job, Freddie," I said.

"Now we know the Guernseys are involved in four out of the five cases. Not sure it amounts to anything, though."

He returned to his desk and sat in his chair. There was a coffee mug in front of him. Several times he brought it to his lips but did not drink. Eventually he set the mug on his desk.

"What I can't figure out is what's taking so long," he said.

"What do you mean?"

"NIMN. The hacker said he was going to send the intel he swiped to NIMN. Shoulda taken 'im all of ten seconds. Only it's been six days since the lawyers received the emails and nothin'. What's the holdup?"

"According to the website, NIMN makes sure to authenticate—"

"Six days? How much time does it take to authenticate a

selfie of some shithead raping a girl?"

"Most news organizations refuse to identify victims of sexual assault."

"NIMN isn't a newspaper. Besides, publish the pics and the punk goes to prison. Keep 'em quiet and he gets away with it. Which outcome do you think the victim would choose?"

I placed my index finger against my cheek.

"Hmm," I said.

"Hmm, hmm, what the fuck does hmm mean?"

"Maybe NIMN is letting the victim make that decision."

"Big of 'em if that was true."

"Maybe we should ask."

"In the meantime, what about the other shit?" Freddie asked.

"I don't know."

"I'm starting to think the hacker never sent the intel to NIMN, that he's sitting on it."

"That could be true, too, especially if it's extortion like you first thought. But man, you're right. It's been six days. What's he waiting on?"

"If it's a hacker for hire, maybe he's waiting to get paid," Freddie said.

"Unless he's already been paid."

"That requires explanation."

"Someone hires the hacker to get the goods on the Guernsey family's business dealings. The Guernseys hear about it and make him a better offer."

"Why the Guernsey family? Why not the lawyers?"

"If it were the lawyers, they wouldn't need us. As far as we know, the Guernseys have the most to lose and the most to pay."

"The Guernseys gain with DIVORCE, lose with CLASS ACTION, split with BRIBE, there's nothing connecting them to MURDER except a distant acquaintance, and nothing connecting them to RAPE at all. If Puchner and the others are telling the truth, they don't know about any of this yet."

"As far as we know."

Freddie began to chant "Thin, thin, thin, thin, thin," until he grew tired of the word.

"I'm open to suggestions," I told him.

He didn't have any. Instead, he stared out the window and I stared at the bulletin board.

"Steve said we're not being bugged," Freddie said. "Came in yesterday and swept the place, did I tell you? So there's that. Also, the software, whatever he put on our computers to catch the hacker if he tried to hack us—nothing."

"Any progress on locating the hacker?"

"He said if it was easy everyone would do it. I'm starting to worry about him, her. When it's Sara, she's all sunshine and lollipops. But Steve, he's all intense and, what's the word? Brusque?"

"They're probably having an identity crisis. I know I am."

"Oh yeah?"

"You met my father. He never wanted me to be a police officer, much less a private investigator. He wanted me to go into business like him, like my brother. I'm starting to wonder why I didn't."

"You know my mother. She wanted me to be an actor. Named me Sidney Poitier Fredericks like somehow that was goin' to get me a part in *Raisin in the Sun* or the lead in a remake of *Lilies of the Field*. 'Course, she coulda been onto somethin'. I'm prettier than he is."

"Yet here we are. What a great disappointment we must be to both of them."

"Speak for yourself, man. Ever since I made her a grandma, I've been the old woman's favorite child."

"All it would take is a couple of anonymous phone calls to the cops. I know I'd feel better. How 'bout you?"

"If it was just us, yeah, but it ain't just us. Is it?"

"No."

"It ain't sayin' much, Taylor, if I'm the responsible one in this here organization."

I laughed because I remembered when it was the other way 'round. But then Freddie married Echo, a Chinese woman with long, gleaming black hair, classical Asian features, and an aura of wicked sensuality that I had never, ever commented on for fear that Freddie would shoot me, and he would have; the man was very protective of his wife, and his son, too, for that matter. Now he was the one who took the time to reason it all out and I was the loose cannon.

"Okay, are we done hating our jobs?" I asked.

"Speak for yourself, partner."

"How 'bout this? You take the girls. Learn what's there, if anything. I'll concentrate on Todd Kendrick and James Cowgill, see where that takes me."

"What about the Guernseys?"

"That's one of the things we're trying to find out, isn't it? If this is really all about them?"

The Kingfield neighborhood in Minneapolis wasn't named after Martin Luther King Jr., despite the fact that there was a park that bore his name on its eastern border. It was actually named after Colonel William S. King, an ex-congressman who lived in the area and was active in the antislavery movement before the Civil War. Dana Kendrick lived on Wentworth Avenue, not far from the park. If you're known by the company you keep, that meant she was middle-class comfortable but had nowhere near the income level of the Guernsey family.

I knocked on her front door.

A lot of PIs like to flash gold coplike badges with the words DETECTIVE, PRIVATE DETECTIVE, or PRIVATE INVESTI-GATOR embossed on them because they think it makes them seem more impressive. Freddie and I use simple ID cards that meet the demands of the Private Detective Board—name, name of our company, address, our photographs and physical description, date issued and date expired. But the IDs also have the word PRIVATE printed across the top and INVESTIGA-TOR across the bottom, both in block letters reversed out of black, along with the seal of the State of Minnesota in glorious color. Very cool, if I do say so myself, although Dana didn't seem to think so.

I flashed the ID at her when she opened the door. I carry it in a thin wallet so I can flick it open the way they do in 1950s cop movies. She glanced at it, at me, back at the ID. She had a small tight mouth that looked as if it had forgotten how to smile, if it ever knew. She asked "What do you want?"

"Mrs. Kendrick—"

"Ms."

"Ms. Kendrick, my name's Taylor," I said. "I'm working with Douglas Jernigan."

"That doesn't answer my question. What do you want?"

"We're both trying to help your son."

"This is all supposed to be over and done with. What that woman said about Todd, there was no evidence that he ever did those things. The prosecutor said so."

"I know."

"Todd didn't do anything wrong. How many times do we have to say it?"

Dana couldn't have been more than forty, hardly old enough to have a son in his third year of college, with a delicate loveliness to her face and bright color to her eyes. The beauty had been overlaid with a hard veneer, though, a coat of shellac worn thin and marred by years of abuse. I doubted that anyone had ever called her a girl, even when she was a girl.

"If I could have a moment of your time," I said.

She sighed dramatically. It happened often when I was a cop and only to a lesser extent as a PI, how people became suspicious in my presence, how my questions sometimes triggered a fight-or-flight reflex. It meant I needed to find a way around the defensive posturing if I was going to get anywhere. I was wondering how to play Dana when she opened the door wide and told me to step inside. I did. She closed the door as if she were afraid it wouldn't shut unless she put some muscle into it.

She led me deeper into the house until we were standing in a living room. It was comfortable but not lavish, with traditional furniture purchased to accentuate the fireplace, hardwood floors, and arched entryways. There were photographs on the mantel and tables, all of the same subject—Todd Kendrick, I assumed—marking his passage from infancy to college age. He was good-looking, but the wicked often are. Along with the photographs, there were several original paintings mounted on the walls, all of them unframed, the kind you buy directly from the painter. I squinted to read the signature of the one nearest me.

"That's mine," Dana said.

"Very nice."

"The others were painted by friends and acquaintances."

"You're an artist."

"Starving artist. I sell at the festivals and craft shows."

"Hardly starving," I said.

Dana glanced at her surroundings as if she were suddenly embarrassed. I couldn't imagine why.

"Since you're here," she said, "you can explain it to me. Mr. Jernigan called the other day, but he didn't make any sense. He said someone stole some photographs off of his computer. He said the photos were of my son and that woman. There are no photos, though. There couldn't be. My son didn't do anything."

"Where is your son?"

"At college."

"Where?"

"In Texas. Todd had to go all the way to Texas to go to school because of what that woman said. He couldn't stay at home anymore. The school sent him a letter. It said they were refusing him continued admission because he had violated the school's code of conduct. Todd didn't even know the school had a code of conduct, and even if it did, he didn't do anything wrong, so why can't he go back there? It's just what that woman said."

"Ma'am—"

"Todd is in Texas and I'm all alone. It was just the two of us all these years. He didn't know his father. I barely knew him. Now he's gone and I'm alone."

"I'm sorry."

"Don't tell me you're sorry. You don't care. Why would you? Just ask your questions and go."

"Did you know James Cowgill?" I asked.

"Jim? He's a friend of Todd's. Was a friend. From school. They hung around together. At least...They stopped speaking when the woman said those things. Most of his friends stopped talking to him after she said those things, another reason why he went to Texas."

"We believe that your son took selfies of himself and Rachel Rozanski on a camera owned by Cowgill."

"No. It's just what the woman said."

"We believe he returned the camera to Cowgill and that Cowgill then used the selfies to blackmail him."

"It's not true. It can't be true. If it were true, why didn't it come out during the investigation?"

"We don't know."

"You say blackmail. For what? Todd doesn't have any money."

"Did you pay Cowgill?"

For a moment she resembled the terrified bank tellers in all those black-and-white heist movies. Her voice became small.

"What are you saying?" it asked.

Tears began flowing from Dana's eyes, slowly at first, gently, and then with greater persistence. As I watched them stain her cheeks, watched as she tried to brush them away with her knuckles, it occurred to me that she had believed every word her son told her, that Dana hadn't known about the photos until Jernigan called, and now she didn't know how to react to the news. Photos meant her son was guilty. Photos meant he was a rapist.

The tears also told me that whoever Cowgill found to pay for the photos, it wasn't her.

"Why are you here?" Dana said. "Why can't you just leave us alone?"

"Believe it or not, I'm on your side."

"I don't believe it."

"Ms. Kendrick, Cowgill was killed yesterday. The police think it was an accident."

"Killed?"

"Jernigan and I aren't so sure."

"Killed?" she repeated. "I'm so sorry to hear that. Jim wasn't a bad boy." Her head came up. The tears had stopped. "I don't think."

"We're afraid if the police investigate, one thing might lead to another."

I paused for a few beats while she considered my meaning. The way she stared at me, I guessed she had come to a conclusion. To be sure, I asked, "Do you understand?"

"Yes."

"Can you think of anyone who might have bought Cowgill's photographs?"

"I think you should leave."

"Ms. Kendrick—"

"Now."

I knew arguing wouldn't do any good, so I apologized for causing her such grief and excused myself. Dana saw me to the door and stood watch as I crossed the street to my car. She didn't close the door until I was halfway down the street.

Kingfield was an old-fashioned neighborhood, one that still had alleys. I drove slowly down Dana's alley until I reached her garage. The garage was old, pre-fifties or at least built before people knew better than to put windows in them. I got out of my car, went to the window, and cupped my hands against the glass. There was more than enough light to make out the red four-door Honda Civic, about three years old, parked inside.

I didn't press my finger against my cheek, but I hummed the word anyway—"Hmm."

It wasn't her car that ran down Cowgill. I didn't think it would be. A three-year-old Honda, though, a house in King-field, a son attending college out of state, no husband, her income apparently generated from selling paintings at art festivals? It all made me wonder—where did Dana get the money to pay for all this, much less the hourly rate of an attorney of Jernigan's stature?

"What do you mean where did she get the money?" Jernigan asked.

"How did she pay you?"

"By check."

"Personal check?"

"Yes, I think so."

"You don't know?"

"Jesus, Taylor. The firm sent her an invoice. She sent us a check. Do you want me to ask Accounting?"

"If it's not too much trouble."

"This better be important."

Jernigan put me on hold. The hold music was a poor instrumental version of "I Will Always Love You." I used to like that song. Now I hate it. There are a lot of things that I've grown to hate that hadn't bothered me before. I was forced to listen to it two and a half times before Jernigan rescued me.

"Personal checks written on her account at Minnesota River State Bank," he said. "Why is this a thing?"

"I've been to Dana Kendrick's house. I've seen her car. She

shouldn't be able to afford them. She shouldn't be able to afford you, Doug."

"What do you mean you've been to her house?"

"She sure as hell can't afford to pay blackmail."

He paused long enough for my point to sink in.

"Someone did," he said.

Jernigan and I argued after that about how far down this road I could go before I violated attorney-client confidentiality. It was decided not very far at all. He emphasized the fact that I was not to contact the St. Paul Police Department under any circumstances. He kept repeating it until I finally said, "You can trust me, Doug," meaning *I will not involve you in any of this.*

"I know I can," he replied, meaning *You had better not.*

Anne Scalasi gave me a little wave when she walked into the restaurant. She was dressed in a crisp white shirt and blue tie, blue skirt, and blue jacket, a gold badge glimmering off her left breast and a single gold star pinned to each shoulder as befitting an assistant chief of the St. Paul Police Department in command of Family and Sexual Violence, Property Crimes, Homicide and Robbery, Youth Services, Special Investigations, Gangs, Narcotics and Vice, and the Safe Streets Task Force. Everyone watched as she made her way to the table, but she was used to that, and not just because of the uniform.

I stood when she arrived, and we hugged each other. Feeling her body pressed against mine gave me a thrill of memory that I quickly beat down. We're friends, I told myself. Friends.

Anne sat. A waitress was by her side before she settled in.

"Coffee. Black," Anne said. The waitress looked my way. "I'm coming from a luncheon," Anne added. "Chicken. Everyone serves chicken. Anyway, I'm not hungry, but you go 'head and eat."

I pointed at the near-empty glass of bourbon in front of me and said, "Again."

The waitress departed.

"Drinking your lunch, are you?" Anne asked.

"I'll grab something on the way back to the office."

"How are you, Taylor? I haven't seen much of you since you decided to give me the cold shoulder."

"Is that what I did?"

"Wasn't it?"

"How's His Lordship these days?"

Anne frowned at the reference.

"Ashley Leighton Redman, the famed architect who was born in Des Moines but behaves like he's the Prince of Wales? Beijing, I think, building something for the Chinese. I haven't seen or spoken to him for nearly two weeks."

"Why are you still married?"

"I don't want to put the kids through another divorce."

"You'd think they'd be used to it by now."

"Funny."

The waitress returned with Anne's coffee and a fresh Maker's Mark on the rocks for me.

"We never had a chance, did we?" Anne asked.

"No. We were just pretending."

We had kept our distance for nearly twenty years. Anne was single when we first met, a schoolteacher engaged to a patrolman who rolled with the Midway Team, and I was newly married to Laura. Fourteen years passed. By then Anne was not only married, she had three kids. She was also enjoying a meteoric career. After being trained at Quantico and doing a stint with the Minnesota Bureau of Criminal Apprehension, she was made a lieutenant and put in command of the St. Paul homicide unit. I was her ace investigator, or so I thought of myself at the time. After Laura was killed, though, I was no longer sure why I was doing the job. Alcohol became an issue as well. I worked and I drank. That was my day. Every day.

To save myself, I resigned and went private. A short time later, Anne had divorced her husband, who had grown increasingly resentful of her with each passing promotion. Unfortunately, by then I was in a committed relationship with the attorney who would later crush my heart. When that relationship finally ended, Anne was married to His Lordship. Everyone knew the marriage was doomed to failure except Anne, of course. But she always was an optimist.

"I wasn't pretending," Anne said.

"A lot of people are lobbying to make you the first female police chief in the history of St. Paul. A lot of people are lobbying against it. What would have happened if you were caught sleeping with your ex-partner?"

"Nothing good, but don't tell me that's why you quit me."

"Don't tell me you haven't divorced because of the kids. They don't even live at home anymore."

"The youngest one does."

"Annie, I quit because I love you and always will. You're the best friend I'll ever have, and you deserve a helluva lot better than a guy who would sleep with another man's wife."

"If I wasn't married?"

"I expect you to call me the very minute your divorce is final. If you divorce."

"If? One day I expect to get a text from Singapore or some goddamn place telling me that His Lordship has found someone else. It would make my life so much simpler. Taylor, I have enemies on the city council. Men can carry on with impunity, but women? I've been fighting the double standard my entire life. I'm so tired of it. That's why I care about you so much, one of the reasons, anyway. You always treated me as an equal."

"Oh, honey. You're not my equal. You're my better."

Anne smiled at that.

"The best investigator I've ever known."

She smiled some more.

"All right, Taylor," she said. "I'm primed. Why did you call me?"

"There was a hit-and-run yesterday."

"In Hamline-Midway. I get eBriefs every morning."

"You should tell the detective in charge of the investigation to check the young man's bank accounts to see if he had come into any money starting around seven months ago." The time of the sexual assault, I thought, but didn't say.

"What reason would I have for telling him that?"

"Nostalgia."

"Excuse me?"

"Pat his shoulder and tell him that back in the day when you ran an investigation, you never left a single stone unturned."

"Uh-huh. Just how would he justify a search warrant?"

"He won't need to justify it. Murder victims have no presumption of privacy."

The mention of murder caused Anne's eyes to brighten, but then it always did. She had been trained at the FBI's National Center for the Analysis of Violent Crime to investigate mass murders and serial rape killings. She had been very good at it.

Anne took a long sip of coffee while I studied her. It was always a joy to watch her work out a problem; you could actually see her think.

"What would he find, I wonder?" she asked.

"I don't know, but I would sure like to."

CHAPTER ELEVEN

While I was pursuing the Cowgill angle, Freddie was busy interviewing the legal reporters. He started with Andromeda Wohlworth. The way he told it:

She was a pretty little thing, and young, wearing a wispy kind of dress like she pictured herself standing on a high bluff overlooking an ocean harbor, the wind blowing through her long hair and clothes while she waited for her man to come home from the sea. Yet when he found her she was sitting at a table and staring at her cardboard coffee cup, an expression of disillusionment on her face as if life had let her down. Her head came up when the door to the coffeehouse opened and she saw the handsome black man for the first time. "Is this him?" she wondered. "The man who sounded so desperate to meet me?" He walked toward her, moving deftly for a big man as he maneuvered around tables and chairs without once taking his eyes off of her. His smile was confident and sure. She could feel her heart pounding in her chest as he approached her...

"Really, Freddie?" I said. "Really?"

"Do you want to hear what happened or don't you?"

"Do you need to make it sound like you're reading a Julie Klassen novel?"

"I don't know who that is."

"Klassen. Local girl. Writes Regency romance novels."

"Whatever she does, that's fiction. This here's the truth."

"If you say so."

"Ms. Wohlworth?" His voice was a rich baritone and sent shivers up her spine.

"Yes," she said.

He reached for her hand. She gave it to him. It seemed so small in his.

"I'm Sidney Fredericks. Thank you so much for agreeing to meet me."

She smiled brightly. "The pleasure is mine," she said.

He gestured at the chair opposite her. "May I?" he asked.

"Of course."

He settled in, again without taking his eyes off of her. She found his gaze disconcerting. Nervous warmth started in her stomach and spread in both directions.

"Ms. Wohlworth," he said.

"Andromeda. My name is Andromeda."

"Andromeda. That's lovely. Named for the Greek princess or the constellation?"

"Both, I think. Although—" She pointed at the word a barista had scribbled on her coffee cup. "My friends call me Andi. I would like it if you called me Andi, too."

"You honor me."

"Oh, for God's sake," I said.

"It just kills you, doesn't it, that women find me more attractive."

"First off—no. Second, this isn't *Masterpiece Theatre*."

"I don't watch that."

"I don't believe you."

"You want me to tell the story or not?"

"Just get to the point, wouldja?"

"Am I in trouble, Mr. Fredericks?" she asked.

"Freddie."

"Freddie." She repeated the name like it was an invitation.

"No, no, you're not in trouble at all, of course not," the handsome black man assured her. "I'm here because we're hoping you can help us."

"You said on the phone that you're with the NCRA."

"NCRA?" I asked.

"Andi, you hold a Registered Professional Reporter Certificate issued by the National Court Reporters Association."

"Yes."

"You appreciate, then, that we're not only deeply involved in promoting the profession of the court reporter, we maintain a stringent code of ethics for our members. Chief among these, and I'm quoting now, 'preserve the confidentiality and ensure the security of information, oral or written, entrusted to the member by any of the parties in a proceeding.'"

Andi began to shift uncomfortably in her seat. "You don't think—" she began.

Freddie cut her off. "Andi, please. We came to you because your reputation is impeccable."

Andi liked hearing that, although up until that moment she didn't know she had a reputation—at least not as a court reporter.

"We're hoping you can assist us," Freddie quickly added.

"In what way?"

"We have heard rumors that some reporters have been a little too free with the information they hear at reported proceedings. If this is true, then we feel we must somehow not only remind our members of their obligations but also strengthen our certification requirements. The NCRA must guard against not only the fact but the appearance of impropriety."

"I appreciate that," Andi said. "I just don't know what I can do to help."

"We would like to understand how this information is getting out. Is it by design or simple carelessness? Do you have friends in the profession?"

"Yes, I do. Some from when I went to Anoka Technical College and others I met along the way."

"You meet with them? An attractive woman like you, you must go to parties."

Andi felt the warmth move up her throat to the face. She knew she was blushing. *"Parties,"* she said. *"Dinners. Just hanging out."*

"What have you seen? What have you heard?"

"I don't know what you mean."

"What do you and your friends talk about? Do you talk about your jobs?"

"All the time. Mostly, though, it's about the people we work with, judges, lawyers."

"Do you talk about the proceedings you record?"

"I don't."

"Of course not, but others?"

"Sometimes. We talk about the stories we hear."

"You repeat the stories?"

"We never name names." It was clear that Andi was now talking about herself. *"We never say what case it is, just sometimes things we find funny or odd."*

"One case in particular that we're aware of, a sexual assault in Hennepin County that didn't go to trial because of insufficient evidence. Something about photographs…"

"Selfies."

Andi's hand flew to her mouth as if she wished she could catch the word and put it back.

"Yes," Freddie said. *"Selfies. You heard that as well?"*

She nodded.

"Can you tell me the circumstances?"

Andi shook her head.

"I'm not interested in names, Andi. No one is going to be in trouble. We're only interested in fixing the problem, possibly

through the continuing education courses members must take to maintain their licensure."

"It was just an acquaintance, I don't remember her name, complaining that a rape victim claimed her attacker took pictures but no one would believe her. She wasn't talking about the case so much as the rape culture, the fact that no one seems willing to believe the victim."

Freddie reached across the table and took Andi's hand. He gave it a gentle squeeze.

"I understand," he said. "I'm upset about it, too."

Andi smiled in return. Maybe he does understand, she thought. He seems so compassionate.

"She said that, did she?" I asked.

"I could see it in her eyes."

"Uh-huh."

"Who else was there?" Freddie asked.

"What do you mean?"

"In the room with you."

"It was her and me and—we weren't in a room. We were in a car driving to a club that we like. Me, her, and another friend who was driving."

"So, no one could have overheard you."

"No."

"Did your friend repeat what she said to anyone else?"

"If she did, I wasn't there," Andi said. "And I know her. She wasn't an acquaintance like I said. She's my friend, and she's even more conscientious than I am. She's not one to spread rumors. It was just that one time because she was angry."

"You can see why revealing confidential information like that is unacceptable."

"I do."

"I want to thank you for your time."

"Is that all?"

"We're hardly conducting an inquisition, Andi. We're just

looking for ways to strengthen our certification process."
This time she squeezed Freddie's hand. "Must you leave so
soon?" Andi said
"There are important meetings I must attend."

"Important meetings?" I said.
"I'm married, remember? Otherwise..."
"Yeah, yeah, yeah."

Freddie rose from the table, much to Andi's obvious disap-
pointment. Almost as an afterthought he asked her, "Do you
know anything about computers?"
"Me? No. Why do you ask?"
"I tried to use my laptop before I came over. I think I caught
a virus."
"Oh, no."
"Do you know anyone who could help?"
"I really don't. Sorry. Although there's this place near where
I live that does computer repair."
"I'll figure it out. Good-bye, Andi."

"So what do you think?" Freddie asked me.
"The narrative voice sucks. Other than that—it doesn't look
too promising, does it?"
"No, but I went to see Lisa King just in case. Want me to tell
you about it?"
"Do I have time to get popcorn first?"

The first thing the receptionist saw when he stepped off the
elevator was a black man. Not a tall man, or a handsome man,
or a man wearing a tailored sports coat from Men's Wearhouse.
He was a black man, and his smile did nothing to dissuade her
anxiety as he approached. Not that she was a bigot; she had
voted for Barack Obama twice. She had been raised in Minne-
sota, which was only six percent African American, though.

Black people made her nervous.

"You knew what she was thinking?" I asked.

"Yes, Taylor. All I had to do was look in her eyes and I knew what she was thinking."

I didn't argue with him.

"May I help you?" She was speaking a little too loudly, but, she told herself, he didn't look like a client.

"I have an appointment to see Lisa King," Freddie said.

"Does she know you're coming?

"I have an appointment," he repeated.

"May I see your identification?"

Freddie gave her a good look at his ID. Her eyes went from the photograph printed there and back to his face. It was only then that she picked up a phone.

"Ms. King," she said, "an African American person named Sidney Fredericks to see you."

Words were exchanged.

"Are you sure?" the receptionist asked.

More words.

"As you wish."

The receptionist put down the phone.

"I'll escort you to her space," she said.

"You can never be too careful," Freddie said.

Her head snapped around so she could get a good look at him. Did he just call me a racist? she wondered. Well, I never.

She led him down one corridor and up another. They stopped at a closed door. The receptionist knocked, waited a couple of beats, and opened the door. A woman was inside seated in front of a stenograph machine. She was wearing headphones that she removed when the black man entered the office.

"Mr. Fredericks?" she asked.

"Ms. King?"

"Lisa." She extended her hand. Freddie shook it. "Thank

you, Agnes."

The receptionist looked from the black man to Lisa and back again. She stepped out of the office, started to close the door, thought better of it, and made a production out of making sure it was opened all the way.

"I'll be at my desk," she told the woman.

Lisa smiled and said thank you. Once the receptionist was out of earshot, she turned her smile to Freddie.

"I'm sorry," she said.

"For what?"

"Never mind. So, Mr. Fredericks—"

"Freddie."

"Freddie, what can I do for you?"

The black man gestured at the stenograph. "I hope I'm not interrupting anything important," he said.

"Just doing some transcriptions."

"I'm surprised at the size of your offices."

"The firm's been expanding," Lisa said. "It's owned and operated by a half-dozen court reporters. We're basically all partners offering"—she smiled as if she had written the speech herself—"cutting-edge reporting and legal services provided by trusted, vetted, and professional court reporters with over a century of combined experience."

"Cool."

"We also do closed captioning. You said on the phone that you were with Associates and Kaushal?"

"We're deeply concerned that confidential information concerning the Peterson murder trial might have been leaked to the public."

"I don't know why you came to me. I've never worked with Kaushal. I don't think any of my partners have, either, although if you put in a good word for us we'd appreciate it."

"You weren't involved in the case, but you know those who were."

She stared at the black man as if she were trying to read his mind.

"Mr. Fredericks—" she said.

"Freddie."

"Mr. Fredericks, I have always strived to maintain the highest standards of confidentiality in my profession. So have my partners. So have my colleagues outside these walls. Do you expect me to say otherwise?"

"No."

"Is there anything else?"

"Lisa, I don't know from court reporters or legal stenographers. I don't know what you guys talk about or don't talk about, and I don't really care one way or the other. But information has been leaked all over the damn place, not just about the Peterson case but several others as well, including one I know you did work, Rozanski-Kendrick in Hennepin County. We don't think there are any reporters involved directly. We do think that maybe things mighta been spoken outta turn that coulda been picked up by someone else. That's what we're interested in. The someone else. Cuz if this stuff does get out people are gonna go apeshit, and all this—" Freddie gestured at the walls. "If your integrity is questioned even a little bit, what's that gonna do to your business?"

"Is that a threat?"

"No, Lisa. That's just me beggin' ya to tell me if anything you and Andi Wohlworth and April Herron said to each other could have been overheard by someone else."

Lisa was obviously jolted by the names of her friends. She thought about it for what seemed like a long time before she answered.

"I assure you, Mr. Fredericks, that anything that might have passed innocently between us stayed between us."

Freddie thought that was a good answer, but not what he was hoping for. They spoke some more, but the answers never got any better.

"We should take their index cards off the board," Freddie said.

"They take depositions in divorce cases, don't they? I'd like to find out who worked with David Helin and Brooke St. Vincent before we decide."

"According to Puchner, the reason Standout Investments settled out of court was to avoid depositions, so..."

"There must be something else that connects these five cases," I said.

"Different courts, lawyers, and judges. One was federal, two were in Ramsey County, the others in Hennepin. Only two of the cases actually saw the inside of a courtroom. One went to jury and one ended up before the Court of Appeals. I don't know."

"Once you eliminate the impossible, whatever remains, no matter how—"

"Swear to God, Taylor, you quote Sherlock Holmes I'll smack you right in the mouth."

I might have finished the quote just to see if he was serious, only my ringing cell phone interrupted. Probably for the best.

I checked the caller ID.

"Mr. Siegle," I said.

"He's back. The man who was watching yesterday, who you chased away? He's back. He's sitting out there—wait. There's another car—another man. Dressed all in black. He's walking to the first man's car."

"Mr. Siegle."

"The second man is standing by the first man's car, and now—he's looking at me. He sees me standing at the window. Oh my God, he's coming toward the house."

"Call 911," I said.

"Taylor—"

"Hang up the phone. Call 911. I'll be there in a few minutes."

I hung up my own phone and headed for the door. Freddie followed close behind.

"What?" he said.

"Maybe nothing," I said.
Only I didn't believe it.

CHAPTER TWELVE

I drove recklessly. It didn't matter. It was rush hour in Minneapolis, and traffic moved at the breakneck speed of a glacier. It took us five minutes to get my Camry out of the parking lot, another ten to get on the freeway, another ten to get off the freeway in Richfield, and five more to reach Clinton Siegle's house. Thirty minutes all told. By then the place was swarming with members of the Minneapolis Police Department.

We parked and ran to the house. A cop stopped us before we reached the door.

"What happened?" I asked.

"None of your business."

Freddie and I both reached into our pockets. The officer dropped his hand to the butt of his Smith and Wesson M&P. Freddie brought his hands up and held them palms out in front of the officer, to prove that they were empty. I kept digging, found my ID, and flicked open my wallet to let the officer get a good look at it. He curled his fingers a couple of times while watching Freddie, and I rested the ID in his hand. He pointed the ID at Freddie, still gripping his duty weapon, waiting for a reason, any reason, to draw.

"You," he said.

"My identification is in my left inside coat pocket," Freddie told him.

"Hold your coat open; take it out slowly."

"Are you fucking kidding me?" I asked.

Freddie pulled the left side of his sports coat open with his left hand and slowly reached into the pocket with his right. "Now's not the time. Taylor," he said. Freddie retrieved his thin wallet and held it up with two fingers.

"Give it to me," the cop said.

Freddie did as he was told.

"You two wait here." The cop disappeared inside the house.

"Let me guess," Freddie said. "You're one of them thinks racism went away when Obama was elected president."

"No, but—"

"Look at the man they elected after. It only got worse, man. Much, much worse."

I didn't know what to say to that, so I didn't say anything.

It was growing dark, and the flashing red and blue lights of the police cars gave the neighborhood a weird sense of movement. Neighbors emerged from their homes and watched from their stoops, wondering what happened, wondering if it could happen to them. Yellow ribbon went up—POLICE LINE DO NOT CROSS. Officers and technicians came and went. What genuinely surprised me was the lack of media coverage—no trucks, no lights, no cameras, no reporters shoving microphones into our faces asking, "How do you feel?" Give it time, I thought.

An airliner passed overhead much too low for comfort. Neither Freddie nor I bothered to look at it. A few minutes later, the police officer exited the house, followed by a plainclothes detective. The detective returned our IDs. The cop stood close enough to listen to the conversation while pretending not to.

"Sergeant Nathan Vanak." I noticed the detective didn't show us his ID. "Explain yourselves, please."

"What do you mean?" Freddie asked.

"You're not a couple of buffs chasing calls on a police scanner. You're here for a reason. What is it?"

If you watch a lot of TV, movies, read the books, you might

come to the conclusion that police and private investigators don't get along—that they're always at loggerheads. That's not necessarily true. Most PIs used to be cops or worked in some other branch of law enforcement. That's where they received their training and the 6,000 hours of experience required before they can get a license. As a result, there's a kind of loose camaraderie between the two groups. I have many friends who carry badges, and, as unlikely as it might seem, so does Freddie. We mostly have a quid pro quo relationship. Help me out and I'll help you out when the situation allows. Except most of my friends were in St. Paul. I didn't know Sergeant Vanak.

"Can you tell us about Mr. Siegle?" I asked.

"He's dead."

"Ahh, Christ," Freddie said.

"Now, gentlemen, why don't you start talking to me?"

There were things I couldn't tell him, so I started with what I was sure he already knew.

"If you check the log on Mr. Siegle's cell phone, you'll know he called us," I said. "He told us that he was being watched. He told us that a man was walking toward his house. We told him to call 911. Did he?"

"Yes," Vanak said. "Just in time for the operator to hear the two shots that killed him."

"What about his wife? Her name's Linda."

"She wasn't home. Did Siegle identify his assailant?"

"No."

"Why was he being watched?"

"I'm not at liberty—"

It hit me. Freddie, too. We both turned and gazed down the street.

"Dammit," I said.

Another passenger plane passed over us. Vanak said something, but I couldn't hear him over the noise of the jet engines.

Freddie and I started moving in the direction of Walter O'Neill's car. It was parked on the far side of the street about four houses down.

"Dammit," I repeated.

I began moving quicker. The uniformed cop jumped in front of Freddie and blocked his path. His hand went to his Smith and Wesson again.

"Taylor?" Vanak asked. "What is it?"

By then I was in a dead run. Vanak was chasing. Neighbors watching us seemed alarmed. Some of them slipped inside their homes.

It took me only a few seconds to reach O'Neill's car, yet the effort caused me to gasp for breath. Either that or the shards of window glass on the pavement reflecting the streetlights that had come on. Vanak was right behind me. We stopped together.

O'Neill was slumped against the driver's door of his car, a bullet hole in his head.

I leaned down, my hands resting on my knees.

Freddie came up from behind us. I heard him chanting.

"Fuck fuck fuck fuck fuck…"

There are images cached in the back drawer of my memory like YouTube videos, ready to be played with HD clarity at the tap of a button. I knew the sight of Walter O'Neill's dead body, the spectacle of forensic pathologists and evidence techs examining every centimeter before transferring it to a black vinyl bag, would become one of them. What would be the trigger, though? Richfield? The sight of it, the mere mention of its name? Or would it be the roar of a jet engine like those that screamed past us with maddening frequency? The triggers for the other videos that haunted me…With Amy Lamb, a beautiful young woman I had failed to save, it was silk scarves. With Tom Storey, it was the sight of a black Ford Explorer, of all things.

I tried not to dwell on it. Instead, I listened intently to every word Sergeant Vanak had to say. The media had arrived in force by then. Four local stations were represented by TV vans with garish colors and huge logos. Their cameras were aimed at the house, though, and O'Neill's car, not at us.

"I don't suppose you're going to make a spontaneous confession," Vanak said. "I'd settle for an excited utterance, anything that can be used in court."

"Sorry," I said.

His partner came up. He had been interviewing Freddie on the other side of the street, Freddie leaning against a prowl car with arms folded across his chest while the first police officer we met stared at him intently.

"Black dude won't answer any questions with or without an attorney," the detective said. "He said he always leaves it to his partner to talk to the white man's police department."

Vanak's response surprised me. "Do you blame him?" he said.

The detective shrugged.

"Did you threaten him?" Vanak asked. "Tell him we'd bring him up before the Private Detective Board, get his ticket pulled?"

"He said, 'Good luck with that.'"

"That's what we like, a cooperative citizenry."

"What should we do?"

"That's a good question. Taylor, what should we do?"

"My hands are tied by the rules of attorney-client privilege," I said.

"Nice try. The rule doesn't apply to third-party consultants."

"It does if the communication between an attorney and his private investigator is for the express purpose of creating work product."

"I have two dead, Taylor, and you're arguing goddamn semantics?"

"You could call my employer, ask him to give me permission to answer your questions."

"Who would that be?"

I told him. "Although," I added, "Cormac Puchner went to Harvard Law School."

By the way he swore I figured Vanak knew exactly what that meant.

"'Course," I said, "there's another option."

"Yeah."

"Ask Mr. Siegle's wife, Linda, why he was fired from Standout Investments Worldwide."

Vanak started writing in his notebook. "Standout Investments?" he said.

"Ask her if she remembers a girl with tattoos who spoke to her husband at the Twin Cities Jazz Festival."

Vanak kept writing.

"Ask her if she knows what Siegle and I spoke about the other day."

Vanak looked up at me, pen poised over the notebook. He knew I was tap-dancing along a very fine line.

"Also, there's Walter O'Neill," I said. "He was a professional. A professional private investigator. Which meant he kept detailed notes about what he was doing for his clients, and since he no longer has a presumption of privacy…"

"It would be so much easier if you just answered my questions."

"If I could, I would. I used to work the job you have now in St. Paul about ten years ago. I know how pissed off you must be."

"Not as pissed off as I was five minutes ago."

"For what it's worth, I'm as upset by all of this as you are."

"Yeah, but you get the big bucks."

"Truthfully? I took home more money when I was with the cops. There were the benefits, too."

"I have your card, Taylor. When I call, you had better answer."

Freddie didn't want to go home just yet. Neither did I. Instead, we drove back to downtown Minneapolis. We didn't speak to each other except for a brief exchange as we left 35W for the

Eleventh Street exit.

"O'Neill was an asshole," Freddie said.

"Yes, he was."

"He was married, too, wasn't he?"

"Divorced."

"Kids?"

"Two."

Freddie nodded and said nothing more. I knew he wasn't thinking of them. He was thinking of his own wife and child.

I parked the car. We entered the Butler Square building and took an elevator to our floor. I unlocked the door to our office, opened it, and turned on the lights. The two of us stood there, looking around as if we had never seen the place before.

My cell phone rang. The caller ID listed Cormac Puchner.

"Goddammit, what do you want?" I said. Then I answered the phone. "Counselor."

"I just had a very frustrating conversation with a Minneapolis detective named Nathan Vanak. I'm thinking of filing a complaint against him."

"Okay."

"He said you gave him my name."

"Cormac—"

"What part of keeping this off the books don't you understand?"

"I didn't have a choice in the matter."

"Hell you didn't. You know what, never mind about that right now. That's not important. I can deal with the cops, but the detective, he told me that Clinton Siegle had been shot and killed. Is that true?"

"Why would a man lie about something like that?"

"I'm asking, Taylor."

"Yes. Siegle was murdered in his home early this evening. Along with a private investigator named Walter O'Neill. He might have been working for the Guernsey family. We don't know for sure."

"The Guernsey family? What the hell do they have to do with it?"

I made my way to my desk. Freddie opened the refrigerator and pulled out a couple of Grain Belt beers. He held one up for me, and I nodded. He opened the bottle and set it on my desk.

"What the fuck, Taylor?" Puchner said.

"What do you want to know, Cormac?"

"Everything."

I told him, including how the Guernseys were connected to four of the five cases. At the end of my briefing, I added—just to be safe—"Siegle told his wife, Linda, why he was fired by Standout and probably what he and I spoke about the other day. She'll tell Vanak; of course she will. Vanak will also take a hard look at O'Neill's notes. I didn't tell him what I was doing for you, but he knows his business. By this time tomorrow, he'll probably have it figured out."

"Just as long as it doesn't come from us, that's the main thing. It's not coming from us, is it?"

"Vanak asked you to give me permission to answer his questions, didn't he?"

"Yes."

"Well, then?"

"The answer is no."

"That's what I told him."

"Look, it's late. I'll talk to you tomorrow. All right?"

"Sure."

"Good night, Taylor."

Puchner hung up. I took a long pull of the Grain Belt, wishing it were something stronger.

Freddie moved to the bulletin board and pinned up another index card labeled MURDER and ran a length of red yarn to O'NEILL and SIEGLE.

"This helps Standout Investments, doesn't it, Siegle's killing."

"It removes the possibility of him authenticating the memo that was stolen, if that's what you mean."

He tapped the card labeled COWGILL.

"Blackmailer getting killed probably lessens the chance that the selfies the rapist took will see the light of day, too."

"Unless the cops uncover them. I kinda sorta dropped a hint to Annie Scalasi over lunch, today."

I thought Freddie might give me a lecture about breaking the rules, but he didn't. Instead, he drained his beer and stared at the bulletin board some more.

The phone rang again. My first impulse was to reach into the pocket where I carried my cell. Only this time it was our office landline that was ringing. The caller ID read ANONYMOUS, never a good sign. I answered the phone anyway.

"Fredericks and Taylor Private Investigations."

A voice I didn't recognize said, "Which one are you?"

"Taylor."

"You were there tonight. You know what can happen, don't you?"

"Who is this?"

"Walk away, Taylor. You and your partner. Walk away or start looking over your shoulders, because one day I'll be there."

"Do you promise? I ask because of the hundreds of people who have threatened us over the years, only one actually meant it. 'Course, he's dead now. Hello? Hello?"

I hung up the phone and told my partner what was said.

"Who does that?" Freddie said. "Calls a man and threatens his life? You want to do somebody you just do 'em. Why the fuck give 'im a warning that you're coming?"

"I couldn't say."

"Whoever it is, he knows who we are and what we're doing. Who knows who we are and what we're doing?"

"Besides the people who hired us?"

"Maybe I should call Sara and have her sweep the office again."

"Something else. He doesn't think we're a threat to him. At

least not yet."

"But if we keep going…"

"What do you mean, if?"

"I'll tell you this, Taylor. No one's gonna do me like they did O'Neill."

I believed him.

"If I die, I ain't dyin' alone."

I believed that, too.

Freddie rubbed his face with both hands like a man who was tired yet knew he wasn't going to bed anytime soon. When he finished, he moved to the safe, worked the combination, and yanked the door open. He reached in and retrieved a nine-millimeter Beretta semiautomatic handgun and a loose maga-zine. He held them up to me. I took them from his hands and set them on my desk.

He pulled out his own gun and went through the ritual of loading it.

"You gonna call Dave Helin and the others or should I?" he asked.

"And tell them what?"

"That we want more money."

CHAPTER THIRTEEN

I left the apartment early, already regretting the sleep I didn't get. I had parked on the street instead of in the lot out back because I thought it was safer. Amanda Wedemeyer was standing at the curb in front of the building dressed in her soccer uniform, an equipment bag slung over her shoulder. Claire hovered nearby.

"You're embarrassing me," Amanda said.

Claire didn't respond.

Amanda saw me and called my name. "Tell her, Taylor," she said. "Tell Mom I'm not a child anymore."

"You're my child," Claire said.

"None of the other kids have their mothers waiting for the school bus with them."

"I don't care about the other kids."

"Taylor, tell her."

"Did it ever occur to you, Mandy, that your mother loves you more than her life and wants to spend every moment she can with you?"

My answer surprised both women. To be honest, it surprised me, too.

"When I was your age, the only time I went to school on a Saturday was when I was in trouble," I said.

"Daylong soccer camp," Claire said.

"Were you in trouble a lot?" Amanda asked.

"It seemed so at the time."

By then the yellow school bus had arrived and opened its folding door. I stood facing the street and watched while Amanda did something I didn't expect considering the circumstances. She hugged and kissed her mother before scampering up the steps. The door closed and the bus pulled away. Claire waved at it.

"You're a good mother," I said.

"No, but I'm trying. Lord knows."

"Listen, I don't want to alarm you, but—"

"Alarm me?"

"If you happen to see someone hanging around who shouldn't be here, I want you to call me or call the police, whoever's closer."

"What do you mean, hanging around?"

"Standing on the street corner, sitting in a parked car, driving up and down the street, around the block…"

"Is this about the private investigator that was killed in Minneapolis?" Claire asked. "I read in the paper—"

"Not necessarily."

"Did you know him?"

"I knew him."

"Was he a friend?"

"Just keep your eyes open, okay? If you see someone who makes you feel uneasy, then feel uneasy. Don't try to talk yourself out of it. We have instincts for a reason. Trust them. If you see anyone—"

"Like those two men?"

"What men?"

I spun away from the street toward the sidewalk. Two men were approaching from different angles, both wearing jeans and sports coats. They wore sports coats for the same reason that I did. To hide their guns. I reached for mine.

The closest man beat me to the draw. Instead of a gun, though, he swept open the bottom quarter of his coat to reveal a gold badge that resembled a warrior's shield fixed to his belt. It gleamed in the morning sun.

"St. Paul PD," he said.

I brought my hand out from under my coat and showed him that it was empty.

"Taylor," he said.

It wasn't a question, yet I answered it anyway. "Yes."

"I'm Sergeant Tony Weiss," he said. "My partner, Sergeant Thomas Manske."

The two policemen flanked me just the way they had been trained.

Weiss lowered his head toward Claire and touched his right eyebrow in a kind of salute.

"Ma'am," he said.

"I need to get some shopping done before Mandy comes home." Claire squeezed my arm. "Be careful."

"It's the life I chose," I said.

She moved cautiously around the two detectives and made her way to her car parked in the lot behind the apartment building. Weiss touched his eyebrow again as she passed.

"I have half a pot of coffee upstairs if you're interested," I said.

Weiss glanced at his partner.

"I could stand a cup," Manske said.

Manske had a hard time getting past Ogilvy.

"Damnedest thing I ever saw," he said. "Rabbit for a pet."

"They're nowhere near as needy as a dog and more affectionate than a cat," I said.

"Do they poop around the house?"

"They use litter boxes like a cat, but you need to train them not to chew on your computer cords. Ogilvy chewed on mine until he took hold of an electrical cord by mistake. That cured him."

We were standing around my kitchen counter, none of us actually drinking the coffee I had poured.

"There was a hit-and-run on Snelling near Hamline University a couple days ago," Weiss said.

"I know."

"I know you know. You were there to see it."

"Who told you that?"

"The video camera at the coffeehouse across the street from where you were parked for an hour before it happened. You jumped out of your car like any concerned citizen might, thought better of it, and went back. You seemed upset, pounding on your steering wheel the way you did before you drove away."

"You know I'm a private investigator."

"Yeah, I know. I also know you used to be one of us, that you worked homicide with Assistant Chief Scalasi back in the day." Weiss raised his cup, wet his lips with coffee, and returned it to the counter. "You gonna answer my questions?"

"I was retained by an attorney named Douglas Jernigan."

"We know Jernigan," Manske said.

"He sent me to speak to James Cowgill."

"Our victim."

"I can tell you that much. My problem is that I can't tell you why I was sent to speak to Cowgill."

"No," Weiss said. "Your problem is that if you don't give me something I can use I might be tempted to spread it around the Griffin Building. We both know how much private investigators depend on the police."

"Almost as much as the police rely on private investigators."

"If everybody is nice to everybody else, especially if you're nice to us, we all get along. That's the way it works. If you're a dick, though, and the word gets out, hell, man, you might as well set up practice in Iowa for all the help you're going to get from here on in."

Yeah, the eternal dance, I told myself. Except Weiss was leading, and if I stepped on his toes...I gave it some thought before I answered. "Just out of curiosity, gentlemen, did anyone take a look at Cowgill's bank accounts?"

The two detectives glanced at each other.

"Odd you should ask," Manske said. "Chief Scalasi passed the word that she had received an anonymous tip telling us to do just that."

"Is that right?"

"It's just a coincidence that you and Scalasi are pals."

"I wouldn't say pals exactly."

"Turns out our boy was depositing $9,990 in his savings account the first of every month since March first," Manske said.

"Just below the cash amount banks are required to report to the Financial Crimes Enforcement Network."

"Look at you, knowing how the system works."

"Where does a college student get that kind of dough?" I asked. "He didn't have a job as far as I knew."

"Can you think of any possibilities?"

"Yes, but I have a vivid imagination and a generally low opinion of my fellow man."

"Indulge us."

"Blackmail. 'Course, I'm just guessing."

"Who would Cowgill have been blackmailing?"

"I couldn't say."

Weiss didn't like the answer, yet he knew he wouldn't get a better one. It was Manske who asked, "What would he have used for leverage?"

"What do most blackmailers use?" I said. "Pictures. Possibly taken with a digital camera. Possibly located on his computer. I'd bet at least one or two pics were sent by email to his victim from his computer and then deleted. I'm just speculating, you understand."

"What would the pics have been of, I wonder?" Weiss said.

"Off the top of my head? I'd say it was a criminal act of some sort."

* * *

When they left, Manske said he was going to look into the possibility of getting a rabbit for his kids. Weiss didn't say much of anything. I rinsed out the coffee cups and placed them inside my dishwasher. Ogilvy came bounding into the kitchen and stared at me with those big eyes of his.

"Life is full of compromises," I told him. "You do the best you can and hope it's good enough."

He didn't seem to believe me, but then again, he wasn't confronted with many moral dilemmas day to day.

Freddie was sitting behind his desk when I walked into the office. He made a production out of looking at his watch.

"Nice of you to drop by," he said. "I was startin' t' think you were takin' the weekend off."

"I was detained by detectives from the St. Paul Police Department."

"Wha'd they have to say?"

"They admire us for our professionalism. Steven, good morning."

Steve Vandertop was sitting in one of our chairs facing the window. There was nothing feminine about his attire; his blond hair was tied back in a ponytail and tucked under his back collar. The bag hanging from his shoulder when he stood up made him look like he was heading to a gym to play basketball. We clasped hands and hugged with our fists between us the way men do so witnesses won't think there's anything gay about it.

"We could use some good news," I said.

"He wouldn't tell me without you being here until I threatened his life," Freddie said.

"I like surprises," Steve said.

"Surprise me."

"I tracked our computer hacker all the way to Uzbekistan.

Then I lost him."

"Surprise," Freddie said.

I settled in behind my desk, put my feet up, and stared at the bulletin board.

"Well, dammit," I said.

"So I turned my attention to the emails," Steve said.

"What emails?"

"The emails that were sent to the lawyers. Those were easy to trace."

"You didn't tell me that," Freddie said.

Steve spread his hands, and for a moment he was Sara again.

"Ta-da," he said.

"Who?" I asked.

"I don't have a who, but I have an IP number. I have a location."

Freddie and I both stood up.

Steve sat down.

"You know, guys, we never did discuss compensation," he said.

"I thought we were paying you your hourly rate," I said.

"You thought?"

"Fuck," Freddie said. "This is the kinda thing I'd expect from Sara."

"Steve," I said, "if your intel pans out, we'll give you a third of Freddie's and my take. If it doesn't, we'll cover your hours and that's it."

"Fair enough."

"Fuck it is," Freddie said. "But okay."

It rarely occurred to me how much bullshit Freddie must endure every day that I don't. Sitting at a table inside the coffeehouse while pretending to play with my smartphone, I had plenty of time on my hands to speculate.

The coffeehouse was actually a café-slash-bookstore called

the Library, and when I entered, no one paid me any mind, including the young barista who needed to finish a text before taking my order—café mocha and yes I'll have whipped cream with that. The name she wrote on my cardboard cup was spelled T-A-I-L-O-R.

Most heads turned when Freddie entered. Some of them leaned toward other heads and whispered in a way that would have made even the most confident person suspicious. I suppose location had something to do with it. In the Twin Cities, the seriously wealthy generally resided in one of three areas: North Oaks, Sunfish Lake, and one of the affluent, lily-white zip codes surrounding Lake Minnetonka. The Library was located about a quarter mile from the western shore of the lake in the City of Mound, birthplace of the Andrews Sisters, Kevin Sorbo, and Tonka Trucks, if those things matter to you. Freddie simply did not blend in.

The concerned looks and anxious conversations ceased, though, when Steve Vandertop entered shortly after Freddie. They shook hands and smiled and sat together after getting their orders filled. The customers were apparently relieved that Freddie had a white friend who could vouch for him. Suddenly he seemed less of a threat.

The Library was doing brisk business. Besides the coffee-house patrons, there seemed to be a nice crowd meandering among the stacks beyond the arch where the café ended and the bookstore began. A bank of three computers was mounted on a counter against the coffeehouse wall near the arch with bar stools arranged in front of them. A sign told customers to help themselves but to please limit their activities to only thirty minutes so others might also use the computers. Another sign said that access to inappropriate sites had been blocked without mentioning what those sites might be. What interested me most, though, was the small print reading *Browser history and passwords are deleted immediately after use to ensure the privacy of our customers.*

I wondered what Steve could do to bypass that little security feature. Probably a lot, I decided, being such a clever $150-an-hour fellow. He and Freddie seemed to be having a grand old time at their table. Eventually they both stood and made their way to the computer bank. Steve sat on one of the stools. Freddie leaned in, effectively blocking everyone's view of Steve's activities. I sipped my coffee and waited.

If Freddie's presence caused a stir, it was nothing compared to the collective sigh when she entered—a young woman, maybe eighteen, maybe not, her hair stringy and unwashed to match her clothes and the backpack she carried. She had piercings in her eyebrow, nose, lip, and ears and several tattoos on her bare arms. She looked as if she lived beneath a bridge, yet when she approached the counter, the barista smiled and said, "Hayley, hi."

Hayley ordered the less expensive daily brew and doctored it with the free honey and cream set up next to the napkins and stir sticks. She paid for it with an American Express card, and I remembered what Clinton Siegle told me about the woman with the ink and piercings who had approached him at the Twin Cities Jazz Festival. *She was young and looked like she was trying hard not to be pretty, you know?*

After modifying the coffee to her liking, Hayley pivoted toward the computer bank and stared at Steve and Freddie a long moment before dropping her backpack on a table and taking a seat with a clear view of their backs. She was waiting for them to leave, I told myself.

I shifted noisily in my chair, but it wasn't enough to attract their attention. I had convinced myself that Hayley was the person we had come to see, and I wanted Freddie and Steve to abandon the computers so we could discover what she was up to. Except I was afraid that she would notice any gesture I made that they might also notice, and I didn't want to give up my anonymity. It took a minute before it dawned on me—you have a cell phone in your hand, dummy.

I began preparing a text, typing one letter at a time with my index finger.

I don't know what it was that caused my eyes to snap upward from the screen. When they did I saw a man standing in front of Hayley. He was at least a decade older than she was and good-looking with the aging frat-boy, I-own-a-boat-on-Lake-Minnetonka panache that some guys have. His dark eyes were filled with intense emotion. He leaned on her table and brought his head down close to hers. Hayley's eyes flicked across the room as if she were seeking assistance from someone, anyone. He spoke. I couldn't hear his words or the sound of his voice, but his expression was harsh, his eyes menacing. Give the girl credit, though. Once he started talking she never looked away.

The frat boy straightened up.

Hayley didn't move.

He gripped the sides of her table again, leaned in, and gave another speech.

The frat boy straightened up again.

This time, Hayley pulled her backpack off the table and flung it over her shoulders as she stood. She glanced toward the barista as if she wanted to say something, but the girl was busy with her phone. The man gestured toward the door. He waited until Hayley started walking and fell in behind her. I didn't think it was a matter of courtesy. It struck me that the frat boy was attempting to block any escape attempt.

I dropped the phone into the pocket of my sports coat and followed them out the door.

They were off the street by the time I got outside. I circled the bookstore to the asphalt parking lot. I paused when I saw a van parked between two rows of cars, its engine running. It was one of those white panel jobs, no windows. Nothing was painted on the sides to indicate that it belonged to a business. The side door was opened. A second man about the same age as the frat boy and dressed just like him stood by the door. He was gesturing for Hayley to enter. She didn't want to. The frat boy was behind her. He pressed her forward. She leaned back. He grabbed her shoulders. She spun away. He grabbed her arm. She tried to free herself from his grip and failed.

"Leave me alone," she said.

"Give it back and I will," he said.

"It's mine."

"It could set me up for life."

"That's not what I want."

"I don't care what you want."

"That's why I took it."

"We'll talk in the van."

Hayley tried to kick him in the groin, but she was standing too close to him and only grazed his leg.

"Get in," the second man said.

"No."

The frat boy yanked Hayley toward him and slapped her hard across the face. Her response was to try to hit him back. He ducked the blow, though, and wrapped his arms around her. He attempted to lift and carry her to the open door of the van. It was hard because of the backpack and because she was kicking and screaming.

The second man grabbed for her legs.

By then I was running hard.

The second man didn't see me until I leapt up and slammed into him full bore.

He went flying about six feet into the side of the van and splashed against the asphalt.

I lost my balance yet managed to stay on my feet.

The frat boy was surprised enough that Hayley was able to squirm out of his grasp.

As soon as her head cleared out of the way, I slammed the heel of my right hand against his nose.

There was a satisfying crack and he fell backward. Both hands went to his nose. Blood seeped between his fingers. I was thinking about punching him again when he went to his knees.

I glared down at him and thought, is that it? One punch and you're done? My excitement was intense, bordering on pure joy. I often felt it during moments of action, and I didn't want it to end. It was both stupid and careless of me, of course, thinking that way, because while I was feeling heroic, the second man scrambled to his feet and pulled an automatic that he pointed at my head. I might not have noticed at all except the girl screamed.

I shifted my head out of the line of fire. At the same time, I grabbed the second man's wrist and pushed the gun up and away. It went off. I drove my knee just as hard as I could into his groin and punched him just as hard as I could in the throat. He dropped the gun and fell to his knees. I kicked the gun beneath the van.

By now the frat boy was up. He threw a punch at my head. I blocked it with my wrist. I brought my other hand up and hit him below the eye with the back of my fist. I followed up with a punch to his solar plexus. Frat boy went down again.

Hayley began running across the lot, dodging between the parked cars.

A second mistake: I followed her.

"Miss," I called. "Stop. Miss? Hayley?"

The frat boy began shouting, "Go, go, go."

I turned in time to see him rise to his feet, take two steps, and dive into the open van.

At the same time, frat boy's partner also scrambled to his feet and dashed around the van to the driver's side. He climbed inside and gunned the engine. Until that moment, I didn't know you could make a van's tires squeal.

The frat boy, blood pouring from his nose, rolled the door shut as the van peeled out of the parking lot.

Somewhere behind me, I heard a car engine followed by the roar of hard acceleration. I turned my head just in time to see a BMW 640i coupe flying out of the parking lot. Hayley was behind the wheel.

Freddie and Steve rounded the corner. She nearly hit them.

I moved to the center of the parking lot and picked up the automatic that I had kicked beneath the van. It was a Colt .38. I unloaded it and dropped it into my pocket.

Steve and Freddie approached me, but no one else did. There was no throng of curious onlookers; no one had alerted the cops or the media. Apparently I was the only one who knew that a kidnapping attempt had just taken place.

"What the hell?" Freddie said.

"Tell me you saw the Beamer."

"I did."

"Tell me you got the license plate."

"I didn't."

I explained what happened. Freddie said, "Tell me you got the license plate of the van."

"I was preoccupied."

"Tsk, tsk, tsk."

"For what it's worth, the emails were absolutely sent from here," Steve said.

I thought about it for a few beats. "The barista," I said. "She seemed to know the girl, called her by name. Let's talk to her."

"No," Steve said. "You don't need to run the license plates or talk to the barista."

"We don't?"

"I know who the girl is."

He didn't say anything more.

"Steve?" I said.

"About our arrangement."

"We said you'd get a third," Freddie said. "What? We gotta put it in writing?"

"Her name is Hayley O'Brien," Steve said. "I met her at a party my family threw around Christmas."

"Go on."

"She's Robert Paul Guernsey's stepdaughter."

CHAPTER FOURTEEN

Brooke St. Vincent crossed her long, sleek legs at the knee as she sat on the sofa. There were photographs mounted on the wall behind her. Brooke cradling a rifle, a dead deer hanging from the branch of a tree between her and a man I assumed was her father. Brooke holding a shotgun and a looped bird carrier with her limit of ducks. Brooke in a Minnesota Twins T-shirt and a floppy hat displaying a record-sized walleye. Brooke with another rifle, this time dressed for a shooting competition.

She's an outdoor girl, I told myself. Of course she is, the way she looks, all that blond hair and those sharp blue eyes. The Office of Tourism should use her in its ads. Explore Minnesota.

"What can I do for you, Mr. Taylor?" she asked.

I dismissed the adolescent answers her question inspired and spoke bluntly. "How well do you know Hayley O'Brien?"

"Is she in trouble?"

"I think so. A little bit."

I explained what had happened an hour earlier.

"Those men were trying to kidnap her?" Brooke said. "Do you think they worked for Robert Paul?"

"I don't know, but she clearly knew who they were. Would he resort to kidnapping his own stepdaughter?"

"The way the old man looks at it, Hayley is his property the same way that I was Kurt's property. What kind of man would he be if he couldn't keep what's his?"

"I'd like to speak to him."

"Good luck with that. He never leaves Axis Mundi. Hasn't for years, anyway."

"If I call, do you think he'll answer the phone?"

"I'd be surprised if you could get their home number. The Guernseys are very private people. Very secretive. Ahh, now I understand why you came to me."

"Do you have the number?"

"Unless they changed it after I divorced Kurt because they were afraid I'd give it out."

"Seriously? Would they do that?"

"Of course."

Brooke lived in a corner apartment on the top floor of a building in Edina. Half of her windows faced I-494, and the other half gave her a bird's-eye view of the luxury shops located in the Galleria. She left the sofa and moved to the picture window facing the shopping center. She was wearing white shorts and a filmy off-white blouse that caused me to once again question my rule against becoming involved with a subject of an ongoing investigation. I reminded myself that Dr. Alexandra Campbell had been a witness for the prosecution whom I had been hired to discredit, and that worked out. A woman named Caroline who had been a witness for the defense actually seduced me and not the other way around. I quickly flashed on Cynthia Grey, though, and asked myself, do you want to go through that again?

"I can't," Brooke said. "I can't give you the number for Axis Mundi. It would be a violation of trust—no, I can't do that."

"I understand. Can you put me in touch with Hayley?"

"I haven't spoken to Hayley since the day I walked out on Kurtis. When I met her...Kurt and I had dated for about eighteen months before we married, so at the time Hayley must have been what, twelve? Thirteen? Every time I went over there she would attach herself to me because I was the only one besides her mother who would actually talk to her, ask her about school, ask about her friends. The others—most of the time they didn't seem to acknowledge that she existed. I felt sorry for her. I told Melissa she should treat her better, that Hayley was family. Lissa's answer—'She's not my family.'

"It all goes back to Robert Paul. He taught his children to think that there were two kinds of people in the world. You're either a Guernsey or you're a loser, and Hayley wasn't a Guernsey. She was the daughter of a father who committed suicide and a mother who married a man forty years older for money."

"What about the piercings, the ink?" I asked.

"Are you asking me to play psychologist? I'd say they're cries for attention. They started at about the same time my marriage was disintegrating. I wish I had been there for her, but I was too concerned with my own problems. I feel bad about that. On the other hand, I wasn't her mother."

"Tell me about her mother."

"First thing you notice about Maura—she's stunning. She makes me look like trailer-park trash. Makes me feel that way, too. She's Robert Paul's third wife. The first wife, Catherine, she was Kurt's mother, and Lissa's and Robert Jr.'s, too. She died young. Cancer. Apparently all the money in the world couldn't save her. The second wife—Robert Paul married her about a year and a half after Catherine died because he thought his kids needed a mother. The oldest son was six at the time. They divorced a year and a half later. The family never talks about her, but I got the impression that she's the reason it's so obsessed with prenuptial agreements.

"Robert Paul waited thirty-five years before he married again. The children were not happy about it, either. Kurt once asked me, 'How would you like to have a stepmother who's two years younger than you are?' Maura and Melissa were born three months apart, both of them thirty years old when Maura married Robert Paul. That was ten years ago. Eleven. From what I've seen, Robert Paul has become dependent on Maura, especially now that his health is deteriorating. He's eighty, after all. The kids don't like that, either."

"Did she sign a prenup?"

Brooke thought that was awfully funny. She was laughing when she returned to the sofa and curled her legs beneath her.

"Of course she did," Brooke said. "I'm guessing it's just as bad as mine or Maura would have left years ago. Either that or she's betting on the fact that Robert Paul doesn't have a last will and testament."

"He doesn't? You'd think a man in his position would know better."

"Yes, you would. But that's not my problem anymore."

"Was it ever?"

"Kurt would talk about it constantly. Who's going to inherit what? It would have been a big topic of conversation over dinner except every time someone mentioned it, the old man would get angry and threaten to leave the entire estate and all his businesses to charity. The kids think its Maura's doing. I spoke to the man, though, during those few times when he wasn't treating me like something you wipe off the bottom of your shoe with a stick. I'm an economist, after all, and I love to talk about money. Robert Paul doesn't have a will because he doesn't want to go to the trouble of divvying up the estate, giving one child one thing and the other child something else. He said he tried and it was too hard. He said it was impossible to make it fair to everyone and he didn't want his family to think he loved one person more than the other. At least, that's what he told me. He's such a detestable human being, it's hard to think that love is a factor in anything he does.

"Under Minnesota law, if Robert Paul dies without a will, his wife is guaranteed to inherit half of his estate and his children will split what's left. Let them all work it out like adults, he decided. So unless his kids can convince the old man to disinherit Maura for being an adulterous whore, which she isn't—Robert Paul had her investigated once just to be sure. He actually hired a private eye, I don't remember his name. Walter something. I think he periodically investigates all of his children. He'd make announcements at dinner, 'I hear you saw so-and-so, I see you met with such-and-such,' and demand an explanation. He never called out Maura, though, at least not while I was there. I guess she hadn't strayed an inch since she married the old man. With seven hundred million dollars on the table, would you cheat?"

"How did Guernsey and Maura meet?"

"From what I was told—I'm getting this secondhand, you have to remember. From what I was told, Maura's first husband had worked for Robert Paul for many years. At least a decade. His name was Charles O'Brien, everyone called him Charlie, and he owned a highly regarded landscaping company. If you ever get a chance to visit Axis Mundi, the landscaping, the elaborate gardens, the arboretum, the maze, that's all Charlie's doing.

"Even though he ran the business, and I think he had twenty employees, Charlie enjoyed getting his hands dirty, literally digging in the dirt to plant the flowers and trees and do what had to be done. Robert Paul admired him for that. Also, the wealthier Robert Paul became, the more isolated he became. Like I said, he almost never leaves Axis Mundi now, instead making Fisk or his kids run any errands for him that need to be run. The old man enjoyed hanging out with Charlie and his gardeners. Of course, he spent time with Maura, too. She was an accountant, but she often worked with Charlie. I know the old man sent them an elaborate gift when Hayley was born. Melissa told me that Maura reminded Robert Paul of Catherine, so there was that, too.

"Anyway, Robert Paul would send Charlie and his people on his private jet to take care of his properties around the country, his business campuses, second houses. It was while he was in San Francisco that Charlie killed himself. From what I was told, he seemed like the happiest guy in the world, both friendly and considerate. People who knew him were shocked when he put a gun in his mouth. His death had a profound effect on Robert Paul, too. He was over seventy at the time, growing more and more isolated, and he started worrying about his future, about dying alone. He actually told me that once. After Catherine died, he said, he was always afraid of dying alone."

"What about his three children?"

"It wasn't the same as having a good woman at your side, that's what he told me. Anyway, after Charlie died, the old man became very solicitous toward Maura, and one thing eventually led to another. They married in a quiet ceremony six months later. The kids weren't invited to the wedding. They didn't even know it was taking place until after it was done. The only people invited were a business associate of Robert Paul's—he and his wife served as best man and bridesmaid, witnesses. Hayley, too. She was six years old."

"That must have been hard on her. Did she even understand what was happening?"

"I don't know. Hayley is ungodly smart. She also has great pride and terrible anger, a bad combination. I thought she might be bipolar the way she's so easily offended, but then everybody at Axis Mundi seems a bit off. Was she really involved in the computer hacks?"

"In my business, you never accept a coincidence. We know that the emails—did David Helin tell you about the emails that were supposedly sent by NIMN?"

"Yes."

"We know they were composed on a computer at the Library in Mound. Somehow that doesn't strike me as NIMN HQ. We were checking it out when Hayley walked in and someone tried to snatch her. So, yes, I'm going to say she's involved. I just don't know how or why."

"You said you want me to arrange an introduction?"

"Or at least put us in touch."

The hiss that came from Brooke reminded me of a slowly

deflating tire.

"I just want to ask some questions," I said. "You're welcome to be there when I do. In fact, I wish you would be. Tell Hayley she can pick the location and bring as many friends as she wants to make her feel comfortable."

"If she's responsible for the computer hacks, then she's the one threatening to terminate my three-point-seven-million-dollar divorce settlement with her stepuncle."

"I admit there's a certain amount of irony to what I'm asking."

Brooke laughed loud and heartily. "Is that what you call it?"

Once again I found myself challenging my rules about fraternizing with subjects of an investigation, reminding myself that they weren't rules so much as guidelines.

"I'm going to phone Dave Helin and ask what he thinks," Brooke said. "If he says it's okay, I'll try to contact Hayley. I'll call you later to tell you what she says."

"I appreciate it. Do you still have my card?"

She nodded and stood up. I stood with her.

"This reminds me of a story," Brooke said. "I don't know how true it is. A teenager in California, I think, was left home for the weekend by his parents. Naturally, he threw a party even though his parents told him not to. The party got way out of hand and there was a lot of damage. The teenager panicked. Apparently his parents were ultraconservative, ultrastrict. To cover up what he had done, the teenager set the house on fire."

"He did what?"

"'Course, the fire department quickly discovered it was arson, and the insurance company refused to pay damages. What I never heard and always wondered—what did his parents do?"

I returned to the office. Freddie was preparing to call it a day.

"What did the divorcée say?" he asked.

"She'll get back to us."

I gazed at the bulletin board. Freddie had been busy with his red yarn, connecting an index card labeled HAYLEY directly to HACKER and a card labeled THUGS to HAYLEY. He'd also run a length of yarn from HAYLEY to GUERNSEY FINANCIAL INC.

"It's starting to resemble postmodern art," I said. "Something you'd see at the Walker Art Center."

"Never been there," Freddie said.

"You're not missing much."

Freddie held up four pink message slips.

"While you were out," he said. "Calls from Scott Mickelson, Doug Jernigan, John Kaushal, and Cormac Puchner's secretary."

"What, no David Helin?"

"They're all anxious to know what progress we've made."

"I'm surprised they aren't constantly calling our cells."

"I think they're trying to keep it professional."

"What did you tell them?"

"That we have it under control."

I gazed at the bulletin board some more and laughed.

"Sure we do," I said.

"I got a question. If this Hayley O'Brien girl, Guernsey's stepdaughter, if she's responsible for the hacks, what do we do about it? Stop the hacker any way you can, the lawyers said. 'Cept Hayley ain't some antisocial punk livin' in her parents' basement, you know? Well, maybe she is. The thing is, if we lean on her, the whole damn world could fall on us."

"If it's her and we can prove it, I say we tell the lawyers and let them figure it out. Half of them work for the Guernseys in one capacity or another anyway."

"What about the guys who tried to snatch the girl?"

"I don't know. Brooke St. Vincent wondered aloud if they might not be working for old man Guernsey."

"If they do, it's another reason to be thinkin' about an exit strategy."

"What if they don't, though?"

"I don't know."

"At least we're consistent."

I drove to the apartment. My cell phone rang. I answered it.

"David wasn't thrilled with the idea," Brooke said. "In fact, he told me not to do it. I contacted Hayley anyway. I'm worried about her. I told her who you were and that you wanted to meet. Should I quote her?"

"Please do," I said.

"'Screw that old man.'"

"Old?"

"She seemed genuinely happy that I called, though. She said she'd love to spend time with me. She even made suggestions where we could meet. If you want—"

"I know what you're going to say, Brooke, and I appreciate it. But I won't ambush her. At least not yet. I think Hayley and I need to have a conversation eventually, whether she likes it or not, only I'd just as soon we not be enemies when we meet if I can avoid it. Besides, she'll think you betrayed her. I don't want that, either."

"Thank you, but what I was going to say—should I ask her about the computer hacks?"

"Did you tell her that you knew about what happened outside the Library?"

"Yes."

"I bet a nickel it'll come up in conversation again. Let it. Then take it where it goes."

"I'll call you afterward."

"Whether she agrees to speak to me or not, she's in danger. The guys who tried to force her into the van—Hayley needs to talk to somebody about that. Make sure she understands, okay?"

"I'll tell her."

"Brooke?"

"Yes?"

"Your ex-husband is an idiot."

"Yes, he is."

After hanging up the phone, I carried it to my front window and looked down on the street. Claire Wedemeyer was waiting dutifully at the curb for her daughter to return from soccer camp, and I thought, damn she's pretty. Not that I hadn't thought so before. Seeing her caused me to flash on Laura, followed by Anne, Caroline, Cynthia Grey, and, for just a moment, Brooke St. Vincent. It occurred to me that I've been intimately involved with a statistically improbable number of attractive women. Lucky me.

My cell phone rang in my hand, startling me for a moment. I glanced at the caller ID. Dr. Alexandra Campbell.

"Hell yes, I've been lucky," I said aloud.

I stepped away from the window and answered the phone.

"Are you coming over?" Alex said.

"I was just going to call and ask if you wanted to get something to eat and maybe catch that new Denzel Washington thing."

"Dinner and a movie? You know, Taylor, you don't need to work that hard. I have Netflix and the phone numbers of every decent take-out joint within a two-mile radius."

"I'm fond of ritual."

Alex thought that was funny.

"Okay," she said. "'Course, that means I'll have to put some clothes on."

"Let me take a quick shower and I'll be right over."

"You could come over right now and take one with me. The average shower uses seventeen-point-two gallons of water. You know I'm big on conservation."

"I doubt we'd conserve much. Besides, this is the land of

11,842 lakes. Water's not an issue here."

"That's a very narrow-minded attitude, Taylor. Must I give you a lecture on environmental consciousness?"

I drifted back to the window and gazed out again. Claire was still standing there, only now her arms were draped over Amanda's shoulders in a protective embrace.

Clark Peterson was standing in front of them.

"I'll call you back," I said.

Claire was the first to see me coming out the door. She smiled slightly and her body seemed to relax, and I thought, that's one of the nicest compliments I've ever received. Peterson turned his head. He smiled, too. A disarming smile. If I hadn't known him I would have liked it.

I moved casually to where the trio was standing—casually, dammit—and worked hard to keep the anxiety out of my voice.

"Hey," I said. "How was camp?"

"Exhausting," Amanda said. For emphasis, she slumped her shoulders and dropped her equipment bag on the ground as if it weighed ten thousand pounds. "Kicking a soccer ball is hard."

Claire saw her chance to escape.

"Let's get you upstairs," she told her daughter. She nodded at the man standing in front of her. "Mr. Peterson."

"Clark, I said to call me Clark."

She didn't. Instead she retrieved Amanda's equipment bag and walked around him, making sure that she was between Peterson and Amanda as they headed for the building.

"Friends?" Peterson asked.

"Neighbors," I said.

"Very pretty. Both of them. The mother doesn't seem very trusting, though. I merely inquired if this was where you lived, if she knew you, and all of a sudden she starts cross-examining me. Who am I? Why am I here?"

"Let's walk to your car and you can tell me all about it."

"Do I make you nervous, too, Taylor?"

"Isn't that why you came to my home without calling first, to make me nervous?"

We started down the street.

"I don't know why people get jumpy when I'm around," Peterson said. "There's only one person I wanted to kill, and she's dead, so…"

"Why are you here?"

"I wanted to know if you've made any progress finding our little hacker, if you have any names you'd like to share."

"Not yet. In any case, I don't work for you, Peterson. I don't report to you. I work for John Kaushal."

"Way I look at it, since I'm paying Kaushal's bills, yes, you do work for me."

"I don't see it that way."

"I don't care how you see it."

We reached a purple Bentley Continental GT convertible, the top down. I estimated the retail value in excess of two hundred thousand dollars.

"Is this your car?" I asked.

Instead of waiting for an answer, I yanked open the door and held it for him.

"Why are you being like this?" Peterson didn't give up his smile, but his eyes had a put-upon look as if he were a puppy that had been kicked for no apparent reason.

"I'm antisocial," I said. "Ask anyone."

"You can see why I'm anxious, though, can't you?"

"Whatever the hacker reveals, if he reveals anything, can't be used against you in a court of law. As far as the state is concerned, you got away with murder. So, no, I don't see why you're worried."

"You should have my problems, Taylor. You really should."

Peterson slipped into the driver's seat. I closed the car door and leaned against it.

"Is this the part where you threaten my life?" he asked. His eyes brightened as if he were looking forward to the prospect.

"Funny you ask. A guy called the other day and threatened my partner and me. It wasn't the first time that happened, or even the twentieth, and we joked about it. See, if we wanted to kill someone, we would never warn them first. I bet you didn't warn your wife, did you? One day, though, you could be walking down the sidewalk and hear footsteps behind you and start to turn, or a car might pull up next to you at a stoplight and you'll lean over to look at the driver, or someone holding a clipboard will knock on your front door and you'll open it and say, 'Can I help you,' and—boom. It's that simple, that easy. You of all people should know that."

"Don't try to scare me, Taylor."

"I'm not. I'm telling you, Peterson, that you're scaring me. See, I don't care if you live or die or move to New Orleans like you said. You mean nothing to me. Unless you threaten the people I care about. Then you'll become the most important person in my life. Are you threatening the people I care about?"

"Why would I do that?"

"I don't know. Cuz it's not in your best interests."

"All I want is to collect my inheritance and get the hell out of here with as little muss and fuss as possible."

"I don't blame you a bit."

Peterson started the Bentley. I stepped back.

"Very nice car," I said. "A little flashy for my tastes, though. It's easy to spot from a long way off."

Peterson put it in gear.

"It's why I like it," he said.

CHAPTER FIFTEEN

My cell phone woke me at about nine Sunday morning. It was on the nightstand next to the bed, and I had to reach across Alexandra Campbell's naked body to fetch it. She bit my shoulder when I did.

I read the caller ID. It listed the name of a woman I didn't recognize. I lay back against the bed before I accepted the call. Alex rolled on her side toward me and started teasing my neck, shoulder, and chest with her lips and tongue and fingers. I thought if I ignored her she'd quit, except she didn't.

"This is Taylor," I said.

"Mr. Taylor, my name is Heather. I'm an assistant to Mayor Mary Feeney."

I decided that short answers were best considering what Alex was doing to me.

"Yes," I said.

"Mayor Feeney would like to discuss a matter with you that she says you are already familiar with."

"Okay."

"Can you meet her for brunch at ten thirty?"

"Where?"

I was surprised by the location Heather suggested because it was in St. Paul.

"I'll be there."

I hung up the phone.

By then Alexandra had moved to my ear.

"Honest to God, Alex," I said.

"Who was that?"

"An assistant to the mayor of Minneapolis. I've been invited to brunch."

Alex moved her hand between my legs and gripped me tightly.

"What about my breakfast?" she asked.

Mayor Mary Feeney was sitting alone at a table next to a window at the Louisiana Café on Selby Avenue when I arrived. She wasn't wearing sunglasses or a big floppy hat; she hadn't disguised herself at all. Yet she went unrecognized in the busy restaurant, and I thought—context. No one expected to see the mayor of Minneapolis in a Cajun joint in the Summit-University neighborhood of St. Paul, so they didn't. It didn't hurt, either, that instead of business attire, she was wearing tight jeans and a V-neck shirt that made her look younger than she had in the offices at Hannum, Hillsman, and Byers.

She was studying the menu. When I reached the table, she looked up at me and smiled as if she were surprised to see me there.

"Mary," I said.

She smiled some more and gestured at the chair across from her. "Thank you for coming."

I sat. A waitress appeared. The mayor said, "I'm ready to order, but I'm sure my companion will need more time."

"Actually, I've been here before and I already know what I want."

Feeney ordered Zydeco French Toast and iced tea. I had the blackened catfish filet, three fried eggs, hash browns grilled with green peppers, onions, and portobello mushrooms and topped with cheddar cheese, Russian rye toast, a side of Cajun andouille sausage, and coffee. Yes, that was a lot of food, but after spending the night with Alex, I needed all the nourishment

I could get.

The waitress retired.

"Thank you for not using my title," Feeney said.

"You're welcome."

"Sometimes I hate it. Sometimes I want to get as far away from it as I can."

"So you crossed the mighty Mississippi and came all the way to St. Paul?"

"It doesn't seem like it should make much difference, yet it does."

"I don't think you get to be the mayor of Minneapolis unless you want to be the mayor of Minneapolis."

"Be careful what you dream."

Always good advice, I thought but didn't say out loud.

"When I started in politics, it was because I wanted to make the world a better place," Feeney said. "I'm not joking. I was that naïve."

"Or idealistic."

Feeney smiled at the word.

"That, too," she said. "Lately, though, it seems all my energy is devoted to keeping my job. 'Course, you can't make the world a better place if you're not in office, can you?"

"Mary, why am I here?"

The waitress reappeared before she could answer. The service at the Louisiana Café was that fabulous. Our conversation switched to food. We chatted about it as we ate. I was pushing the remains of my eggs and browns around the plate with a slice of toast when we returned to the original topic.

"My impression when we were in Scott Mickelson's office was that you don't care for Bryan Daggett," the mayor said.

"He's a bully."

"You don't care for me, either."

"Does it matter?"

"It does. You see, I want to lobby you into joining my side."

"I thought we were already on the same side."

"I'm the one who'll get tossed down a well if things go badly."

Not that you don't deserve it, I thought but again didn't say.

"Ryan-Reed is owned by the Guernsey family," Feeney said. "Are you aware of that?"

"I wasn't then, but I am now."

"The Guernseys intend to buy as much of Minneapolis—of Minnesota—as they can get their hands on. I went along with them because I needed the money. My last election was both brutal and expensive. The seven-point margin I won by? It was bought and paid for by the Guernseys."

"Now you're suffering buyer's remorse," I said.

"In a manner of speaking. I want to separate myself from the Guernseys as much as I can. It's important that the voters in Minneapolis know that I am not in the pocket of the one percent."

"How can I help?"

"Have you identified the computer hacker yet?"

"No."

"When you do, I would like you to impress upon him the fact that he has friends in high places."

"You?"

"All I ask in exchange is that he be a friend to me."

"In what way? Just in case he should ask."

"There's a treasure trove of scandalous information concerning the Guernseys, Ryan-Reed, and Minnesota River State Bank that I'd be willing to let him find."

"If, in exchange, he loses your notes," I said.

"You know how these things work."

"I was just guessing."

Feeney leaned back in her chair.

"Plus," she said, "if he has any legal problems, he should know that I can be relied upon to make them go away, especially if they originate in my city."

"I'm sure he'll be happy to hear it."

"I can't make the world a better place if I'm not in office,

Taylor."

"You said that before."

"I'll pay you five thousand dollars to deliver the message. There's another five for you if you convince the hacker to accept my offer."

"Okay."

"Okay? Just like that?"

"Sure. Why not?"

"You have no quarrel with the price? It's a fair price?"

"It's a very fair price."

"I'll have the first installment delivered to your office tomorrow morning."

"You don't have it on you, Mary? I'm disappointed."

The mayor grinned as if I had made a wonderful joke.

The deal I made with Alexandra Campbell to let me leave her bed unharmed to see another woman was that I'd return immediately after. When I did, I found her on her backyard patio surrounded by a wide assortment of plants and shrubs that she had planted herself. Most of them had stakes in front with tiny cards listing their Latin and common names. She was wearing form-fitting yoga clothes and going through a variety of poses. I sat on an iron chair in front of a round iron table with a hole in the center to accommodate a huge umbrella and watched.

"See anything you like?" she asked.

"Nope. Not a thing."

Alex smiled as best she could while on her knees, her back arched, the top of her head pressed against the ground, her arms thrust above her, her fingers interlaced.

"This is called a grounded tipover tuck," she said. "Good for headaches."

"Do you have a headache?"

She didn't answer. Instead, she went into a stretch position, one leg back and one leg front, her torso leaning forward and twisted so that her head was looking straight up and she was able to press the palms of both hands together above her shoulder.

"It wouldn't hurt for you to get into shape," she said.

"I am in shape."

She grinned like she thought I was kidding myself.

"I run three to five miles nearly every day," I said. "I do martial arts training at a gym in downtown Minneapolis."

"How often?"

"As often as I can."

"Can you do this?" Alex asked.

She stood on one leg, reached behind her for the second leg, and raised it well above her head while thrusting her other hand straight out in front of her.

"No, I can't do that," I said.

My cell phone rang.

"You're not going to answer that, are you?" Alex said.

The caller ID read BROOKE ST. VINCENT.

"Business," I said and swiped right.

"Taylor," Brooke said.

There was a lot of ambient background noise on her end, and I told her that it was hard to hear.

"I have you on speakerphone," she said. "We're at the Minneapolis Institute of Art, and they have some kind of children's event going on today."

"Hi, Taylor," a second voice said.

"That was Hayley O'Brien," Brooke said.

"Hello, Ms. O'Brien," I said.

"Brooke said you wanted to talk. Since you helped me yesterday, I said I would."

I stood and pivoted away from the patio because Alex had assumed a position in which her hands and feet were planted firmly on the ground, her back curved, and her breasts and pelvis pointed at the sky. I found it very distracting.

"I appreciate it," I said.

"Brooke is my friend, and she said you're a good guy."

"Where can we meet?"

"Here. Meet us—it's really noisy in here. Meet us on the front steps near the lion."

"I'll be there in twenty minutes."

I hung up the phone and turned back toward Alex. She was now sitting on her heels, her back perfectly straight, the crown of her head pointed upward, her forearms resting on her thighs, the fingers of both hands curled into an "okay" gesture. The scoop neck on her Lycra top gave me a nice view of her breasts.

"Don't move an inch," I said. "I'll be right back."

"Where are you going now?"

"I'm leaving you for another woman. Actually, two of them this time."

"Kinky."

In fact, the Minneapolis Institute of Art had two carved lions in front of it, with a long flight of concrete steps between them that led to a seldom-used front door flanked by Greek columns. Brooke St. Vincent and Hayley O'Brien were sitting on the steps near the first lion and gazing out on Washburn Fair Oaks Park across the street. It was a peculiar sight, Brooke with fair, unblemished skin and golden hair, dressed as if she were visiting, well, the Minneapolis Institute of Art, sitting next to Hayley with her piercings, tattoos, and stringy hair up in a kind of Princess Leia hairstyle, dressed as if she were cleaning out the basement.

Hayley's backpack was resting on the concrete step. She dragged it closer when I mounted the steps. Although I stopped a few steps below them, my head was even with theirs.

"Taylor," Brooke said. She offered her hand and I shook it. "This is Hayley O'Brien."

I offered to shake her hand, but Hayley was using it to clutch her backpack.

"How are you doing?" I asked her.

"Fine."

"You had a bit of a scare yesterday."

"I wasn't scared."

"I was."

Hayley tilted her head and looked at Brooke as if she thought I was lying and wanted to know if her companion agreed.

"I'm sure you two have plenty to talk about," Brooke said.

She attempted to rise. Hayley grabbed her wrist and held her in place. When she was sure Brooke wasn't going anywhere, she turned back to me. A troubled expression touched her eyes and mouth.

"Why were you following me?" Hayley asked.

"I wasn't."

"Then why were you at the Library the same time I was?"

"Coincidence."

"I don't believe it."

"Neither would I if I were you. You don't know me well enough to trust me." I glanced at Brooke. "Neither do you."

"We have friends in common. They trust you and I trust them."

I appreciated the sentiment very much, although I knew from experience not to embrace it too tightly. To her credit or detriment, depending on your point of view, Hayley remained unconvinced as well.

"Tell me why you were there in the first place and I might believe you," she said.

"Have you ever heard of NIMN—Not in Minnesota?"

"Yes."

"Someone from NIMN apparently sent an email to my employers using the computers at the Library."

"I never touched those computers."

"I never said you did."

"Why did you follow me into the parking lot?"

"You looked frightened. You looked like you needed help."

"Oh yeah, and you go around helping complete strangers."

"Yes, sometimes I do. That's the way I'm wired."

Hayley hesitated for a moment, her eyes clouded with emotion.

"My father was like that." She spoke as if she were speaking to herself. "What I remember of him. One time we were driving in the rain and there was a car broken down along the freeway, and my father stopped to see if he could help. Turned out it was this real old couple that ran out of gas or something. My mother stayed angry at my father for a week after that. She said by stopping he put us all at risk of being murdered or raped or I don't know. That's how I remember it, anyway. My father..."

Brooke leaned toward the girl and whispered into her ear. Hayley's response was to hug her tightly. I felt uncomfortable watching the exchange yet held my ground.

Brooke eased the girl away. "I'll see you again real soon," she said.

When Brooke stood, she was several feet taller than I was. She descended the stairs until we were able to look into each other's eyes at the same level. She gripped my forearm.

"Hayley is my friend," Brooke said.

"Then she's my friend."

"Call me later." Brooke glanced back at Hayley. "You, too."

She was at the base of the concrete staircase and heading toward the parking lot on the corner before Hayley spoke.

"Brooke's the only one in the entire family who cares about me, and now she's not in the family," she said.

"I'm sorry."

"What do you know?"

"Only what I've been told."

"What have you been told?"

I decided the best way to play Hayley was to tell her the truth as bluntly as possible.

"Your father died when you were six years old," I said. "Your mother married Robert Paul Guernsey shortly after. No one in the Guernsey family likes her or you."

She paused again, and I thought, this is a girl who slides in and out of her head frequently, using events from the past to translate the present.

"I don't believe my father committed suicide," she said. "He was always so happy."

"Sometimes people who are deeply depressed seem that way."

"You don't know anything about it."

"It's a subject I know quite well, as a matter of fact. Hayley, you can feel only your own sadness. It's impossible to know the unhappiness of others. If you have another reason to believe your father was killed—"

Hayley stood abruptly. She muscled her backpack over a shoulder.

"Brooke said you wanted to help me," she said. "Is that true?"

"I'm here to help my employers. If I can help you at the same time I will."

"Your employers? The Guernseys?"

"No, although a couple of them have had dealings with your family."

"It's not my family. Let's go."

"Where?"

"Anywhere. Just go."

We moved down the concrete steps, crossed the street, and entered Washburn Fair Oaks Park. It was pretty lame as parks go in Minnesota, just a square block of green surrounded by Victorian mansions that had long ago been converted to apartment houses and offices for small businesses and nonprofits. A homeless man had staked out one of the benches. Hayley looked at him as if it were her bench only she didn't want to make a fuss about it.

"When were you home last?" I asked.

"Do you mean Axis Mundi? It's not my home."

"Are you hungry? Would you like to get something to eat?"

"I'm not starving, Taylor. I have a credit card. I'm not homeless, either. I have my car. If I get in trouble, I also have my cell phone."

"So you're running away in style."

"I'm not...You don't know me."

"Want some advice?"

"No."

"See the girl in the bright yellow dress?"

The girl was standing near the bus stop on the corner. Hayley found her quickly.

"What about her?" she asked.

"I didn't tell you where she was, yet you found her right away. Do you know why? Because she's wearing a bright yellow dress."

"I don't get it." Hayley looked down at herself, at her clothes, her ink; she touched the rivet in her nostril. "I'm not running away and I'm not hiding, so what I look like doesn't matter."

"Your mother, the Guernseys, are they searching for you?"

"I get a text every day, Taylor. One text, usually at about ten A.M. Come home, it says. It's like I'm an item on a to-do list. Ten o'clock, text Hayley. Then they forget about me. They always forget about me."

"What about the two men who tried to kidnap you yesterday? Were they sent by your—" I said "people" because she didn't seem to like the word "family."

"No," Hayley said.

"Not Fisk?"

"If it had been Fisk I would have run like crazy. He frightens me."

"More than the two men in the parking lot?"

"Sean and Chad? They don't scare me. Anyway, that was

about something else."

"Someone hacked the computers of five local attorneys, stole secret information, and threatened to expose it on NIMN. Is that the something else?"

"We live in a parasitic capitalist culture."

"That's beside the point."

"No, it *is* the point. The super-rich have political access; they control economic policy, social networks, media outlets; they control the reality everyone else lives in. They're rich and they make sure everyone else stays poor. It's the way they want it. Something else. They control the law. They lie, they cheat, they steal, they murder, and nothing is ever done about it because the law and the courts are set up to protect them. They sit up there on that goddamned hill thinking it really is the center of the world. When was the last time you saw a millionaire go to jail for anything? Anything?"

"Hayley—"

"Are you going to tell me I'm wrong? That the world is a wonderful place? Or are you going to tell me that's there's nothing to be done about it, that you refuse to do anything about it? Which one are you, Taylor? A self-deluding romantic or a gutless defeatist?"

"Do I have to be one or the other?"

She quoted Edmund Burke. "The only thing necessary for the triumph of evil is for good men to do nothing. Or good women."

"Okay."

"We need to fight back."

"Is that what you're doing? Fighting back?"

Hayley didn't answer. By then we had crossed the park at a diagonal and were standing on the sidewalk across the street from the Hennepin History Museum.

"The two men yesterday," I said. "I could check the traffic cameras in the area to get the license plate of the van they drove, but to do that I would need to involve the police. I don't want to do that. How 'bout you?"

"I haven't done anything wrong."

I grabbed her by the forearms and shook until she was glaring at me.

"Then why did they try to kidnap you?" I said.

"Greed. Pure greed. And stupidity. Do you know why people support tax breaks and other benefits for the super-rich even though it hurts them? Because in the back of their minds they dream of being super-rich themselves. That's what Sean and Chad are hoping for. Like there's any way the super-rich will let that happen."

Hayley pulled her arms out of my grasp and looked down at the sidewalk. So I looked down, too. If I hadn't been looking down I might have missed it—the subsonic round that bore into the concrete, the impact creating a small crater.

My mind registered what was happening before my body could react. I literally had to scream the words "Get down" before I could make myself move.

I wrapped my arm around Hayley's shoulders and shoved her hard. We crossed the thin boulevard and collapsed on the street between two parked cars, my body falling on top of hers.

Two more bullets flattened into the ground, tossing up chunks of grass and dirt.

We rounded the rear bumper so that our backs were against the car and facing the street.

"Someone is shooting at us!"

I don't know if I was shouting at Hayley or myself. In either case, the girl stared as if I were speaking a language she had never heard before.

I thought I heard the dull thud of two more gunshots, thought I saw where they came from. I brought up the Beretta, gripping it with two hands like I had been trained, and peered over the top of the trunk of the car, yet I couldn't find a target.

"What's happening?" Hayley asked. "Why don't I hear anything?"

"Subsonic rounds. Bullets fired at less than the speed of sound. They don't break the sound barrier; they don't make that loud crack. Fired from a weapon with a suppressor, you'll never hear them coming."

"Who's doing this?"

"I think it's your friends from yesterday."

"No. Killing me won't get them what they want."

"What do they want?"

"You're interrogating me? Now? This is because of you, isn't it? This is all your doing."

"What are you talking about?"

"You're one of them."

"One of whom?"

Hayley didn't answer. Instead, she secured her backpack and began making her way down the street in a low run along the line of parked cars, keeping them between her and the park, using them for protection.

I made a grab for her, but she was too quick.

"Stop," I said.

She wasn't listening.

I was afraid she would draw fire, so I brought up the Beretta again with the idea of giving her cover. Again I couldn't find a target to shoot at.

I stayed behind the parked car.

Nothing happened.

I looked for Hayley.

She had disappeared up the street.

Two couples walked across the park toward me. They were laughing at a joke that must have been pretty funny.

A Lexus worked itself into a parking space behind me.

A third couple walked along the sidewalk as if they didn't need to be anywhere in a hurry.

I crawled out from behind the car, moving cautiously. No more shots were fired. I holstered the Beretta and walked up the street, searching for Hayley as I went. I didn't see her or her

BMW. Finally I reached my own car.

"What the hell just happened?" I said out loud.

CHAPTER SIXTEEN

I explained it all to Freddie early Monday morning. His response was to pin another index card to the bulletin board, this one labeled SNIPER, and connect it to Hayley with red yarn.

"Subsonics," he said. "Very professional."

"Or a gifted amateur."

"That, too. Question is, who was the sniper shooting at? You or the girl?"

"The girl."

"You know this because?"

"I'm pretty sure she was behind the computer hacks."

"Why?"

"Just a guess—to punish her family."

"If she has the goods, why doesn't she send 'em to NIMN like she promised?"

"I don't know."

"Who were the two guys who tried to snatch her from the Library?"

"Their names were Sean and Chad. Beyond that, I don't know."

"Why was the sniper trying to kill her?"

"She's a loose end. Look." I gestured at the bulletin board. "It might be smart to also run yarn from SNIPER to O'NEILL, SIEGLE, and COWGILL. In each case, the killing tied up a loose end that might have been detrimental to the Guernsey family."

"Except the Peterson murder and the rape, the Guernseys don't have a horse in them races, do they?"

"I don't know."

"Jeezus, the amount of shit we don't know. Okay, let's say the Guernseys really did send a sniper to kill one of their own. That ain't got nothin' t' do with us."

"I like her. Hayley. I like her. She's so damned committed."

"It sounds to me like she should *be* committed. Look, I've seen this before, another damsel in distress you want to protect."

"She's confused and hurt, and she seems so alone."

"She's not our client, Taylor. She's not our concern. What we were hired for—"

"What about O'Neill?"

"Man was a professional. He took his chances just like the rest of us."

"Are you going to his funeral? I doubt it's been scheduled yet, but when it is, are you going?"

"Why would I?"

"He was one of us."

"I get that, Taylor. Only it ain't our job is what I'm sayin'. Same with Hayley."

"I know, but—"

"But what?"

The office door was knocked on. I opened it. A woman, about thirty, overweight yet fashionable in business attire, stood in front of me.

"Are you Taylor?" she asked.

I said I was. She reached into the bag hanging from her shoulder and withdrew an envelope.

"I'm supposed to give this to you."

I took the envelope. The woman left without speaking another word. I watched as she made her way to the elevators while I opened the envelope. It was filled with cash.

I stepped back into the office, closing the door behind me.

"Who was that?" Freddie asked.

I answered by tossing him the envelope. He looked inside.

"My, my, my," he said. "I do like the color green."

"It's a down payment from the mayor of the City of Minneapolis."

"Bless 'er heart. What do we need t' do to earn it?"

"Find Hayley O'Brien, if she really is the hacker, and deliver a message."

"Like the kind of message we delivered to the punk that was stalking our client last year?"

"No, no, no. This one is strictly verbal. Not even a threat. Just an offer of mutual assistance."

"Sounds like the mayor is trying to cover her ass." Freddie dropped the envelope on his desk. "Whaddaya know? Turns out the girl's our concern after all. What do we do next?"

We were surrounded by lawyers in a smoke-filled room found deep in the bowels of an utterly exclusive club located on the edge of downtown Minneapolis. Only this time no one offered us cigars or alcohol.

We sat in the same chairs around the same table as a week earlier while I carefully explained everything that had happened in the past seven days, although I did fail to mention the mayor's bribe and the fact that I had bent the rules of client confidentiality by talking to the cops on three separate occasions.

"You should see our bulletin board," Freddie said.

What caught me by surprise was the realization that whenever the conversation bent to one lawyer's case, the other four attorneys seemed to purposely tune out. I didn't know if it was out of courtesy or apathy.

Cormac Puchner was the first to speak when I finished, no

surprise there.

"Can you prove that Hayley O'Brien is responsible for the computer hacks?" he asked.

"You mean in a court of law?" I asked. "No."

He gestured with his hands as if that were all he needed to know.

My partner said, "By a preponderance of the evidence—"

"Have you been going to law school at night without telling us, Freddie?" Douglas Jernigan asked.

Freddie shook his head.

"Let's hurry this along. I need to be in court in less than an hour."

"I have a hundred meetings," said Puchner.

"Let's assume, for argument's sake, that you're correct about Guernsey's stepdaughter," Scott Mickelson said. "Is that a door we want to open?"

He was speaking to Freddie and me, but the question was meant for his colleagues.

"Obviously the girl is in danger," John Kaushal said.

"We don't know that," Puchner replied.

"The word of Sidney Fredericks and Holland Taylor has always been good. Don't you agree?"

Puchner shrugged as if he didn't have an opinion.

"If Hayley is responsible for the computer hacks, the family will want to know," Kaushal said. "If she's in danger because of the hacks, they'll want to know that as well. If she's in danger from her family, then knowing that we know about it might forestall the Guernseys from doing something unspeakable." Kaushal paused. "Don't you agree?"

"No, I don't agree," Jernigan said. "We hired Fredericks and Taylor to keep the stolen information from reaching the public. So far they've done that."

"All we've been doin' is watchin' the bodies pile up," Freddie said.

"That has nothing to do with us."

"There're two ongoing police investigations, one in St. Paul, one in Minneapolis. Could be eventually it'll have a lot to do with you."

"Not me," Mickelson said. "Or you either, John."

Kaushal didn't react to the remark. It was if an ongoing police investigation didn't matter to him one way or the other. If Jernigan and Puchner objected to the suggestion they might be tossed under the bus, they didn't show it.

Puchner said, "I've already dealt with the police. They're no longer an issue."

"They're always an issue, man," Freddie said.

"What exactly do you two want from us, anyway?" Jernigan asked.

"Besides more money," Puchner said.

"An introduction to the Guernseys," I said. "We can't reach them on our own."

"Although more money is also good," Freddie added.

"Oh hell," David Helin said. It was the first time he'd spoken. "If that's all…"

He had dealt personally with members of the Guernsey family because of the Brooke St. Vincent divorce case, so Helin had several contacts he could reach out to and several numbers he could call. He told Freddie and me that he would get back to us as soon as he had something concrete to report, which surprised us. Of all the attorneys in the room, he was the one with the most to lose if the Guernseys should ever see what the computer hacker stole from them.

Freddie and I retreated to the office. First thing Freddie did was check for phone messages and review our emails. I watched him do it.

"What?" he asked.

"I was just wondering, does Hayley have a laptop in her backpack? I bet she doesn't, the way she throws it around. If she did, she wouldn't have needed to use the computers at the Library."

"What are you thinking?"

"Maybe that's why she hasn't sent the intel she stole to NIMN. She doesn't have a computer."

"Or she didn't want her emails and whatnot traced back to her."

"No. Her cover's blown. If she didn't know that before, she'd've figured it out after what happened yesterday."

"How does that help us?"

"Why don't you stay here and take care of business while I drive out to Mound, buy a good book at the Library, something by William Kent Krueger—"

"I don't know who that is."

"Get a cup of joe. Hang around a bit. See who drops by."

"Do you really think Hayley will return to the scene of the crime? No one does that, man. It's a myth. Mostly people stay as far away from the bad thing as they can get."

"We seek comfort in what we know. The fact the barista knew her by name, it's obviously a place she's familiar with. Don't forget the free computers, either."

"What about the divorcée?"

"I think we torched that bridge yesterday. If Hayley thinks I was responsible for the attack, Brooke probably will, too."

"Wouldn't hurt to give 'er a try."

"Okay. In the meantime—"

"If Helin calls, I'll let you know."

That's when the cops knocked on our door.

"You gonna talk to us or what?" Detective Sergeant Nathan Vanak asked. He was sitting in one of our chairs, his legs crossed at the ankles and his feet resting on our low round table, his hands locked behind his head as if he owned the place. His partner was leaning against the door, his arms crossed over his chest, a bored expression on his face.

"Wanna cup of coffee?" Freddie asked.

"No, I don't want a cup of coffee," Vanak said. He glanced at his partner. "You want a cup of coffee?"

"Depends. They got decaf?"

"Do you guys have decaf?" Vanak asked.

"No," I said. "We don't have decaf."

"They don't have decaf," Vanak said.

"Never mind, then," his partner said. "Gotta say, though, it doesn't seem hospitable not having decaf."

"It doesn't, does it?" Vanak agreed. "What about visitors who don't want caffeine? Don't you care about them?"

"Yeah, me and Taylor have an act, too," Freddie said. "Banter back and forth 'bout nothin' to confuse and confound suspects and such. So let's pretend we're both confused and confounded. What the hell?"

"Clinton Siegle's wife, what's her name?"

"Linda," I said. Vanak was aware of the name, of course. He just wanted to know if I was emotionally invested in the case.

"Linda, right," he added just to be sure. "Nice woman. Having her husband killed like that, a real tragedy."

"It was."

"Linda confirmed Siegle's involvement with Standout Investments. She told us about the mysterious memo that the company is supposedly trying to suppress. The company would only speak to us through its attorney, though. What was the name of that Harvard prick?"

"Cormac Puchner," Vanak's partner replied.

"What kind of name is Cormac?"

"Irish," Freddie said. "Ancient Irish."

"How do you know?"

"Musta been TV or somethin' like that, cuz you know us brothers can't read."

"Don't give us shit, Freddie."

"Not me. Wouldn't wanna confirm no racial stereotypes you

might have."

"No, you wouldn't want to do that."

"Sergeant Vanak." I purposely used his title because I wanted to snap him up. "If you're upset about something and you want to take it out on us, I can live with that *if* you tell us why you're upset."

"Puchner is obfuscating like crazy. Refuses to even acknowledge that Siegle and Walter O'Neill were actually killed, much less that Standout was somehow involved."

"Obfuscating," Freddie said.

"You like that word, Freddie?"

"Gonna teach it to my kid soon as I get home."

"What else?" I asked.

"We spoke to Mrs. O'Neill. She's devastated by what happened to her ex. Have you met Mrs. O'Neill?"

"No."

For a moment, it looked like Vanak was going to say something besides the words that actually came out of his mouth. "She gave us permission to search his office. It was a small space in one of those business malls you see along the highway. Not opulent like your digs. I'm told that the average PI makes about forty-five thousand a year. What do you two pull down? A lot better than that, I bet."

Neither of us cared to admit that we were in the ninetieth percentile when it came to income, but I noticed Freddie slowly take the mayor's envelope off his desk and slip it into a drawer.

"You went to Walter's office," I said.

"Someone had broken in," Vanak said. "His computer was stolen. We couldn't find any written notes. Nothing to indicate what he was working on. Nothing that could tell us who he was working for. What does that tell you?"

Neither Freddie nor I had an answer.

"Want to know what it tells us?" Vanak's partner said. "It tells us that Siegle might not have been the target. Up till now we were working under the premise that O'Neill was killed because he just happened to be sitting there when the hitter went after Siegle. Now we're wondering if O'Neill was the primary, because he found out something he shouldn't have, and Siegle was killed because he was a witness. According to your statement, the last thing he said before you told him to call 911"—he didn't consult his notes, yet he quoted me accurately—*"He's looking at me. He sees me standing at the window. Oh my God, he's coming toward the house."*

"What do you have to say about that?" Vanak asked.

"It hadn't occurred to me."

"Give us something. I'll settle for a name."

"I can't."

"You mean you won't."

"I mean I can't."

"He was your friend. Are you telling me that you won't help us find his killer because of some fucking rule? Taylor, Freddie, I promise it won't come back on you."

"He wasn't our friend," I said. "That's beside the point. We can't give you anything because we don't have anything. O'Neill's clients aren't our clients. If we knew who he was working for, what he was doing, we would tell you, but we honestly don't know. I thought this was about Standout, and now…"

Vanak rose from his chair and went to the door. His partner opened it. He paused before crossing the threshold.

"I'm going to leave this for now." He wasn't looking at us as he spoke. Instead, he gazed into the corridor. "I'm going to leave it because I know about you two. I know you're going to pursue this on your own. I know that you're going to tell me whatever you learn."

Vanak and his partner left, closing the door behind them.

"Are we going to tell them if we learn anything?" Freddie asked.

"Apparently that's what we're expected to do."

"We always do what's expected, don't we?"

CHAPTER SEVENTEEN

We were upset that we might have misread the murders of Clinton Seigle and Walter O'Neill, only we didn't know what to do about it. We decided it was best to stick to the original plan. So, while Freddie held down the fort, I made my way to the lot where my Camry was parked. Along the way I called Brooke St. Vincent. She told me that she had lost contact with Hayley.

"I don't know what to do," Brooke told me. "I keep calling, but she must be swiping left."

I told her I was sorry to hear it.

"I tried calling Axis Mundi. No one answered. I left a message. An hour later, Maura called. She said that Hayley left home eight days ago and she hasn't seen her since. She said she's very concerned."

Eight days ago, I told myself, would have been Monday, two days after the lawyers received the emails from NIMN.

"What happened after I left the Institute of Art?" Brooke asked.

I explained.

"I don't understand any of this," Brooke said.

"Hayley's made a lot of enemies."

"Why? Who? It can't be her family, can it?"

"I don't know." God, how I hated those three words.

"I'll keep calling," Brooke said.

"If you would give me her number—"

"No."

"Okay."

"Not without her permission. I'm sorry, Taylor."

"No. That's a good thing. Be loyal to your friend. She needs it."

"I can't give you the number at Axis Mundi, either."

"I understand."

"If I reach Hayley, I'll tell you."

"I appreciate it."

"Where will you be?"

"For now I'm heading to the Library just in case she tries to use the computers there."

"You're a good person, Taylor. When all this is settled, I hope you'll call on me."

As quickly as a lightning strike I flashed on the times I could have hit on Brooke and didn't, and now she was telling me what I had wanted to tell her. There's a lot to be said for the slow game, I told myself.

"I will," I said. "Count on it."

I had consumed four twelve-ounce cups of coffee and a turkey pesto sandwich by early evening with no sign of Hayley O'Brien.

There are tricks to staying alert while conducting surveillance. One of them is to stay active. The worst thing you can do is just sit still and watch a doorway for eight hours or more. If you don't actually fall asleep, your mind will meander to the point where a polka-dot elephant could wander past without you noticing it.

I wondered if that was what had happened to Walter. If he had allowed his concentration to drift. If that's why his killer was able to approach his vehicle without him noticing. Or did he notice? Did Walter know his killer?

I shook the questions from my head and instead focused on

the job. I conducted my surveillance from inside the café itself, the parking lot, the bookstore, and outside again with numerous stops in the café's restroom. I wore a couple of different hats and jackets so no one noticed me. At least no one bothered to call the cops to complain about the stalker who was now sitting in a Camry on the far side of the street with a clear view of the Library's entrance.

It helped that I was able to park in the shade. It was sunny and seventy degrees outside, about average for the Twin Cities in late September. Yet it slowly climbed to over ninety degrees inside my Camry with the tinted windows up. Windows up make it harder for the subject to see you while you're seeing them.

I was thinking that trading the furnace for a table inside the café again wasn't a bad idea. There had been a shift change. The current baristas hadn't seen me before, and the Library was busier now than it had been earlier in the day. I slipped on a light jacket, no hat, and opened the car door. That's when I saw her.

I ducked back inside the car.

Hayley was wearing the same clothes as the day before and carrying the same backpack. She paused at the door, looked up the street and down, and stepped inside. I crossed the street in a hurry while wondering what she was going to do when she saw me—fight or flight?

She did neither. Instead, she closed her eyes and sighed as if I were a bad habit she just couldn't shake.

"Would you please leave me alone?" she said.

I rested my hand on her shoulder. "I am so relieved to see that you're okay. Brooke St. Vincent will be, too."

Hayley shook my arm away. "Why wouldn't I be all right?"

We were standing inside the café in front of the bank of computers.

"You're kidding me, right?" I said. She couldn't possibly be that naïve. "Someone was shooting at you."

"I don't know that. It could have been you."

"Lady, I'm just a hired hand. You're the one making people angry. Angry enough to kill."

"Are you going to protect me from them?"

"I'm trying."

"Why? You're not my father."

"I used to be a father. My daughter died in a car accident. She'd be about your age if she had lived."

"Is that true?" Hayley said. "Or just something you're telling yourself?"

"Does it matter?"

"Once I do what I came to do, everything will be fine."

"No, it won't."

"You don't know."

"What are you? Eight? This is grown-up shit that you're doing, and it's dangerous. Three people have been killed already. I knew one of them personally."

"What?"

"Goddammit, Hayley. Will you do what I ask? Will you let me help you?"

I didn't realize I was shouting until I felt the silence that followed. It seemed everyone in the café had quit their own conversations and was now staring at us. Hayley was staring as well, at some point far off in the distance. Something must have clicked inside her head. She suddenly lost her defiance and started trembling, to the point where she seemed to be bouncing up and down like a tennis ball.

"None of this was supposed to happen," she said. "People being killed. Your friend, you said your friend…"

A young man sitting with a young woman at a nearby table abruptly stood up. "Are you okay?" he asked. He was speaking to Hayley, but I noticed he kept glancing down at his date, and I thought, he's not the first guy to do something foolish to impress a girl.

Hayley's eyes refocused. "Do I look like I'm okay?" she said.

"If he's bothering you—"

"Bothering me?"

I rested my hand on Hayley's shoulder again. "Please," I said.

Hayley nodded her head. At least I think she nodded her head. In any case, she didn't stop me from grabbing hold of her elbow and leading her out of the Library. The young man did nothing to stop us.

As I opened the door for her, I moved to relieve her of the backpack.

"No," she said and clenched it to her chest.

It wasn't quite night, yet most of the vehicles zipping by had their headlights on. We managed to cross the street without getting run down, but it required effort. When we reached the sidewalk, I nudged Hayley in the direction of my car. That's when frat boy and his friend stopped us.

"Hayley," frat boy said.

She was startled enough to curl into me so that her face was pressed against my chest. My left arm went around her shoulder. My right went slightly behind my hip not far from where the Beretta was holstered beneath the jacket.

"I knew you'd come back," frat boy said. "Where else were you gonna go? You don't have any friends."

"I thought you were my friend," Hayley said. She refused to look at him.

"Me? I'm just the guy who was fucking you."

"Why are you doing this, Sean?"

Now you know who's who, I thought.

"For the money, why else," Sean said. "Now give me the files."

"No."

"They belong to me."

"No. Taylor?"

"You heard the lady," I said.

"This ain't got anything to do with you."

That came from Sean's pal. I pivoted so that he was on my left and Sean on my right with the street at my back.

"You were wrong before, Sean." I used his name as if we had known each other for a thousand years. "Hayley does have friends."

"Yeah, like who?"

"Me, to start with."

"Who are you?"

"I'm the one with a hand six inches away from the butt of a nine-millimeter Beretta semiautomatic handgun."

Hayley's head came off my chest. She looked at me as if she couldn't believe what I was saying. Sean seemed confused as well. His fingers went to his puffy nose and probed for a bit before he slowly dropped his hand.

"You're the guy from before," he said.

"That's right."

His friend took a step forward. I remembered the Colt he had pulled the other day, the one that was now locked in my office safe. I wondered if he had another gun and decided, why wouldn't he? It's easier to get a gun in this country than a driver's license. I watched his hands carefully.

Sean seemed to sense the danger. "Chad," he said.

His friend stopped moving.

We stood there for a second or two without speaking.

Sean said, "We can make a deal."

"I love deals," I said. "What do you get?"

Hayley spun in my arm until she was facing Sean.

"No deals," she said.

"What do you get?" I asked again.

"Taylor—"

"I get the files," Sean said.

"What do we get?"

Sean and Chad exchanged looks. From the expressions on their faces I could tell we weren't going to get anything except the wrong end of the stick.

"That's what I thought," I said. "Hayley and I are leaving."

"Not until she returns my property," Sean said.

"It's mine." Hayley's confidence seemed to be returning. "It belongs to me."

"I'm the one who did all the work to get it."

"You wouldn't have known where to look if I hadn't told you, and I told you so we could post it on the internet, not use it to blackmail my family."

"What difference does it make? You hate your family."

Hayley clenched one fist, the other holding tight to the backpack. My left hand continued to rest on her shoulder. My right was touching the hem of my jacket.

"It makes a big difference," she said.

"Give me the files."

"Make me."

"Okay," I said. "We're done here."

"Hell we are," Chad said.

He moved his hands too much for my comfort, so I filled mine with the Beretta. I pointed it at his face. I didn't like shooting with one hand, a snap shot from the shoulder, but he was just seven feet away and I figured my chances were good.

Sean spread his hands wide.

"No, no, no," he chanted. "No, no, no. No. No, no. Stop it."

Chad froze in place. His eyes grew wide and fixed on the muzzle of the gun.

"I said we're leaving," I told them. "You got a problem with that?"

"Leave, then," Sean said. "We don't want any trouble."

I turned my head just in time to see a red dot center on his chest.

I screamed, "Get down."

Sean's chest exploded.

There was very little noise. Just a kind of thud. Sean didn't cry out. Neither did Chad.

I pushed Hayley down on the sidewalk and covered her body with mine.

Sean's body fell backward against the concrete.

Chad stared down at him, a bewildered expression on his face.

"What did you do?" he asked.

"Get down," I told him.

He went to Sean and cradled him in his arms.

"What did you do?" he asked again.

I half pulled, half carried Hayley as quickly as I could, following the line of cars parked along the street until we reached mine. I didn't look back, not even when I heard another thud followed by a loud, slow exhale.

We took cover behind the vehicle that was parked directly in front of my Camry. Hayley was breathing heavily, her shallow breaths infused with soft whimpers.

I holstered the Beretta and pulled the key fob from my pocket. I used it to unlock the car doors. I grabbed Hayley's hand.

"Ready?" I asked.

She didn't know what I was talking about.

I pulled Hayley to the rear door on the driver's side, keeping to the street side of the Camry, using it as a shield. I opened the door and stuffed her inside.

"Stay down," I told her.

I shut the door and opened the driver's door and squeezed inside, keeping as low as possible while still being able to see over the steering wheel. At the same time, I glanced down the sidewalk. Chad was slumped over the body of his friend. Neither of them was moving.

I started the car, worked it out of the parking space, executed a tight U-turn, and accelerated hard down the street in the opposite direction from the sniper. At least I hoped it was in the opposite direction. Once again, I hadn't seen him.

Why them? I wondered. Why did the sniper shoot Sean and Chad? Why didn't he shoot us? He had tried to shoot us in the park, hadn't he?

Hayley had rolled into a tight ball on the floor directly behind my seat. I couldn't see her in the rearview mirror, so I glanced briefly over my shoulder. She was shaking like tall grass in a hard wind.

She kept asking herself, "What did I do, what did I do?"

I curled my hand behind the seat and tried to give her a reassuring pat but couldn't reach. Hayley became quiet.

By then we were on the freeway, and I was trying hard to keep the speedometer at the posted limit. I wanted no dealings with the police. Yeah, I was a material witness to a homicide, and the Private Detective Board has rules about that sort of thing, only I didn't want to explain what happened outside the Library until I was able to sort out Hayley's involvement in it—unless the cops came knocking on my door and asked, of course, in which case I'd spill my guts. They might, too. The City of Mound has its share of traffic cameras like everyone else.

"We need to talk," I said.

Hayley didn't answer, and I didn't press the point. All I wanted to do at the moment was get as far away from the Library as possible.

We drove without speaking until we were in Minneapolis. The bright freeway lights illuminated the inside of the car. Hayley stayed on the floor, but her head came up and she looked at me for the first time.

"Where are you taking me?" she asked.

CHAPTER EIGHTEEN

Dr. Alexandra Campbell found us on her doorstep.

"Can we come in?" I asked.

She looked down at Hayley, at her piercings and tats and stringy hair and dirty clothes and backpack, and then she looked up at me with an appraising smile as if she had discovered something about my character that she hadn't known before.

"Of course," Alex said. She held the storm and inside doors open for us, and we passed into her house.

"Alex, this is Hayley O'Brien."

Alex offered her hand and said, "How are you?"

Hayley's response was to clutch the backpack to her chest.

"Hayley," I said, "this is Dr. Campbell."

"Are you a medical doctor?" Hayley asked.

"No," Alex said.

"Oh."

"When was the last time you had a hot meal?" Alex asked her.

"Five o'clock. Why does everybody think I'm homeless?"

Alex turned her eyes on me. All I could do was shrug.

"It's a long story," I said.

"Please. I'd love to hear it."

"I'll tell you later. For now—Alex, I need your help. We need your help. Hayley is in danger, and I need to hide her."

"What kind of danger?"

"Mortal."

"Seriously?"

"I'm standing right here," Hayley said.

Alex and I turned to face her.

"I hate it when people talk as if I'm not in the room," Hayley added.

"I apologize," Alex said. "Are you in mortal danger?"

"I guess."

"Why?"

"I'm trying to tell the truth."

"That is dangerous. Please, take a seat."

Hayley found a chair and sat with her backpack resting on her lap.

"Alex," I said, "I'm hoping you can put her up for a few days while I try to sort it all out."

"Why not take her to your place?"

"The police could knock on my door at any moment. Besides, she's, you know, and I'm—"

"She's a young woman and you're a man? For goodness sake, Taylor. What a prude you are."

Considering our relationship, I didn't think that was a particularly accurate description, yet I refused to argue the point.

"What do you want to do?" Alex asked.

The question seemed to jolt Hayley. It was if no one had ever asked her opinion before.

"What?" she said. "Me?"

Alex squatted in front of Hayley and rested her hand on the girl's knee. "Do you want to stay here for a few days?" she asked.

Hayley's gaze flickered across the room without lingering on anything for very long until her eyes rested on Alex's. "I don't know you," she said.

"I'm a schoolteacher."

"Schoolteacher?"

"University of Minnesota. Are you in school?"

"No. I...I was enrolled at...I was supposed to start classes at UC Berkeley in August, but things happened."

"If I'm not mistaken, they don't start their spring semester until the second week of January." Alex reached up and brushed a lock of hair out of Hayley's eye. "Plenty of time to decide what to do."

"Dr. Campbell?"

"Call me Alex."

"I don't have anywhere else to go."

"You're welcome to stay here, if that's what you want."

"You have no reason to help me."

"You need help. What more reason do I require?"

"You could get in trouble."

"Oh, I don't think so. Besides, that's what we have Taylor for."

Maybe it was the sound of her voice, or the look in her eye, or the slight smile on her lips, or even the way she caressed the girl's knee with her hand, but something about Alex gave Hayley permission to let go. Tears flooded her eyes, and a long, low moan of anguish escaped from deep inside where it had been held prisoner by her rage. She leaned forward and wrapped her arms around Alex's neck. Alex's arms circled Hayley's waist. The backpack slipped off the girl's lap and thudded on the floor. They stayed that way, hugging each other while Hayley wept, for what seemed like a very long time.

While they hugged, Hayley began to tell us her story.

It came out in bits and pieces, a tale short on affection and long on neglect. Hayley had everything money could buy but none of the answers to the questions that constantly invaded her sleep. Why did her beloved father put a gun in his mouth and pull the trigger? Why did her beloved mother marry a man old enough to be Hayley's grandfather? Why did her stepfather treat her like a porcelain doll, something to be seen and not heard? Why did her stepbrothers and stepsister ignore her very existence except for those times when they berated her for being an ugly, ungrateful, and spoiled bitch? Why did her mother let them do it?

Why did every friendship end in sorrow?

Why had she ever been born?

"They forgot my fourteenth birthday," Hayley said. "Even my mother forgot. They were all apologetic when they realized what had happened. I was given a lot of money. Toys. They also forgot my seventeenth birthday. I got a car that time. A BMW. My stepfather said the color matched my eyes. What color are my eyes, Taylor?"

"Light green."

"What color is my car?"

"Dark blue."

"They just want me to go away. All of them. Even my mother. They'd be happy to pay my bills, college tuition, rent, whatever I want, if I would just go away. Go to California. Oh, and stay out of trouble. At least the kind of trouble that gets into the media. It's okay just as long as my name isn't connected to the Guernsey name."

"It can't be that bad," Alex said.

"I knew a girl in high school. She was caught drinking underage. Her parents grounded her, took away her car, her smartphone, her privileges. All she was allowed to do was go to school and come home for three months. She complained bitterly whenever I saw her. Said she hated her family. I would have given everything to have a family like that. I got piercings, I got tattoos even though it was illegal because I was under eighteen at the time, and no one cared. Except Melissa. She said I looked like a slut."

"The computer hacks," I said. "That was payback?"

"Have you ever done anything for revenge, Taylor?"

"Yes."

"Sweet, isn't it?"

"Actually, I found it to be very unsatisfying. A total waste of my time."

"We'll see."

"Make me understand what you hope to accomplish."

"Knowledge is power. Do you believe that, Taylor? Knowledge is power, but only if it's one-sided. When secrets are revealed, power is lost or transferred to someone else. If the public finds out what despicable people the Guernseys are, they'll lose their power over the rest of us. They'll never survive it. Power is their beating heart."

"Half of the hacks have nothing to do with the Guernseys."

"Yes, they do."

"I saw what the lawyers—"

"Lawyers? You believe lawyers?"

"I saw what they showed me."

"Did they show you everything?"

"You tell me."

Hayley slid off the chair and sat on the floor next to Alex. Alex took her hand in both of hers as Hayley spoke in a voice that made me think she had told her story many times, at least in her head.

The entire Guernsey family lived at Axis Mundi on Lake Minnetonka. Apparently it was the size of a resort. The members were expected to dine together each night, even Hayley. Servants would serve them the way they did in Downton Abbey. The old man wanted it that way. That's what they called him behind his back, the old man. To his face it was Father or, in Hayley's case, Stepfather, always reminding herself and everyone else of her place in the family hierarchy.

"My mother calls him Robert Paul," Hayley said. "Nearly everyone else does, too. Never Robert. Never Bob. Always Robert Paul, both names together."

During those dinners, conversations frequently veered to the family's many business endeavors.

"The things they said," Hayley told us. "They spoke effort-lessly about bribing the mayor and defrauding the government like it was...like they were discussing the weather. Will we get our building permits? Will it rain? I would think, if only people could hear them. Then I thought, maybe they should."

"So you hacked the computers of their lawyers," I said.

"I didn't. Sean did. He knew computers. I didn't. I guess he made money stealing people's identities."

"How did you hook up with him?"

"I met him at the Library. He bought me coffee. Later, he took me to a bar and bought me a real drink."

"Did he know you were underage?"

"Yeah, but he didn't care, and neither did I. Then we fucked."

She used the word for dramatic effect, yet the moment she spoke it, Hayley turned her head away. It was obvious that she didn't give a damn what I thought of her, but I could tell she cared about Alex's opinion. The older woman squeezed her hand tighter. Hayley found Alex's eyes. I knew another crying jag was about to begin.

"They kept telling me I was a slut and then I decided I wasn't but I was...and Sean—I just wanted someone to hold me. He was good to me, too. Treated me better than my own family until...Later, he shared me with his friends, and I let him."

The tears fell. "Somehow I got it in my head that I could hurt my family by hurting myself."

There wasn't much talking after that. I left the room. Alex gave me a look that suggested I was being a jerk, but what was I supposed to do? Pat Hayley on the back and say, "There, there?"

When I returned, Alex was brushing the tears off Hayley's cheek with her thumbs. She was smiling.

"We learn as we go," Alex said, and I thought, isn't that what I always say?

"You told Sean whose computers to hack," I said.

"Uh-huh," Hayley replied. "Because of what was said at dinner I knew the names of the lawyers, of the law firms. "Sean—I knew he was just using me for sex. I decided to use him, use his skills at tracking computers and stealing identities. I told Sean I wanted to steal the information from the lawyers and put it up on the web, on NIMN. He thought that was funny. 'Course, he was already planning to betray me."

"Why those lawyers? Why those cases?"

"You really don't know, do you? It was because...Listen, the thing with Standout Investments. That wasn't about violating the Telephone Consumer Protection Act. Remember a couple years ago they caught Wells Fargo committing massive consumer fraud to make it seem like the bank was bigger, more successful than it really was, creating all those fraudulent accounts, forging customer signatures, sending out unwanted credit cards. There was a big scandal. The government fined them like one hundred and eighty-five million dollars. The bosses were dragged before a Senate subcommittee. Well, Minnesota River State Bank has been doing the exact same thing. The president of Wells Fargo said that every customer should have eight accounts whether they wanted them or not because 'Eight Is Great.' Stepfather wrote 'Four or More' in emails to his managers and directors. That's what they're trying to hide. Who cares about sending ads to people's cell phones? Jesus. They were afraid that if they allowed the suit against Standout to go forward, all this other stuff would come out.

"The thing with Mayor Feeney—it was Robert Jr. who actually gave her the envelope filled with cash. Fifty thousand dollars. He gave it to the mayor personally and told her that if she cleared the poor people out of the neighborhood on the North Side where Ryan-Reed wanted to build its new plant, there would be more money where that came from, and the mayor wrote it all down verbatim. When Robert Jr. told us this at dinner, do you know what the old man said? He said Robert Jr. should have negotiated harder. He called him a pussy and said that if he was half as smart as him, Robert Jr. could have bought the mayor for ten or fifteen thousand less. That's what I want the people to know."

"What about the Dawn Peterson murder case?" I asked.

"Melissa was sleeping with Clark Peterson. She was Dawn's friend. They went to school together. Somehow Lissa was introduced to Clark, and the next thing she was fucking his brains out behind Dawn's back. When Dawn disappeared, Melissa was all 'Is this my fault? Did Clark kill Dawn because of me?' The old man, Stepfather, he was furious, kept calling Lissa a whore, which I guess she was, sleeping with another woman's husband and all. The old man didn't care that people might believe Melissa was somehow involved in Dawn's disappearance, that she was in it with Peterson. Instead, he kept telling her that if his name—his name, not Melissa's—he said if it came up at trial, if it was connected to the murder, she'd regret it big-time. If her name had been O'Brien instead of Guernsey, he wouldn't have cared. Only the Guernsey name didn't come up. I don't know why. The defense lawyer knew Lissa was screwing Peterson because he questioned her about it. He came to Axis Mundi. I saw him. But the Guernsey name was never mentioned, Dawn's body was never found, and Peterson got away with it. He got away with murder. It wasn't the only one, either. Taylor, according to the notes we stole from his attorney, Peterson confessed that he had killed three or four other women over the years and hid their bodies where no one could find them just like he did with Dawn. He's a fucking maniac."

I sat in one of Alex's chairs. It seemed very big. Or maybe I was feeling very small. Clark Peterson had lied to me, no surprise there. But John Kaushal, too? Peterson obviously told him about his affair with Melissa. The information must have been in the notes that were stolen.

I asked myself, what else don't you know? The words seemed tiny when I uttered them aloud. "The Todd Kendrick rape..."

"He's my stepbrother," Hayley said. "Only no one knows that. Kurtis got this college girl pregnant like twenty years ago. He didn't want to marry her, or at least Stepfather didn't want him to marry her. Instead, to avoid a scandal and because Stepfather told him to, Kurt agreed to pay her off. Not a lump sum, though. A salary instead. That way the Guernseys had control over her life in case she should change her mind. Kurt deposited money into her bank account at Minnesota River every month as long as she kept quiet about his son. Then Todd was accused of rape, and his mother—what was her name? Diane?"

"Dana," I said.

"Dana said she didn't have the money to defend Todd in court, but Kurtis did. The blackmailing began at the same time because there were pictures. Todd had taken selfies of him raping that poor girl. The old man was apoplectic, but he told Kurtis to both help Dana and pay the blackmailer. He thought paying up was better than having his bastard grandson go to prison and maybe having his name dragged into it, screw the victim."

"Okay."

"Okay? Is that all you have to say?"

"Why didn't you send it all to NIMN like you promised in the emails?"

"Because Sean betrayed me, I told you. Once he hacked the information, he decided to use it to blackmail the family. I found out at dinner Saturday night. Each one of them— Stepfather, Robert Jr., Kurtis, Melissa—each one of them received an email telling them to pay up or else. Oh my God, Taylor, it was awful. They were so angry. Remember at the Library when you said I made people angry enough to kill? I just sat there shaking. My mother looked at me and said, 'Honey, are you all right?' and I'm like, 'Are you kidding, Mother?' I was terrified that they would find out it was me. I left that night. I threw some clothes in my backpack and ran out of the house. They didn't even realize it until two days later. At least that's when I started getting texts asking where I was.

"I went to find Sean. I wanted to make him stop what he was doing. He wouldn't listen to me. He reminded me that I had started all this to hurt my family. He said, what better way to hurt them than to take their money. But that's not—that's not what I wanted. I just wanted to—I wanted the world to know the truth. This was...blackmail was—I wanted no part of it. I pretended that it was okay, though, that I was okay with it, and Sean fucked me that night, and when he went to sleep, I stole the files.

"Sean told me...I don't know anything about computers, Taylor. I thought if you downloaded something onto your computer it was there forever. What Sean said, he said even if the lawyers had deleted the emails and notes and things, he would still be able to find them. But then he told me that he had managed to put all of the lawyers' stuff on a single thumb drive so if the cops came they wouldn't be able to find the illegal stuff on his own computer. I guess that was something he did while he was stealing people's identities, covering his tracks. Anyway, he must have been telling the truth, because when I ran out with his flash drive, he started chasing me. Why would he do that if he had a backup?"

"You didn't go home," I reminded her.

"I was afraid."

"You didn't upload the information on NIMN, either."

"I was afraid. I guess I didn't really appreciate what would happen until I saw how the family reacted to the blackmail. I didn't know what to do."

"You sent emails to the lawyers," I said.

"No, I didn't. That must have been Sean trying to blackmail them just like he was attempting to blackmail my family. Later—I waited a week, Taylor, an entire week of doing nothing except being afraid, of talking to no one but myself. I finally decided if I uploaded the information, if I gave it to NIMN, there would be nothing to blackmail anyone with. It would all be out there like I had originally wanted, no reason to pay anyone anything. Only I didn't have a computer. I threw clothes into my backpack, grabbed my phone, but I forgot all about my laptop. I thought about buying one, but I didn't really have a place to set it up. Finally, when I was ready, I went to the Library because I used to hang out there all the time and I knew they had free computers. Except Sean stopped me. And then you."

"Okay."

"You keep saying that."

"C'mon, kid. Give me a minute to think."

"What's there to think about? You were hired to stop me from going to NIMN. Well?"

"Well, what?"

"Stop me."

"Could you just relax for a second?"

Hayley pulled away from Alex and stood directly in front of me, both of her fists clenched.

"What are you going to do?" she said.

"I don't know. Alex, what should I do?"

"I bought a bottle of that bourbon you like," she said.

"Now there's a thought."

Hayley lowered her voice. "What are you going to do?" she asked again.

"Have a drink. Do you like bourbon? Normally, I wouldn't offer given your tender age, but honestly, I don't know of anyone who needs it more."

We ended up sitting around Alex's kitchen table.

"I don't want you to upload the files on NIMN," I said. "Partly it's because I was hired to stop you from doing just that. But mostly, Hayley, mostly it's because we might need the leverage those files can provide. Like you said, knowledge is power. Let's keep as much of it as possible for now."

"For now?"

"Promise me. Promise you won't take your information to NIMN until I say it's okay."

"I promise."

"Then I promise to get you out of this mess."

"How are you going to do that?"

"I don't know yet. So far I've been making this up as I go along. Give me your cell phone."

"My cell phone?"

"Please."

"You want to keep me from calling for help."

"No, Hayley. I want to keep the bad guys from tracking you by your GPS."

"I disabled that the first thing. I'm not stupid."

"Did you also do that with your BMW? Do you even know how?"

The question seemed to surprise her.

"I didn't think of that," she said. "Do you think that's how they found me at the Library and yesterday at the park?"

"It's possible."

Hayley slid her phone across the table, but she did it reluctantly.

"If you need to get ahold of me, tell Alex," I said.

"I only have one class on Tuesdays, and I'll cancel it so I can spend the entire day with you," Alex said.

Hayley looked as if she might start crying again, so I finished my bourbon and stood up.

"I better leave," I said. "Wait. One more piece of business. The mayor of the City of Minneapolis said she'd be happy to be your best friend forever if you promised to be hers."

"What does that mean?" Hayley asked.

"What do you think it means?"

"Tell her to go to hell."

"Okay."

"Okay?"

"I was paid to deliver a message. Message delivered. Moving on."

Alex walked me to the door. When we reached it, she said, "Thanks for the surprise. It's what I've always wanted."

"I owe you."

"Yes, you do. I might even make you take me dancing."

"Don't let Hayley anywhere near a computer."

"She said she wouldn't upload the files. Don't you trust her?"

"About as much as she trusts me. Just keep an eye on her."

Hayley called to us from the kitchen.

"You know, I can hear you," she said.

"I'm trying to save your life at considerable risk to myself, my partner and his family, what few friends I have left, and my business. Please don't make it harder than it already is. Did you hear that?"

She hesitated before answering. "Yes."

"Do I get a kiss good-bye?" Alex asked.

I answered with my lips.

"How 'bout me?" Hayley asked.

"Good night, Hayley," I said.

CHAPTER NINETEEN

The police pounded on my door at seven thirty in the morning like I thought they might. I had just finished my run and greeted them in jogging shorts and a T-shirt. Only it wasn't cops from the City of Mound or deputies from the Hennepin County Sheriff's Department. Instead, it was Detectives Weiss and Manske of the St. Paul PD. When I opened the door, they stepped inside the apartment without asking permission and began glancing around as if they expected to see a meth lab set up next to my refrigerator.

"Something I can help you with?" I asked.

"We searched James Cowgill's place," Weiss said. "Guess what we didn't find. We didn't find a computer, a cell phone, or a camera. If it wasn't for the power cords that were left behind, we wouldn't have known he even owned a computer, cell phone, or camera."

"Oh."

"Oh?" Weiss turned to his partner. "Did you hear that? He said 'Oh.'"

"I heard him," Manske said.

"What do you want me to say?" I asked.

"Where the hell are the kid's computer, cell phone, and camera?" Weiss said.

"How would I know?"

"Are you saying you don't know who took them?"

"I don't know who took them."

"Guess."

"I can't."

Weiss turned to his partner again. "He said he can't."

"I heard that, too," Manske said.

"Taylor, you said there were photos."

"I suggested that there were photos."

"The photos are missing."

"I gathered that."

"Who was in the photos? What were they doing in the photos?"

"I've never seen the photos."

"That doesn't answer my question."

I flashed on Douglas Jernigan and what he told me in no uncertain terms.

"That's a line I can't cross," I said. "I want to, believe me. You have no idea how much I want to. I've already told you more than the law allows."

"Taylor—"

"I can't. At least not yet."

"What's that supposed to mean? Not yet? Are we supposed to cool our jets while you wrestle with some sort of ethical dilemma?"

"It has nothing to do with ethics."

"What, then?"

"I can't tell you."

"Look, we know you're tight with the assistant chief, worked homicide with her back in the day. I'm guessing it was you who told Scalasi to tell us to look into Cowgill's finances. Am I right? If you want to tell her on the down low…"

"I can't."

"Taylor, it's murder."

"You wouldn't even have known that much if I hadn't told you."

"You think that makes you a hero?"

Ogilvy bounded into the room. Weiss stared down at the gray-and-white French lop-ear. For a moment, I thought he meant to kick him.

"Where I come from, you know what we do with rabbits?" he asked. "We eat them."

Ogilvy must have been as distressed by the sound of Weiss's voice as I was, because he turned and quickly hopped away.

"Now you've hurt both of our feelings," I said.

Manske slid between me and Weiss.

"We'll give you a couple days," he said.

"What do you mean, you'll give me a couple days?"

"Forty-eight hours. See, I think you want to tell us what we want to know, but you can't without screwing over your client. I get that, Taylor. I really do. So we'll give you forty-eight hours from right now to figure it out. Cowgill's still down at 300 University Avenue." 300 University Avenue is the address of the Ramsey County Medical Examiner's Office in St. Paul. "He's not going anywhere."

"What happens after forty-eight hours if I don't deliver?" I asked.

"I don't know. We'll take a couple days to think about it."

The knock on the door came so quickly after the cops left that I figured they must have forgotten something. Another threat left unspoken, perhaps. It was Claire, though, and that made me wonder if she had known the police were in my apartment and had been waiting for them to leave. She was wearing a white shirt under a blue vest that matched her skirt, and I said she looked great. She ignored the compliment.

"He came back," Claire said.

"Who?"

"That man from the other day, something Peterson."

"Clark Peterson?"

"I saw him drive by while I was waiting with Mandy for the

school bus. He slowed down so I could see him."

"Are you sure?"

"I remembered the car. Purple convertible."

"Yeah, okay. I'll look into it."

"Why is he hanging around?"

"He's trying to annoy me. Guess what? It's working."

After Claire left, I inspected Hayley's phone. The ringer had been turned off, so I hadn't noticed that she received five calls and seven texts. The first came at eleven the night before and the last just twenty minutes earlier. All of the calls were from Maura O'Brien. Apparently Hayley had refused to list her mother as a Guernsey on her contacts list.

I called Alex using my own phone. "How's it going?" I asked.

"Very well. Hayley is a sweet girl, and I like her very much."

"Sweet?"

"She's been on the defensive every day for the past twelve years. Give her a chance to relax and be herself with someone she likes and trusts and she's simply delightful."

"Likes and trusts? Alex"—I glanced at my watch—"it's been less than twelve hours."

"I can't help it if I bring out the best in people. What do you want, anyway?"

"Just checking in. Do you have plans?"

"We're going shopping, going to lunch, making it a girls' day out. I told Hayley not to worry about a single thing, that you would take care of it."

"I would prefer that you stay close to home while I do."

"If anyone ever needed a break, it's her."

Since Hayley started all of this out of anger, I wasn't sure I agreed. Still...

"Let me speak to her," I said.

A moment later Hayley was on the phone.

"Good morning, Holland," she said.

I couldn't remember telling her my first name. "What else did Alex tell you about me?" I asked.

"You really did have a daughter. I'm sorry about what happened to her and your wife. I know, I really do know, how hard that must have been. How hard it must still be."

"Thank you. Listen, your mother seems desperate to reach you. She's called and texted a total of twelve times since last night."

"Do me a favor. Swipe left."

"Hayley—"

"My mother doesn't love me, Taylor."

I thought of all the mothers I've known, starting with my own and ending with Claire Wedemeyer.

"I find that hard to believe," I said.

"So do I."

"If I run into her, do you want me to deliver a message?"

"Tell her—tell her if I had it to do over again, I wouldn't have gotten the tattoos."

Whatever that meant.

I was surprised when I found the door locked. For the first time in a week I had beaten Freddie into the office. I used my key to unlock it. The door swung open to the left. I took one step inside the office and saw a tall man on my right. He was young, about twenty-five, and dressed in a suit. He was also pointing a gun at my head.

"Don't move," he said, so I didn't.

Behind him I could see Freddie sitting at his desk. He was grinning as if the surprised look on my face was worth the price of admission.

"You have no idea how disappointed I am in you right now," I said.

"Me?"

"Letting this punk get the drop on you."

"I was distracted."

"By what?"

"Please close the door," a woman said.

When I did, I discovered her standing on the left side of the office near my desk. I knew immediately that she was Maura Guernsey. Brooke St. Vincent had called her "stunning." The first word that came to my mind was "startling." Her appearance was startling and dramatic in the same way that Grace Kelly, Elizabeth Taylor, Vivien Leigh, Marilyn Monroe, Michelle Pfeiffer, Catherine Deneuve, Charlize Theron, and Hedy Lamarr were startling and dramatic.

I turned to look at Freddie.

"Okay," I said. "I'll give you this one."

He spread his hands wide as if he expected nothing less.

The gunman had moved against the wall. I noticed for the first time that the curtain had been drawn over our bulletin board, keeping the index cards and red yarn from prying eyes. I figured that Freddie must have done it before opening the door to Maura and her boy-toy.

The gunman kept pointing his piece at me, but he was now in a position where he could cover Freddie, too, if Freddie made any sudden movements. I pivoted back toward Maura. I pretended that I didn't know her name.

"What can we do for you?" I asked.

"Where's my daughter?"

I threw a thumb at the gunman. "Missing persons is one of the things we do for a living," I said. "You don't have to threaten us to look for your kid. Just offer money."

The gunman moved up behind me and pressed the muzzle of his weapon against the base of my neck.

"Hands up," he said.

I raised my hands. It took him only three pats before he found my Beretta, yanked it from the holster, and tossed it onto the cushion of one of the chairs surrounding our glass table.

The gun caromed off the cushion and ended up on the floor beneath the table where I wouldn't be able to reach it in a hurry.

By then I was doing a lot of thinking along the lines of how we were going to get out of this mess. None of my thoughts filled me with confidence. Freddie must have been doing some thinking, too, because he said, "Hey."

Gunman and I both glanced at him. He was sitting tall behind his desk, except now his right hand was hidden from view. Like old married couples, sometimes partners know exactly what the other is thinking.

I told the gunman, "Put your piece away before my partner shoots you."

His response was to smirk and tighten his grip on the butt of his gun. He was holding it with one hand about a foot away from my upraised hands. Foolish boy.

"Here's the thing," I said. "We don't usually carry weapons. Why would we? Still, what we do for a living, sometimes we get unexpected visitors like you two. Usually irate husbands who are going to fall hard in a divorce settlement because of some photos we took. They threaten us, sometimes with guns, also like you two. We stash our own weapons beneath our desks in case we need to reach them in a hurry to protect ourselves. Freddie is pointing his at your head right now."

The gunman glanced at Freddie and back at me again. From the expression on his face I guessed that he thought I was bluffing.

"You, lady," I said.

"My name is Maura Guernsey."

"Take a look under my desk. Tell your friend what you see there."

Maura walked behind my desk and leaned over. For a moment, I could peek down her shirt at a pair of perfect breasts encased in a white lace bra. So could the gunman; his eyes followed her every movement. Foolish, foolish boy.

"I don't see anything," Maura said.

I grabbed the slide of the gunman's automatic with my left hand and held it still. With my right, I hammered the gunman's wrist, breaking the strength of his grip on the gun butt. He released the gun. I held it with my left hand, the muzzle pointing in the wrong direction, but it was a simple matter to transfer it to my right hand and point it at the gunman, who now had a stunned expression on his face. The move took about a half second.

"Slick," Freddie said. "All those classes you take must be paying off."

"It wouldn't hurt you to come with me once in a while."

Freddie removed his right hand from under his desk and set his stapler where it belonged.

"Next time maybe I will," he said.

I told the gunman to sit down. He didn't it do it fast enough to suit me, though, so I whacked him on the side of the head with his gun. He stumbled and needed to use the back of a chair to maintain his balance before he sat.

"Geez, Taylor," Freddie said.

"The man invades our space, points a gun at us, he's lucky I don't blow his brains out. You, lady—"

"I'm Maura Guernsey." She repeated her name as if it were a shield that would protect her.

"Sit down."

Maura glided to the chair, smoothed her skirt beneath her well-shaped bottom, and sat, crossing her legs at the knees, resting one arm across her lap so that the fingers of her hand brushed the hem of her skirt where it met her thigh. The other hand she used to caress the single strand of pearls around her pale neck. It was wonderfully choreographed, and I thought, you need to stop noticing these things. In fact, you had better stop thinking about this woman altogether.

I stood away from Maura and her young companion. From where they sat, the gun was at eye level. I casually waved it around in front of me.

"Let's start again, shall we?" I said.

"Where's my daughter?" Maura repeated.

"Who's your daughter?"

"Hayley O'Brien."

"How long has she been missing?"

"Are you trying to be funny?" Maura asked.

"It's a question we ask everyone on a missing persons case. How long—"

"Nine days."

"Actually it's been eleven counting today," I said. "Hayley left two days before you even noticed she was gone. What the hell is wrong with you?"

The color drained from Maura's face, leaving only her expertly applied makeup behind. Standing closer to her, I now noticed she had no lines on her forehead, no creases around her eyes or the corner of her mouth. Hell, even Amanda Wedemeyer had lines and creases. The secret to Maura's beauty was that she was having work done even at her comparatively young age, forty-two if my math was correct. I was less impressed with her. She reminded me of a photograph on the cover of *Vogue* that had been airbrushed until the subject had been robbed of all character, until it was nothing more than a caricature, a wax-museum facsimile.

She spoke in a soft voice, her eyes fixed on the carpet. "She's been spending weekends away lately, and I thought…" Her head came up and her voice increased in volume. "You've spoken to Hayley. You must have. Where is she?"

Knowing Dr. Campbell's shopping habits, she might have been at the Mall of America, Rosedale, Grand Avenue, or Uptown, so I wasn't lying when I said, "I have no idea."

"You must."

"I don't."

"Is she safe?"

"Last time I saw her."

"Please, Taylor, I need to know."

"Why did you come here? How did you and your gunsel come to think that we even knew Hayley?"

Freddie annoyed me by rolling his eyes and repeating the word "gunsel." "You've been reading those old-time crime novels again," he said. "*The Big Sleep. The Maltese Falcon.*"

"Do you mind? I'm working here."

"I've always been a Chester Himes man myself. Walter Mosley."

"Freddie."

"Ask the cop for his ID."

My eyes fell on the kid, who was still massaging the swollen area of his head where I had hit him.

"Cop?" I said.

"Why'd you think I didn't take 'im when he came through the door? He's a cop. I know 'em when I see 'em."

I swung both my eyes and the muzzle of the gun onto the young man's face. I made a gimme gesture with my free hand. He reached into his jacket pocket—very carefully, I might add, not once taking his eyes off me—and retrieved a thin wallet not unlike the ones Freddie and I carried. He handed it to me. I took a glimpse and tossed it to Freddie, who was still sitting behind his desk, so he could take a look, too.

"Officer Arthur Cerise, City of Orono Police Department," Freddie said. "Little out of your jurisdiction, ain'tcha, boy?"

Cerise didn't answer.

Freddie threw the wallet back to me. I handed it to the kid as I drifted past him to the refrigerator, opened it, pulled out a tray of ice cubes from the top shelf, cracked it, and dumped about half the cubes onto a small towel.

"Let me guess," I said. "Orono has a contract with the City of Mound, providing police services."

Again Cerise didn't reply. I twisted the four corners of the towel together, creating a makeshift ice pack, and gave it to the kid.

"You have an arrangement with Mrs. Guernsey," I added.

He pressed the ice against the swelling and remained silent. I held up his gun.

"I can give it back or I can call your chief and have him come over and pick it up. Which works best for you?"

"You can tell him, Artie," Maura said.

"See, now you have permission."

"There was a shooting in Mound last night," Cerise said. "Two men were killed. One of them was named Sean Meyer. We knew, I knew, that Mrs. Guernsey's daughter, Hayley, had been involved with him. She had asked us to keep an eye out for Sean, for the girl. Orono has two full-time investigators. They asked me to check all the cameras in the area while they worked the crime scene. We didn't find video of the shooting, but we do have a traffic camera at the intersection near the Library. I checked the license plates of all the vehicles that passed through the intersection within thirty minutes of the incident. One of them belonged to Hayley's BMW. I found it parked near the Library. Another license plate belonged to a Toyota Camry owned by a private investigator. You. I asked Mrs. Guernsey if she knew your name, and she said that she did."

"David Helin called Monday," Maura said. "He was Brooke St. Vincent's attorney in her divorce case with my stepson Kurtis. He said you wanted to talk to us about Hayley, but Kurtis refused to listen and hung up the phone on him. That's how I knew your name."

"Did you tell all this to the investigators?" I asked.

Cerise didn't answer.

"You told Maura"—I refused to use her surname out of disrespect—"but not your superiors?"

He didn't answer again.

"Did you tell the investigators about Hayley's involvement with Sean?"

He still refused to speak, but at least I got a head shake.

"What about Hayley's Beamer?"

"The family sent someone to pick it up," Cerise said.

"I bet your bosses don't know that, either."

"We pay extra to keep our family safe," Maura said.

"Of course you do."

"Please, Mr. Taylor, tell me where my daughter is. I'll pay whatever you want."

"Now we're talking," Freddie said.

"I need her home. I need her safe."

"Yeah, about that," I said. "Someone tried to murder your daughter. Twice."

"Oh no, no..."

"Was it you?"

Maura ignored the automatic I still held in my hand as she jumped quickly to her feet and slapped me hard across the face. It hurt, yet like Cerise when I hit him, I pretended that it didn't.

"How 'bout the rest of the Guernseys?" I asked.

She hit me again, which is what I would have done if I had been her and innocent—or guilty and didn't want anyone to know it.

Cerise stood.

"Hey," Freddie said.

The young cop looked at him. Freddie shook his head. Cerise sat back down and pressed the ice pack against his temple.

"How dare you?" Maura wanted to know.

"Hayley told me that your family is being blackmailed for all manner of misdeeds. She said you're all angry enough to kill. That's a direct quote."

"So what?"

"She thinks the family is blaming her."

"But why?"

I nearly said, "You know why." Instead, I answered, "You've been treating her like an illegal immigrant for twelve years."

"That's crazy. Everyone loves her. Robert Jr., Kurtis, Melissa—they take turns pampering her. Robert Paul treats her like a princess no matter what she does, and she's done plenty. The tattoos and piercings, it's like she's deliberately trying to provoke him, yet he refuses to discipline her in any way and gets angry when I do. He bought her an eighty-thousand-dollar sports car for her seventeenth birthday, tied it up with one of those giant bows that you only see on TV commercials, and then he apologized because it was blue. He said he wanted to give her a car that matched her eyes but that model of BMW didn't come in green."

Wait, I thought. What?

"Robert Paul is livid about what's happening," Maura said. "He blames his children. They're dishonoring the Guernsey name, he says. He doesn't blame Hayley, though. Why would he? She's not involved in any of the family's business dealings. He doesn't want her to be. That's why he never officially adopted her and changed her name. He wants her to live life as an O'Brien. I think it's because he liked her father so much."

"You married him so soon after Hayley's father died," I said.

"I was shattered by what happened. Robert Paul said he wanted to take care of me and Hayley. I let him. I did it for her. And me. I have no regrets about that."

"Hayley doesn't believe that her father committed suicide."

"I have a hard time believing it myself. Charles was an expert at concealing his depression. Most people wear their hardships like a medal on their chests. Look at me: I'm angry, frustrated, depressed. Not Charlie. Never Charlie. Instead, he concealed it. He always pretended to be the happiest person in the room, always sticking to the positive. He listened to music. Danced whether people were watching or not, exercised, took walks, worked side by side with his employees in the gardens. Not even his best friends knew about the demons he wrestled with every day. Only I knew. Even then, it was difficult for me to recognize when he was hitting a low point. That final trip to San Francisco"—she turned her head so I couldn't see her face—"he wanted me to go with him. I didn't because Hayley was six years old and just starting the first grade. I never told Hayley that, though."

"It doesn't change the fact that someone is attempting to kill your daughter," I said. "The first time, they missed. The second time, I think they might have shot Sean and Chad by mistake. It's hard to know."

"Hayley was involved in the killing of Sean and Chad?" Cerise said. "Are you sure?"

"She didn't do it. That doesn't mean she wasn't involved."

Cerise took a deep breath and exhaled slowly as if a weight had been lifted from his shoulders. I told myself that he had been certain that Hayley had killed Sean and Chad, yet he was willing to protect her for Maura's sake, for her money. Knowing Hayley wasn't guilty after all made him think better of himself.

"Where is she, Taylor?" Maura said. "Are you hiding her?"

"I checked the traffic cam video," Cerise said. "Taylor was the only one in the Camry that I could see when he left the scene."

That's because Hayley was hiding behind my seat, I thought but didn't say.

"Where is Hayley?" Maura asked. "I keep calling her phone, but she doesn't answer."

"I don't know what to tell you."

"Can you find her? You did once. Can you do it again? Please, Taylor. I'll pay whatever you ask."

"Okay."

I think she expected me to put up more of an argument, because she paused for a few beats. Freddie filled the silence.

"We'll need you to sign a contract," he said. He took a sheet of paper from his desk. Maura crossed over to him and filled in the blanks. I stared at Officer Cerise. After a few silent moments, I handed his gun to him, butt first. He took it and wrestled it into a shoulder holster beneath his suit jacket.

"You don't ever point guns at people," I told him. "You're a cop. If you want to scare someone, use your badge. That's what it's for."

"I'll remember."

"How long have you been on the job?"

"Nineteen months."

"And already on the take. Good for you."

By then Maura had finished filling out the contract. I didn't know if she had paid Freddie a retainer or not.

"Please help me, Taylor," she said. "Both of you. Please."

"We'll call you as soon as we know something."

I ushered her and Cerise out the door and locked it behind them.

CHAPTER TWENTY

I stared at Freddie.

"What?" he said.

"You're not sleeping here, are you?"

"What are you talkin' about?"

"You've been in the office early every day for a week."

"Naw, man. You've been late every day for a week. What's your excuse t'day?"

"The St. Paul cops knocked on my door again."

"What the hell, man? They've been t' your place so often you should make 'em pay rent. You know what, though? That story's not high on my reading list right now. Tell me what happened at the Library. Who's Sean? Who's Chad?"

I explained everything in gruesome detail.

"Jeezus, Taylor. Why them and not you? Or the girl? Why not just sweep the sidewalk?"

"I don't know."

I told Freddie that I had Hayley safely squirreled away in the Cities. I told him what she had told me about the hacks, with as many particulars as I could recall. When I finished, Freddie went to our bulletin board, pulled open the curtain, and started putting up index cards. He replaced HACKER with SEAN and CHAD and linked them to HAYLEY and SNIPER after first removing the card labeled THUGS. After I explained it to him, all five of the attorneys' cases, including MURDER and RAPE, were linked to GUERNSEY as well. He nearly removed the card labeled NIMN but decided to let it be.

"You left her with the files," Freddie said. "Why did you do that?"

"Seemed like a good idea at the time."

"The girl could still put 'em up on the web."

"She promised me she wouldn't."

"Do you believe her?"

"Yes. Well, until something happens that makes her change her mind."

"You mean like the wind blowing in a different direction? Where exactly is Hayley, anyway?"

"I'm not sure I should tell you."

"Keeping secrets from your partner, what's that about?"

I explained some more about my visit with the St. Paul detectives that morning.

"They gave you forty-eight hours?" Freddie repeated. "Who talks like that except movie cops? Forty-eight hours before the bomb goes off. Before the killer strikes again. Before the innocent man is sent to the electric chair. C'mon."

"I think they're serious, though, so if it all goes sideways, and it probably will, I don't want to take you with me."

"That's awfully white of you, Taylor."

"Besides, I'll need someone to bail me out of jail."

"Who do you think will knock on our door first, the St. Paul cops or Minneapolis?"

"Minneapolis. They've always been less forgiving. Freddie, let's look at this logically."

"That'll be a change."

I went to the bulletin board myself and started rearranging the index cards and connecting yarn. The cards labeled DIVORCE, CLASS ACTION, MURDER, BRIBE, and RAPE were stacked on top of each other. One length of red yarn connected them directly to the card labeled GUERNSEY, and one length of yarn connected them to another card marked HAYLEY.

SIEGLE, O'NEILL, and COWGILL were linked to the stack with three separate lengths of yarn. SEAN and CHAD were joined to HAYLEY, and SNIPER was connected to all three. NIMN was left floating unattached. I removed all of the other cards from the board.

"Now," I said. "What if..." I used yarn to link SIEGLE, O'NEILL, and COWGILL to GUERNSEY. "The Guernsey family knew exactly what was happening even before the lawyers, because Sean and Chad decided to blackmail them. Except—"

"Except Hayley stole their evidence and they had to put their plans on hold while they tried to get it back."

"The lawyers used the extra time to contact us. What if the Guernseys decided to use the time to minimize the damage that the hacked intel might cause by eliminating loose ends. Cowgill, the blackmailer, is taken off the board, and so are his photos. This protects Todd Kendrick, the illegitimate son of Kurtis Guernsey. Siegle is killed so he can't authenticate the memo that said Standout Investments was knowingly violating the Telephone Consumer Protection Act. This limits discovery by the plaintiffs that are suing Standout and helps hide wrongdoing by Minnesota River State Bank. O'Neill is killed because he's in the wrong place at the right time."

"Except it doesn't explain who hired O'Neill and why he was surveilling Siegle in the first place," Freddie said.

"No, it doesn't. Set that aside for now. Shouldn't we also link SNIPER to GUERNSEY, because he killed Sean and Chad, who were attempting to blackmail the Guernseys, and because he tried to kill Hayley, who wanted to hurt them in her own way?"

"Do you honestly think they tried to knock off one of their own? Disinherit her, I can see that. Toss her out on the street. Or go the other way and buy the girl off, put her on an island in the Caribbean where she can rail against 'em all she wants. Kill her, though?"

"I only know what Hayley told me."

"Lots of contradictions between her and what the mother said."

"More than you'd expect."

"You get the feeling we're being played?" Freddie said.

"Absolutely. The question is—by whom?"

"It's getting to be a long list of possibilities. Oh, before I forget..."

Freddie went to his desk, opened a drawer, withdrew a fat envelope, and tossed it to me. I looked inside. It was filled with cash.

"This came over the threshold last night about the time you were dancing with Hayley and her pals," Freddie said. "David Helin called. Doesn't matter much now, but he said he couldn't help us. He said none of the Guernseys would take his calls, much less ours. Ten minutes later the door was knocked on, maybe a coincidence, maybe not. When I opened it, I found the envelope on the welcome mat and no one around. Ten stacks. Apparently the lawyers took my little joke about wanting more money seriously, although why they couldn't just hand it to me..."

"You get the feeling the boys are trying to keep us motivated?"

"Hmm."

"Considering the many things they neglected to tell us, it's clear we're hanging out with the wrong crowd. Our mothers would be appalled."

"On the other hand, this is startin' to be one of our more lucrative jobs."

"What are we up to? Thirty-five grand?"

Freddie held up a personal check written by Maura Guernsey.

"Thirty-seven five, nearly all of it untraceable. What I'm thinkin', Steve is welcome to a third of the original twenty stacks the lawyers paid us—sixty-six hundred and change. The rest, though, that's all ours. He don't get a share of that. Maybe we don't give the government a share, either."

"I like the way you think, partner."

"So, partner, what's our next move?"

"Remember when this whole thing started, you said we should reveal ourselves and I said the bosses wanted us to keep it quiet."

"Yeah, but my idea was about attractin' the computer hacker and baitin' 'im into hittin' us so Sara could trap him. We don't care about that anymore, do we?"

"What I'm concerned with"—I gestured at the bulletin board—"is Cowgill, Siegle, O'Neill, Sean, and Chad. They were killed because of what they knew. They were killed because someone wanted to keep them quiet."

"Meaning?"

"Let's make some noise."

April Herron approached me in the corridor at Hannum, Hillsman, and Byers with an expression of wide-eyed terror on her face that nearly made me laugh. I also felt a stitch of guilt because I knew I was the one who put it there. As we passed, I startled her by reaching for her hand. The receptionist who was escorting me to Scott Mickelson's office was three strides past us before she realized that I had stopped. She turned just as I said, "Good morning. It's a pleasure to see you again."

April gave me a reluctant smile. "Good morning," she replied.

"I know that you're a stenographer, but I can't recall your name."

"April. April Herron."

"Of course. I hope everything is going your way since I saw you last."

"So far, so good."

"I'm sure your luck will continue. Have a nice day, April."

"Thank you."

I hoped April understood what I was trying to tell her, that she and her friends had nothing to fear from us. She did seem to have more of a spring in her step as she walked off, but maybe that was just me. I rejoined the receptionist, and together we found Mickelson's office. He was sitting behind his desk and reading what looked to me like a brief. He did not stand up; he did not offer to shake my hand. I gestured at the brief.

"I thought we were becoming a paperless society," I said.

"Electronic filing is now required in all eighty-seven counties in Minnesota, but some lawyers simply refuse to join the electronic age. They cling to hard copies the way children embrace security blankets. What did you come here to tell me, Taylor? If you had good news, you would have called."

"When we were first brought us into this, you told Freddie and me that the notes stolen from your computer indicated that the mayor was taking bribes from Ryan-Reed Construction. What you didn't tell us was that they implicated Robert Guernsey Jr. directly. You were holding out on us, Scott. Why? Don't you trust us?"

"The information was on a need-to-know basis, and you didn't need—" Mickelson's head snapped up from the brief. There was tension in his body. He studied me for a few hard beats before he continued. "Have you seen them? Have you seen the stenographer's notes?"

"No."

Apparently my answer gave him reason to loosen up. Mickelson leaned back in his chair and looked across his desk at me.

"Then you can't testify that you had," he said.

"Why would I?"

"How are you aware of this matter?"

"The hacker told me."

"Was it Hayley O'Brien as you suspected? Did you find her? Do you know where she is?"

"Yes, yes, and no."

"What does that mean?"

"It means I found her and we had a long conversation."

"Where is she now?"

"That I don't know."

"What do you mean, you don't know?"

I shrugged in reply.

"You found her and then you lost her, is that what you're telling me?"

"Lost is such a harsh word. It implies carelessness."

"What word would you use?"

"Misplaced?"

"Christ, Taylor. Tell me, is she still capable of uploading the stolen information on NIMN?"

"Yes."

"The threat to my clients, then, is as real as it ever was."

"Yes, but now you know it's a family matter."

"Mayor Feeney and the executives at Ryan-Reed will not agree. I doubt that Robert Guernsey Jr. will agree when the federal marshals come for him, either."

"I just thought you ought to know."

The fact that Scott Mickelson was upset when I left his office didn't surprise me. What did shock me was that Cormac Puchner wasn't. His attitude reminded me of the slogan passed around by Londoners living through the Blitz during World War II—*Keep calm and carry on.*

"Do you understand what I'm telling you?" I asked. "The reason that Standout Investments Worldwide agreed to the settlement is because the Guernsey family was anxious that a prolonged lawsuit would lead to the discovery of fraudulent consumer practices being conducted by Standout's parent company, Minnesota River State Bank."

"Yes, I got that."

"Well?"

"Well, what?"

"Don't you care?"

"Taylor, my law firm doesn't represent Minnesota River State Bank. We represent Standout, and while I'm deeply concerned about how the computer hack might impact that company, I'm really not interested at all in what happens to the bank."

"Even though they're owned by the same people?"

"I'm not an in-house lawyer, Taylor. I don't need to worry about the ethical ramifications. Listen. As a corporation's family structure grows in complexity, an in-house lawyer will face an unprecedented array of potentially conflicting client interests. Take Standout, for example. It's owned by Minnesota River, which is owned by RPG Holding Company, which is owned by Guernsey Financial, Inc., which also owns several other companies, including Ryan-Reed Construction, the Oak Tree Stores, and Minneapolis-Butler. Just figuring out who your client is at any given moment can be a daunting proposition. Fortunately, I don't have that problem. My job is to represent Standout and only Standout."

"The Guernseys might not see it that way."

"You're not listening, Taylor. I don't work for the Guernseys. That little bitch can screw them like a light bulb for all I care, just as long as she doesn't do it to Standout, too."

"That has to be the most singularly self-centered attitude I've ever come across. Or the most practical."

"Taylor, I have one job—protect the settlement, keep it from blowing up into something much bigger. You have one job—keep the intel the hacker stole from falling into the hands of NIMN. Let's not complicate the matter by concerning ourselves with ancillary issues that neither of us is being paid to address."

"Five dead men is not an ancillary issue."

"If you want to find their murderer, do it on your own time. Just don't bring my client into it."

"Standout is your client. Not the Guernseys."

"Now you're catching on."

* * *

Douglas Jernigan gnawed on the stem of his unlit pipe while he worked it out.

"You're alleging that Todd Kendrick is Kurt Guernsey's illegitimate son," he said. "It was Guernsey who allegedly paid the boy's legal fees. It was Guernsey who allegedly paid the blackmailer, James Cowgill, to suppress the so-called selfies that Kendrick allegedly took while he was raping Rachel Rozanski."

"Allegedly," I said.

"Don't be annoying."

"Sometimes I can't help myself."

"Taylor, I don't know how this changes anything."

"It suggests that Kurtis Guernsey had a motive for killing Cowgill."

"If that's true, why didn't he kill Cowgill seven months ago when the blackmailing first began?"

"Maybe he was waiting for his kid to leave for college in Texas, making sure suspicion didn't fall on him."

"Yes, well, it has nothing to do with us."

"You don't think so?"

"Just as long as you keep the selfies that were stolen off my computer from falling into the hands of the authorities. That's what you're being paid to do, isn't it?"

"Yes, sir."

"Is there anything else?"

"What if it's somebody else's selfies?"

"I don't understand."

"The St. Paul detectives told me that someone stole Cowgill's phone, camera, and computer. If they should surface—"

"You've been talking to the police? I thought we had an understanding."

"They've been talking to me; I haven't been talking to them. I think they might try to throw me in jail because I refuse to talk to them."

"If they do, please make sure your one phone call is to me."

"That doesn't answer my question."

"As long as the selfies aren't traced to me. Think of it as a line in the dirt. I can't break attorney-client confidentiality; I can't reveal the existence of the photos. But if someone else does using a different source of information, why should I care?"

John Kaushal circled his desk and went to his office door. He shut the door and leaned his back against it.

"You're right," he told me. "I was holding out on you. I don't know why. I guess I didn't want you to think worse of me than you already did."

"I don't think badly of you, John. I think you're an honest man trapped in an impossible situation."

"It's unlikely that the rest of the world will agree with you. What young Ms. O'Brien told you is true. Clark Peterson confessed that he killed his wife and told me where he hid her body. Since he was in the mood, he also bragged about killing three other women and hiding their bodies over the past twenty years. 'Bragged' is the correct word. I checked the Minnesota Missing and Unidentified Persons Clearinghouse after he left my office. The women were never found; they're still listed as missing persons. I've been left with the exact same dilemma that tortured Frank Armani and Francis Belge."

"If the information about Peterson's wife, Dawn, is revealed, you said it can't be used against him."

"The court will still consider it privileged information. As such, it's inadmissible."

"What about the information concerning his other victims?"

"That's a different matter entirely. You've heard the term 'fruit of the poisonous tree'? It was coined by Justice Felix Frankfurter. It holds that evidence gathered with the assistance of illegally obtained information must be excluded from trial. Since the source of the original evidence—the tree—is inadmissible, then all the additional evidence that it leads to—the fruit—is also inadmissible, whether it was obtained legally or not. However, there's a provision called the attenuation rule. It holds that evidence may be admissible if the connection between the evidence and the illegal method it was obtained is sufficiently remote, or attenuated. What that means is that Peterson's confession is inadmissible because it was obtained illegally. However, if the police, who have no connection whatsoever to the misconduct that obtained the confession, reinvestigate the missing persons cases after reading it and discover evidence directly linking Peterson to his victims, then yes, that can be used against him in court."

"I understand now."

"Understand what?"

"Why Peterson is oh-so-very subtly threatening to hurt people I care about unless I tell him the name of the hacker."

"Why does he want to know the name of the hacker?"

"Why do you think?"

"My God. Taylor, he needs to be stopped."

"I know."

"I don't know what I can do to help. Peterson is no longer my client, yet I remain legally obligated to protect his confidences."

"Tell me about Melissa Guernsey."

"You know about her, too? All right. Melissa and Peterson were having an affair. She was the friend of Dawn's that Peterson was allegedly sleeping with when he killed his wife. I spoke with her. She claimed she knew nothing about Dawn's disappearance. She was also desperate that her involvement with Peterson be kept confidential."

"Which you did, kept it confidential."

"Revealing her name in court would not have helped my client."

"Do me a favor," I said.

"If I can."

* * *

Brooke St. Vincent and David Helin had been standing close together when I entered Helin's office at Stanislav, Kennedy, Helin, and DuBois, yet quickly separated and moved in opposite directions. I pretended not to notice. Greetings were exchanged, and we all sat down.

"You lied to me," I said.

Brooke smiled slightly. "I bet I didn't," she said.

Sean and Chad had attempted to blackmail the entire Guernsey family. I guessed that they had also attempted to blackmail Brooke, and I told her so.

"I didn't lie about that," she said. "I just didn't mention it."

"I stand corrected. Why didn't you mention it?"

"What for? I wasn't going to pay those creeps, and I already made it clear that if the world found out about the email and the prenup, I was prepared to deal with the consequences."

"If you had told me, it would have made my life much easier."

"Making your life easier isn't my—" Brooke nearly said "job" and then thought better of it. "You're right. I should have said something, if not to you then to David. I'm sorry."

"You said that you don't know where Hayley O'Brien is," Helin reminded me. "Is she still intent on sending the email to NIMN?"

"I don't know that, either."

"She isn't," Brooke said.

"Are you sure?" Helin asked.

"I spoke to Hayley at the MIA before I introduced her to Taylor. She told me that she was responsible for the computer hacks. She also told me why she did it. I told her she was going to hurt a lot of people. She said that was the entire point. She also promised me that I wasn't going to be among them. She said she never had any intention of uploading the email. She said we were friends and that I deserved better from Kurtis and her family. She said that she was sorry that Sean and Chad had attempted to blackmail David and me. Now that they're no longer a concern, I guess we're home free."

"Hayley told me something about her relationship with the Guernseys, which you confirmed earlier," I said. "But Maura told me that the Guernseys all adored Hayley, especially the old man."

"The Guernseys aren't very good at expressing affection," Brooke said. "Maybe they do love her in their own way. All I know is that during the time I was at Axis Mundi they were sniping at each other constantly."

"What do you think, Taylor?" Helin asked. "Do you think that Hayley will keep her promise?"

"My impression is that there is only one copy of the files that were hacked. Until Hayley willingly gives it up, I don't know what to think."

I called Freddie. He said, "Now what?"

I said, "Now we wait."

"You're sure about this?"

"I made it clear to the lawyers that we now know exactly what was stolen from their computers. If they haven't figured out that we're also in contact with Hayley, they soon will. One or more of them will contact their clients. I asked John Kaushal to do just that. Eventually someone will contact us and the negotiations will begin."

"What are we negotiating again?"

"We'll return the hacked files."

"Which is what we were hired to do."

"In exchange, whoever is trying to snuff Hayley backs off."

"Which we weren't hired to do, protect the girl. I got no problem with that, though. Should I tell you my problem?"

"Please do."

"Instead of cuttin' a deal, what if they send the sniper instead?"

"I'm just playing this by ear. If you have any suggestions…"

"No suggestions, just another problem."

"My old man used to say, 'Don't bring me problems, bring me solutions.'"

"Yeah? My old man used to say, 'Shut up and listen.'"

"What, Freddie? What's your problem?"

"O'Neill. I hated the racist mother, but someone's got t' pay for O'Neill. Siegle, too. I got no concern for those other dipshits. But like you said, O'Neill was one of us, and Siegle, he was probably the only innocent guy in the room."

"Yeah, I know."

"What are we going to do about it?"

"The best we can."

CHAPTER TWENTY-ONE

Hayley waited for Alex to leave the kitchen before she leaned toward me and whispered, "I'm not sure I like her."

"What's not to like?"

"She's so demanding. This morning, she wouldn't let me have breakfast until I gave her all my clothes and took a shower. While I was in the shower she put my clothes in a washing machine."

"What a bitch."

"I know, right? She let me borrow one of her robes. I saw in her closet. Alex has a Little Bo-Peep dress, did you know that?"

"For Halloween, I'm sure."

"A French maid outfit, too."

"Alex does like her masquerade parties."

"Look at me."

I did. Gone were the piercings and the grungy clothes. Hayley's hair was clean and shiny and cut short so that it just grazed the top of her shoulders. Makeup highlighted her green eyes while obscuring the tiny holes that had been previously filled with metal. She was wearing tight black jeans and a slate-gray crewneck sweater that both revealed her curves and hid her ink. When she'd first come to Alex's door after I arrived, I'd failed to recognize her. I thought she was one of Alex's students.

"She did this to me," Hayley said. "It's like I'm wearing one of those costumes in her closet. She was sneaky about it, too.

Took me shopping. 'Try this outfit on, oh it looks so cute, no don't take it off. When was the last time you had your hair done, oh it'll be fun, we should look at some makeup, too.' She's devious."

"I like your hair," I said.

Hayley brought both hands up and smoothed the back of her head.

"I have curls," she said. "A wave. I never knew because I had always worn my hair long and the weight straightened it out."

"You're very pretty."

Most women would probably have accepted the compliment whether they believed it or not. With Hayley, I should have known better. She stood from her chair and glared down at me. Her eyes flashed defiance.

"I was pretty before," she said. "You didn't notice because you're a conservative old man who expects a woman to dress in a certain way and act in a certain way and then puts her down when she doesn't meet your expectations."

"What do you mean, old?"

"You want to sleep with me now, don't you? I can tell by the way you look at me. You didn't before, but now that I'm presentable—"

"I don't want to sleep with you, Hayley."

"Why not?"

"There are so many reasons I don't know where to begin. How 'bout the fact that you're only eighteen?"

"Are you one of those guys who divides his age by half, adds seven years, and decides that's the limit, that's where you draw the line? By that equation my stepfather was still twelve years too old for my mother. It didn't bother him."

"It would bother me."

"Don't lie, Taylor. Men only want one thing from women."

"That's not true. Sometimes we want them to do other things as well, like clean house and cook dinner."

"Don't make fun of me."

Alex hurried into the room.

"What's going on?" she asked.

"Nothing," Hayley answered.

"Battle of the sexes," I said. "I think I'm losing."

"It's not funny, Taylor. Women are treated like shit in this country and don't tell me it's only a few men who do it. If that were true, we wouldn't need the Me Too movement. No, Taylor, it's tens of millions."

"He isn't one of them," Alex said.

Hayley's eyes flew from me to Alex and slowly came back again. "Then he's one out of a hundred," she said.

I decided it was the closest I'd get to an apology. On the other hand, I didn't really deserve one.

"I met your mother," I said. "She came to my office."

"Mother." Hayley spoke the word as if it were an obscenity. "Did you tell her where I was?"

"No."

"What did she say?"

"She cares about you very much. She wants you home. She wants you safe."

"Did you—do you believe her?"

"There was a guy pointing a gun at me at the time, so yeah, I believed her."

"Was it Mr. Fisk?"

"No. An Orono cop named Cerise."

"I don't know him. Probably a boy-toy."

"Your mother has boy-toys?"

"She's forty-two years old and beautiful and she's married to an eighty-year-old man who hates everyone and everything. Why wouldn't she have boy-toys?"

"Love. Loyalty."

"What are those?"

"You know exactly what they are," Alex said. "Don't you dare pretend that you don't."

"Alex—"

"You keep telling me how badly people treated you. How badly did you treat them?"

"I never meant to hurt anyone."

"Of course you did, Hayley. You left home eleven days ago with the intention of destroying your family. I can't speak for your mother, but if you were my daughter I'd be climbing the walls with worry. I'd be calling the police and the hospitals. I might even point a gun at somebody to make them tell me where you were."

"I'm sorry," she said. I had the impression that she wanted to say more but couldn't make the words come out. That was okay. I thought I knew what she wanted to tell us. That she wished she could get a do-over, a chance to make it right. Only life seldom worked that way.

Alex draped her arm around Hayley's shoulder, and the young woman curled against her chest.

"What am I going to do?" she asked.

"The best you can," Alex said.

Where have I heard that before? I asked myself. I fished Hayley's cell phone from my pocket and slid it across the table and told her what my father had often told me. "It wouldn't hurt to call your mother once in a while. Just don't turn on the GPS."

At the same time, my own phone rang. I checked the caller ID and answered it. I left the room, speaking low so the two women wouldn't hear me.

I understood why she selected the parking lot of the Calhoun Beach Club near the Uptown area of Minneapolis for our rendezvous. It wasn't the kind of place where a chauffeur-driven vehicle would draw attention. The car pulled up to where I was leaning against the back bumper of my Camry. The driver got out and opened the rear passenger door.

"Get in," he said.

The driver was bigger than I was and looked fit. He was dressed all in black, including his shirt, but wore no hat. His sand-colored hair trembled in the wind.

"No," I said.

He looked at me as if I had called him a dirty name.

"Get in," he repeated.

"My mother told me when I was a young boy to never, ever get into a car with a stranger. What about your mother?"

He let go of the door and turned so that he was facing me. There was a discernible bulge in his suit coat beneath his left arm. He flexed his fingers, and for a moment I was transported to the Wild West. Was he really going to draw on me?

"Oh, for God's sake," a woman's voice said.

A moment later its owner appeared. She was wearing a skirt that was short enough that I could see her knees as she swung her legs out of the car and stood up. She was also dressed completely in black except for the single strand of pearls around her neck.

"Are you Taylor?" she asked.

"I am."

She approached, her right hand leading the way. I shook the hand.

"I'm Melissa Guernsey," she said.

"A pleasure."

She tilted her head at the driver. "Mr. Fisk," she said.

"Mr. Fisk," I repeated. I offered to shake his hand, yet he would have none of it.

"Is Hayley all right?" Melissa asked.

"She's fine. Would you like to step into the club and talk?"

"It's such a lovely afternoon; walk with me, Taylor."

Fisk clearly didn't approve of that idea, only Melissa dismissed his protests before he could even make them. "Park the car," she said, and together we strolled toward Lake Calhoun. It was difficult to cross Lake Street during rush hour without getting run down, and by the time we managed it, Fisk had caught up. Melissa and I began to follow the asphalt path around Lake Calhoun, mixing with the joggers, inline skaters, and other walkers. Fisk followed a discreet thirty yards behind us. Melissa glanced back at him.

"Mr. Fisk isn't my driver, despite what you might think," she said. "I have my own car, after all. Nor is he my bodyguard. Nor is he my friend. He's here to keep an eye on me while I talk to you. Father's orders."

"I don't know what to make of that."

"Do you know my father, Taylor?"

"I've heard of him."

"What have you heard?"

"Nothing good."

Melissa thought that was worth a chuckle. "He's not one to suffer fools gladly," she said, a phrase that I immediately translated into a single word—"prick"—but didn't say. "Tell me about Hayley. You said she's okay?"

"She was fine the last I saw her. She gave me a lecture about our sexist society."

"That's my girl," she said. "When did you see her last?"

"Melissa—"

"Taylor, what will it take for you to return her to us? Name your price, and please don't get all large and emphatic. Don't tell me that you can't be bought."

"Of course I can be bought. That's why I had business cards printed up. Melissa, do you people think I kidnapped her? That I'm holding Hayley hostage?"

"She's been gone nine days."

"Eleven. Haven't any of you people been paying attention?"

"She's gone off for a few days at a time without telling any-one before."

"I got that impression. It might interest you to know, Melis-sa, that Hayley's mother hired me this morning to find her daughter."

"She did? Maura didn't tell us. I wonder why."

"My question is, why didn't your family contact the police in the first ten minutes after you realized that she was gone? Why didn't you contact the media?"

"You know why."

"Pretend I don't."

"Don't play games, Taylor."

"Why did you agree to meet me?"

"John Kaushal said you had information regarding the Peterson murder case."

"Is that all he told you?"

"He said you probably knew where Hayley was. If that's true, why don't you bring her home? Do you want more money? I'll be happy to pay it."

"It's a little more complicated than that."

"Why?" I was attempting to come up with a good answer, only Melissa beat me to it. "Hayley doesn't want to come home, does she?"

"She's concerned about the reception she'll receive," I said.

"That girl. We love her so much. I remember the first time I set eyes on her. She was six years old and holding her mother's hand, the prettiest thing I've ever seen, and suddenly I'm Aunt Lissa even though she's technically my stepsister, and all we did from that moment on, my brothers and I, all we wanted to do was spoil her. Yet Hayley fought us every step of the way. She took every compliment as an insult, every gift as a bribe. Simple courtesies like offering ice cream on a warm day were viewed with suspicion. I don't know why."

"Sure you do."

"By all means, Taylor, explain it to me. You've lived at Axis Mundi. You know my family so intimately. Tell me all about it."

"I don't know your family, but I know those who do."

"Who? Besides Hayley, who do you know?" Again Melissa answered her own question before I could. "Brooke. You've spoken to Brooke St. Vincent."

"Your ex-pal."

"No. She's still my...It was the old man's doing. How could I be friends with someone who bests the family, was the way he looked at it. The way he insisted I look at it. 'Course, Brooke cheated. I knew she spoke to a lawyer about her prenuptial agreement because I was in the limo with her when he called that night, the night we went clubbing together before her wedding. She told him to send her an email. I heard it. Only I never—I've always wanted...How is she, anyway?"

"She seems to be doing quite well."

"I wish I could call her, but the old man..."

"Which brings me to my point. You were taught that you were a Guernsey and everyone else was a loser."

"It was my father's way of motivating us. Not Hayley, though. He never spoke like that to her."

"Perhaps not, but she was in the room when he said it to you. She heard it every day growing up. And she's not a Guernsey."

We walked in silence after that, although there was plenty of noise coming from the many other visitors to Lake Calhoun, automobile traffic, and the footsteps of the man following behind us. We were halfway around the lake when Melissa began telling me her story. Like Hayley's, it was filled with emotional abuse and unrealistic expectations. Melissa was taught every day that she needed to be better than everyone else, whatever that meant. She still wasn't sure.

"I asked the old man why he didn't adopt Hayley," she said. "He said he didn't want her to turn out like the rest of us— stupid losers, fat and ugly, brainless, not worthy of love. Imagine hearing that from your father. Imagine being forty years old and living in the same house with a man who says those things."

My cell phone rang. I checked the caller ID—it was Freddie—and swiped left.

"I apologize," I said. "Normally when I'm walking with an attractive woman, I'd turn the damn thing off, but the nature of my business is such right now that I'm unable to do that."

"Don't, Taylor. Don't be one of those men."

"What men?"

"I know that I'm not pretty. I've always known. I'm well aware that every man who flirts with me like you just did, every man who approaches me, is interested only in my money and my name. There are no exceptions. It was terribly painful knowing that when I was growing up. Now, though, I listen to the lies men tell me, pretend that I believe them, take what I need—mostly sex, I won't lie to you, Taylor—and then discard them as soon as they start making demands of me. Clark Peterson was one of them. He hit on me the moment Dawn left the room, arranged secret trysts because he said he couldn't be apart from me for more than a few days at a time. He was entertaining enough, but I wouldn't have given him the price of a gas-station cup of coffee. I told him so a week before he…you know."

"Do you know how messed up that sounds?"

"Yes, I do."

My head filled with the words I could tell the woman, probably should tell her, starting with the simple fact that I wanted nothing from her, not her money or her name or even twenty minutes of her time. I'd begin with that so she'd believe me when I also told her that she was pretty. Not nearly as pretty as Maura or Brooke St. Vincent, or even Hayley, now that I'd seen her without her disguise, but pretty in her own right. She had nice legs. I noticed them when she got out of her car. I assumed they had mirrors at Axis Mundi, though, so she must have known that. If she didn't it was because someone told her she was ugly and kept telling her until she believed it. Nothing I could say was going to alter that fact, so I said nothing.

"What?" Melissa said. "No argument? You're not going to tell me that all I need is the right man to show me how beautiful

I really am?"

"What you probably need is a good therapist."

"Don't be insulting."

"But that's none of my business. My business is with Hayley. Does your family know why she ran away?"

"We didn't at the time. Now...She's responsible for the computer hacks and the blackmail attempts, isn't she?"

"The hacks, yes, but not the blackmail. That was done without her knowledge or consent. When she discovered what was happening, Hayley stole the information from the blackmailers and went on the run."

"That's why there was no follow-through, why the blackmailers didn't contact us after the initial emails."

"Hayley's been hiding ever since. By the way, the men who were responsible for the blackmail attempts against you and your lawyers are dead now. But you already knew that."

Melissa stopped on the sidewalk and pivoted toward me. "No," she said. "I didn't."

I studied her face, not knowing if she was telling the truth or not.

"I didn't," Melissa repeated.

"Several others were killed as well."

I provided details. Melissa's response was to turn and continue walking around the lake. I spoke to her back.

"Someone has been trying to kill Hayley as well," I said. "There have been at least two attempts that I'm aware of."

Melissa spun back toward me. "No," she said. "He wouldn't do that. He's an angry, bitter old man, but he's not a monster. He wouldn't do that."

Melissa looked past me to where Fisk was standing, his hands in his pockets. She walked to him, got within striking distance.

"He wouldn't do that," she said.

Fisk stared into her face. He didn't bat so much as an eyelash.

"Tell me," Melissa said. "He wouldn't do that."

"No, ma'am," he said. "He wouldn't do that."

"Would you?"

"No, ma'am. I wouldn't."

"I'd like to speak to your father," I said.

"So would I," Melissa said.

CHAPTER TWENTY-TWO

Axis Mundi was gorgeous in the same way I imagined that the palace at Versailles and the Taj Mahal were gorgeous, although I'd never been to either of those places. To give you an idea of how my mind worked, though, instead of fixating on the many beautiful plants and trees that I couldn't identify anyway, I took notice of all the security cameras hidden in birdhouses, mounted on outdoor lanterns, and attached to power stakes in the gardens that greeted me at the gate and followed me a half mile to a huge house on a hill.

I parked behind Melissa's car. She and Fisk were already standing in the driveway and speaking to a man who wasn't much older than we were. When I approached, Melissa introduced us.

"My brother Kurtis," she said.

I offered my hand. He ignored it.

"I hear you've been speaking to that bitch Brooke St. Vincent," he said.

I probably should have defended the lady's honor, yet what was the point? She took three-point-seven million off the sonuvabitch. His attitude wasn't going to change no matter what I had to say.

"I'd like to speak to your father," I said.

"About what?"

"Whom. About whom."

Kurtis moved in close, violating my personal space on purpose. I pretended not to be annoyed.

"If you know where Hayley is, why don't you climb in that piece of shit Camry of yours and go get her?"

I thought of many different ways I could have answered him, except half of them would probably have brought Fisk into the fray, and I wasn't ready for that yet. Before I could think of a verbal response, though, the huge front door of the house opened and Maura came out. She sprinted to where we were standing, a difficult and unseemly thing to do in heels and a skirt.

"Taylor," she said, "did you find my daughter? Where is she?"

"Do you know this man?" Kurtis asked.

"He's the private investigator I hired."

"Father said—"

"I don't care what he said."

Both Melissa and Kurtis took a step backward as if they had never heard such defiance coming from her before.

"No outsiders," Kurtis told Maura. "That's what he said."

She wasn't listening. Instead, she rested a hand on my forearm.

"Taylor, please."

"We need to talk," I said. I gestured at Fisk. He was leaning against the car, his arms crossed over his chest. He seemed bored until I added, "We need to talk in private," and then his eyebrows curved upward and his expression changed to one of curiosity.

"This way," Maura said. She continued to hold my wrist as she led me into the house. Melissa and Kurtis followed behind. Fisk remained with the car.

I had never gone without. My old man had made a good living, so growing up I always had what I needed—a nice house, good food, clean clothes, money in my pocket. Yet sitting in the

Guernsey living room, I felt poor.

"What is it you want to tell us?" Kurtis said. "Be concise."

"Where's your father?"

"Talk to us. Then we'll decide if you get to see Father."

"Where's your older brother?"

"San Francisco on business. What difference does it make?"

Maura spoke softly. "Have you seen Hayley?" she asked. "Is she safe?"

"For now."

"What does that mean?" Kurtis said. "For now?"

"Five people are dead. All of them had hurt or were threatening to hurt the Guernsey family. Convince me that Hayley won't be number six."

Maura was on her feet. "What?"

"I told you in my office this morning that someone had tried to kill her twice. Weren't you listening?"

"Yes, but—"

"But what? Someone tried to kill Hayley. Prove to me that it wasn't you and I'll bring her home."

I meant for my words to be both accusatory and shocking, and I expected a loud and angry response. What I received was silence and blank stares. It turned everything inside me to ice, even my thoughts.

Kurtis moved to the huge window and looked out. Fisk had stepped away from the car and found a bench overlooking the grounds. Nothing in his face or posture revealed how he felt or what he was thinking.

"He couldn't do that," Kurtis said. "Not to Hayley. Never to Hayley."

"Are you talking about Fisk?" I asked.

"Fisk doesn't take a deep breath unless the old man…No, I don't believe it."

From their sudden fidgeting, I gathered that neither Maura nor Melissa supported Kurtis's opinion. Finally Melissa said, "It could have been a mistake. You know Father never actually speaks the words when he wants something done. Even when he's talking to us, he just sort of lets his instructions be known in a way that allows him to declare later that he never said to do what he wanted done."

"It has to be a mistake," Maura said. "Yes, a mistake. My baby."

"Are you telling me the sonuvabitch out there actually kills people for that old man?"

"We don't know for sure what he does," Kurtis said.

"Father wants something and the person he wants it from either suddenly gives in or disappears," Melissa said. "How often has that happened over the years? A dozen times?"

"We're discussing your stepsister, your daughter," I said.

"Don't you think we know that?"

"How long has Fisk been employed here?"

"Eleven years or so."

He started at about the same time that Charlie O'Brien was found dead in a hotel room in San Francisco, I told myself.

"Not long after that there was a man my father couldn't come to an agreement with."

"What happened to him?"

"He was killed in a hit-and-run accident."

"This is insane," Maura said. "No one is trying to hurt my daughter. It's all...Taylor. Take me to her, please."

"I need to speak to your husband first," I said. "Where is he?"

Kurtis gestured at a spot outside the window.

"In the maze," he said. "He spends more and more time in there."

"How do I get in?"

"We're not allowed to tell you. Or anyone else. Father's orders. It's where he hides from the world."

"What is wrong with you people?"

* * *

I left the house and moved across the manicured lawn toward what seemed at a distance like a giant wall of green. The Guernseys watched me do it from their window. I passed Fisk sitting on his bench. He watched, too.

As I approached, the wall became a hedge about eight feet high and far too thick to see through. I pulled my cell from my pocket as I approached it. I set it on speakerphone and held it in front of my chest so the Guernseys wouldn't see me using it. I called Alex.

"Hi, Taylor," she said.

"Hi. Put Hayley on the phone."

A moment later, Hayley said, "Taylor, it's me."

"How do I get through the maze?"

"The maze? At Axis Mundi, that maze?"

"Yes. How do I work it?"

"It's easy, except...First of all you need to go through the right entrance. The one facing the lake. There are four entrances, but the one facing Lake Minnetonka is the only one that leads to the center. All the others will have you going in circles."

I changed my route so that I was angling toward the corner of the maze. Lake Minnetonka glistened beyond. I turned when I reached the corner and hugged the wall until I found the correct entrance.

"Now what?" I asked.

"Once you enter, you go right-left, right-left, right-left three times. Do you get that? Three right-left turns."

"I get it."

"After that it's left-right, left-right, and left-right three times. Three left-right turns."

"Okay."

"That will take you to the center."

"Sounds simple."

"Yet people mess up all the time. Stepfather loves it when they do. He enjoys laughing at them. You need to be careful when you reach the center, though. You need to remember which opening you used. There are four exits leaving the center of the maze, and only that one will let you out."

"Thank you, Hayley."

"Taylor? My father built that maze."

"I'll talk to you soon."

It sounded simple, yet it wasn't, mostly because the path through the maze was narrow and the walls were high. The sun was thinking of setting, and I was engulfed in shadow. I couldn't even see the turns until I reached them, but by adhering strictly to Hayley's instructions I reached the center. The sun still had purchase there, and I could easily discern a fountain surrounded by marble benches. Robert Paul Guernsey was sitting on one of the benches. His shoulders were hunched, his hands were folded together on his lap, and his head was hanging low as if he were wrestling with thoughts of a deeply serious nature.

"Mr. Guernsey," I said.

He turned slowly toward me. His eyes took a few moments to focus. I don't know what I had been expecting. What I found was a dilapidated old man with nothing left but hunger.

"How did you do that?" he asked.

"Do what?"

"Walk the maze."

"Was it supposed to be hard?"

"Who are you?"

"My name is Taylor."

"I know you. The private investigator."

"That's right."

"You have something that belongs to me."

"What would that be?"

I wanted him to say the name of his stepdaughter. Instead, he answered, "Stolen files."

"No. I don't have those."

"Liar."

"It's true. What I do have..."

"Hayley." His voice caressed the word, and for a moment his humanity peeked through. It was like someone had opened a door to a dimly lit room and quickly closed it, again. "I gave her everything. Money. Clothes. The best schools. A car. My parents couldn't give me a car. I had to buy my own. I was twenty before I learned to drive. What did Hayley do with all that I gave her? Nothing. She squandered every opportunity, just drifting through life without a care."

"She's eighteen years old. That's her job."

"I was born in the middle of the Great Depression, Taylor. Do you know what that means? Of course not. People today have no idea. My family lived in a shack without heat, without lights, without food more often than not. I used to help my father pull a wagon down the street searching for scrap iron that we could sell for pennies to the government during the war. When I was eighteen I was breaking my back building roads for the park system under the Mission 66 program. No college for me. Now look what I got. What I built. What do you say to that?"

"I don't mind ambition," I said. "Ambition is a good thing. Except when someone else is forced to pay for it."

"What did my worthless children ever pay? Nothing. I provided them with everything. Without me, they'd starve. They'd be on welfare like all those other losers."

"From what I've seen, you took more than you gave."

"You're a fool, Taylor. Hayley, too. I could have raised her up to be a goddess among men. When I'm gone she'll have more money than a goddess."

Wow, I thought but didn't say.

"What did she do?" Guernsey said. "She tried to blackmail me." He punched his chest twice with such force that I was sure he hurt himself. "Me."

"She most certainly did not," I said. "Absolutely not. The two men who did try to blackmail you and your lawyers were friends of Hayley's, that's true. They used information that they picked up from her to decide what law firms to hack, that's also true. But when she discovered what they were doing, Hayley stole the files and went on the run. I was there when they tried to force her to return the information. She refused, and they nearly killed her."

Guernsey's voice, never very loud, became even softer. "I didn't know," he said.

"Now they're are dead. Someone shot them. Who could have done that, I wonder."

"I couldn't say."

"Who tried to kill Hayley?"

Guernsey rose from the marble bench. For the first time his face looked as if there were life in it.

"What did you say?" he said.

"You heard me."

"Are you blaming me?"

"Are you to blame?"

"Hurting Hayley, that wasn't supposed to happen."

"If you say so."

"What do you want, Taylor? Money?"

"What is it with you Guernseys that that's the first question you always think of asking? I'm trying to protect your step-daughter. The question is, am I protecting her from you?"

He moved quickly toward the exit, much more quickly than I would have expected from a man his age. He slowed considerably, though, by the time we departed the maze. Midway across the empty lawn, he had to pause a few moments to catch his breath. He took my arm without asking, and I helped him to the house. His wife and children came out to greet him, but he brushed past them, told them to stay back, and kept moving until he reached the bench where Fisk was sitting. Guernsey gripped my arm tightly either for support or out of anger, I couldn't tell which.

"Tell me about this," Guernsey said.

Fisk was staring at me when he spoke. "There's nothing to tell."

"Hell there ain't."

"I did what I've always done, what you pay me to do. I solved your problems."

"My stepdaughter wasn't one of them."

"I never went near Hayley, never threatened her, and I wouldn't have even if you told me to. There are things I won't do. I told you that when I took the job."

"I don't believe you."

Fisk rose slowly from the bench and moved close. The old man gripped my arm tighter.

"I would never hurt that girl," Fisk said. "Not for money and not for you."

The thing is, I believed him. I believed every word he said. Guernsey, though, didn't seem to.

"You're fired," he said.

"What did you say?"

"I want you out of here. You have one hour to pack before I call the police and have you arrested for trespassing."

"After everything I've done for you, this is how it ends?"

Guernsey's grip grew tighter on my arm. Fisk's eyes kept flicking over me as he spoke, as if he knew I shouldn't be hearing what he had to say, yet he couldn't help himself.

"I took care of that kid with the camera like you wanted," he said. "Made it look like an accident. The memo writer, that goddamned PI—I told you not to hire him. I told you he'd only get in the way, and he did. Now you do this?"

"Your services are no longer required," Guernsey said. "Don't worry, Mr. Fisk. You'll be well compensated."

Fisk glared at me as if he thought I was his replacement.

"I had better be," he said.

Fisk walked into the house like a man in a hurry. Guernsey turned toward his family. He continued to hang on to my arm.

"Maura," he said.

Maura came forward. The others remained where they were. He whispered to me as she approached. "She was the most beautiful woman I had ever seen when we married, and now look at her, pumped so full of plastic."

"Guernsey, you're a fool," I said.

His face clouded with anger, yet he didn't release my arm until Maura drew near. Then he took hers.

"We're bringing Hayley home," he said. "Aren't we, Taylor?"

"If she's willing," I said.

"Please, Taylor," Maura said. "Please."

"I'll call you later."

"Tonight? Please, Taylor."

"Probably tomorrow. I'll call."

"In the meantime, Maura," Guernsey said, "what's the name of that young policeman you've been spending time with?"

"Robert Paul, you don't think…"

"Now, now, honey. I know all about him, know how you hired him to watch out for Hayley. If things went beyond that, I'm just too old to care. But I need to talk to him. Now, honey." Guernsey stared at the entrance to his house. "There's something I need for him to do, unless…Mr. Taylor? Are you for hire?"

"I have way too many clients already," I said.

CHAPTER TWENTY-THREE

"So what we got here is a rich supervillain like in them James Bond movies," Freddie said. "And he's doin' what? Turning on his trusted henchman? You know that's not going to end well."

"The thing is, I believed him. When Fisk said he never threatened Hayley, I believed him. I believed the old man, too. I don't think either of them had anything to do with the attempts on Hayley's life."

"Who did?"

I went to the bulletin board and unpinned the stack of index cards comprising the names of the five lawyers and their cases. I spread them apart and reconnected them to both GUERNSEY and HAYLEY. I sat behind my desk and stared at them.

"What are we missing?" I asked.

"You said Fisk all but confessed to offing Cowgill, Siegle, and O'Neill."

"Yes."

"But not Sean or Chad."

"No, but he didn't deny it, either."

"Did you ask?"

"No, I didn't ask."

"Motive, means, and opportunity—I bet he had 'em all."

"I appreciate you coming over to my way of thinking, Freddie, I really do. Still..." I stared at the bulletin board some more. "Something the old man told me that made me go

'Hmm.' He said that when he's gone Hayley will have more money than God. But Brooke St. Vincent told me that Guernsey doesn't have a will."

"Guy like him, 'course Guernsey has a will. How else can he cut people out of it?"

"If he does, it's a secret between him and his lawyer."

"Which lawyer?"

My cell phone rang as if it had the answer. The caller ID listed Claire Wedemeyer.

"Hi," I said.

"Taylor, you told me to call you if someone—"

"What is it?"

"That man who was at the apartment, he's back."

"Clark Peterson? Where?"

"At Mandy's soccer game."

I quickly got directions and told Claire that I was on my way but it might take me some time before I reached her. I told her not to wait, told her that if Peterson threatened her or Amanda in any way she should call the police.

I hung up the phone. Before I left, I went to the office safe.

"You're not seeing this, Freddie," I said.

"Seeing what?"

I opened the safe and swapped my Beretta for a different gun and a suppressor.

Freddie didn't speak a word as I left the office.

The sports fields at Linwood Community Recreation Center in St. Paul were built into the side of a steep hill and pretty much hidden from view on three sides. They also had a parking problem. There was a lot, but it was too small to be of much use. Patrons were forced to park on St. Clair Avenue, a busy thoroughfare set above the fields, or on one of the narrow adjoining side streets. I found Clark Peterson's purple Bentley Continental GT convertible at the end of a long line of cars where Deubener Place met Benhill Road, which made me question Peterson's judgment. The streets were lined with thick trees and shrubs. The luxury car could easily have been messed with, even stolen, with no one around to see. One the other hand, the isolated location was perfect for me.

I parked my own car one block over and walked to Linwood. I entered through the trees and hovered at the edge of the park behind the cyclone fence, well out of sight of the families that had gathered to watch their daughters play soccer. Night had fallen, and the huge lights lining the field were turned on. It was one of my favorite things when I was a kid, playing baseball under the lights, and I wondered if the girls enjoyed it as much as I had. It took me a minute to locate Amanda on the field. For someone who seemed to find the game to be burdensome, she was flying around at a reckless clip. It was much easier to spot Claire, but then I could have picked her out of a group of ten thousand.

Peterson was standing along the sidelines away from the families. He had his hands behind his back and was rocking back and forth on his heels. His expression suggested that the entire event was being staged for his benefit and he was pleased.

I called Claire with my cell phone.

"I'm sorry," I said. "I'm still in Minneapolis. Are you okay?"

"I'm fine. Peterson is just standing there with a smug look on his face and watching the game."

"Stay close to your friends."

"Taylor, what the hell is going on?"

"I'll explain later. I'm trying to get to the park. Don't wait for me, though. When the game is over, leave with everyone else."

"I will."

I hung up the phone and waited. There was something about watching the kids playing with such fervor that made me feel good about the world, although, the way the two teams reacted when the game was concluded, I realized with a twinge of disappointment that Amanda had lost another one. After slapping hands with the other team, something else that made me confident about the future, she walked to her mother, her shoulders slumped, and I thought, get over it kid, you can't win 'em all.

Claire gave her daughter a hug while the families gathered up their belongings and made to leave. Claire and Amanda departed with them, heading for the long concrete staircase that led to the top of the hill. Peterson stopped them. Once again Claire draped her arms over Amanda in a defensive embrace. Peterson said something to them, waving his arms for emphasis. Claire shook her head and started following the families. Peterson grabbed her arm. Claire shook it free. Peterson put up his hands as if saying no to a second helping of pie. He was smiling. I could almost hear him say, "What? Me lay hands on you? I didn't do that. Why would I do that?"

Claire and Amanda climbed the stairs toward St. Clair Avenue with the others. Peterson watched them. After a few moments, he spun around and walked across the park toward the entrance off Deubener Place. I left my spot at the edge of the trees and moved down toward his car and waited. A couple of families had also parked there. I willed them to hurry, willed them to enter their vehicles and drive away before Peterson arrived, and they did.

Peterson was alone when he reached the Bentley. He was bathed in the light of a streetlamp; I remained hidden in shadow. I spoke his name and emerged from the trees. He smiled when he saw me. It was the same smile he had when he had lied to me in his lawyer's office. He circled the Bentley until it was behind him.

"Taylor." He spoke as if we were old friends and he was glad to see me. "I knew she'd call you. What's her name? Claire? I knew she'd call and you'd come running."

"I was told that it wasn't just your wife. I was told that you made other women disappear, too. How many?"

"If you know that it's because you found the hacker and he told you. Who was it? Make it easy on yourself and tell me, Taylor, or your women might be next. Her or the little girl. Amanda—she's juicy for a girl her age."

I brought the gun up. It was the semiautomatic that I had taken off Chad in the Library parking lot, untraceable to me. I had attached the suppressor to the barrel. They used to be illegal in Minnesota, but now you can buy them over the counter.

Peterson laughed at me.

"Who are you kidding?" he said. "Threatening me with a gun. You're not going to use that. Guys like you have a code." He quoted the word with both hands. "It's like those old Wild West movies. You never draw first. You never shoot an unarmed man. You never shoot anyone in the back. And when you catch the bad guy, you always turn him over to the sheriff. Only what are you going to tell the cops? That I watched some little girls play soccer? That I said hello to one of the moms? What's the crime in that?"

"You didn't answer my question," I said. "How many other women did you kill? Three? Or four?"

"Who keeps count?"

"You're right. I do have a code. A line in the sand that I won't cross. You're on the wrong side of it."

"Taylor, don't be an ass."

"There are things I will do and there are things I won't do. One of the things I won't do—"

"Taylor—"

"I won't let anyone hurt the people I love if I can help it."

Peterson finally caught on. By then it was too late, though. I shot him three times in the chest. The gun didn't go *poof, poof,* like you hear in the movies. Instead, there was a clicking sound like the snapping of fingers.

The bullets flung Peterson against the Bentley. He slowly slid down until he was in a seated position against the passenger door, out of sight of the street. He died sometime during the journey.

I glanced up Deubener Place and I glanced down. I saw no one. I heard no one. I dropped the gun at my feet and walked out of the shadow into the street. I made my way to my Camry, moving slowly yet not too slowly. Along the way, I stripped off the rubber surgical gloves I was wearing and stuffed them into my pocket.

I unlocked the car with my key fob, climbed inside, started it up, and drove off, using side streets to maneuver myself across town. Along with its story on the three hundred and ninety video cameras used by the Minneapolis and St. Paul Police departments, NIMN had published an interactive map showing their exact locations. They were easy to avoid.

CHAPTER TWENTY-FOUR

I had a restless night. It must have shown in my face, because the next morning Alexandra Campbell told me, "You look terrible."

"I've had a lot on my mind," I said. "Where's Hayley?"

Alex called the girl's name, and a moment later she bounded down the staircase.

"Good morning," Hayley said.

I had to admit she looked a helluva lot better than I did in her tight jeans and pink pullover. She was smiling, but I wasn't.

"What is it?" she asked.

"Time to go home," I said.

"To Axis Mundi?" Hayley shook her head as if she couldn't think of anything more distasteful.

"You don't have to stay there," I told her. "You're over eighteen. An adult. But you need to at least make an appearance. Too much has happened."

"They'll never forgive me."

"They already have."

"How could they?"

"Your family knows that you had nothing to do with the blackmail attempts, that it was all on Sean and Chad. They also know that when you discovered what they were doing you stopped them. That scored a lot of points."

"I'm the one who started it all because I wanted the world to know what they were doing."

"Your stepfather and the others don't know that part. They think that you might have spoken out of turn about family business with your friends, and your friends acted on their own. My advice, what they don't know won't hurt them."

"I won't live a lie."

"Hayley, how did you think this was going to end? What did you think was going to happen when you threw your family's secrets up on the World Wide Web? Did you think you would be regarded as a hero? Did you think society would rise up as one to applaud your honorable intentions? Edward Snowden is still living in exile. Julian Assange is in virtual prison in the Ecuadorian embassy in London."

"It was the right thing to do."

"Go home, Hayley. Despite what you think, the people there love you. At least they're trying to. If nothing else, you'll soon have more money than God. Your stepfather told me so himself. Think of what you can do with all that cash, the good you can do. Change the world."

Hayley pivoted toward Alex.

"What should I do?" she asked.

"Taylor's right, you don't have to stay at Axis Mundi. If things get intense, you can always come back here to me."

Hayley smiled as if she couldn't think of anything more wonderful. She moved toward Alex and fell into her arms. They kissed, but not as friends kiss. They kissed like lovers, with passion and hunger, their bodies pressed hard against each other. I wish I could say I found the scene heartwarming. Or even erotic. Instead, I was appalled, my brain screaming, "Alex, what are you doing?"

I tried mightily not to let it show, though, especially when they broke the kiss and Hayley pivoted toward me. She held out her hand. A flash drive was resting in the palm.

"Here," she said.

"Are you sure?"

"Why didn't you take it from me when we were at the Library, or later when we came here?"

"It doesn't belong to me."

"You could have taken it. I wouldn't have been able to stop you."

"That's a poor reason to steal, because you can get away with it."

"It was your job to take these files."

"I like it better that you're giving them to me."

I took the flash drive from her hand and slipped it into my jacket pocket without looking at it. I told myself that Freddie would be so pleased.

"I don't get you at all," Hayley said.

"That's okay. Sometimes I don't get me, either."

"Hayley," Alex said, "don't forget your backpack."

Hayley squeezed her hand and headed upstairs. As soon as she was out of earshot I spoke up.

"Jesus, Alex, what are you thinking?" I said.

"About what?"

"You know about what."

"The girl is over eighteen, Taylor. She's not one of my students. She doesn't even go to the U."

"That's your threshold? That's where you draw the line?"

"Did it ever occur to you that she was the instigator? That Hayley crawled into my bed looking for comfort and not the other way around? For God's sake, she saw two men killed in front of her, men she knew personally."

"That doesn't make any difference. She's a child."

"She's a woman with needs just like the rest of us."

I heard Hayley at the top of the stairs.

"You and I are going to have a talk later," I said.

"Funny, Taylor," Alex said. "You never struck me as the jealous type."

"That's not what the talk will be about."

"I'm ready," Hayley said. She descended the steps, the

backpack slung over her shoulder. It didn't get in the way as she and Alex hugged again.

"I already miss you," Hayley said.

"You know where I live."

"I do."

They kissed again, this time with affection. I opened the door, and Hayley stepped out. I glanced at Alex before following her. Alex gave me a shrug as if to say, "What's a girl to do?"

I maneuvered my Camry to I-94 and eventually to I-394, heading west toward Lake Minnetonka, with neither of us I having much to say until we were in the suburbs.

"I'm sorry," Hayley said.

"For what?"

"For putting you to so much trouble."

"It's part of the job."

"No, your job was to get the files, and you could have done that without helping me."

"I like you, Hayley."

"Even though I stole your girlfriend?"

"Is that what you did?"

"Alex and I slept together."

"I got that impression."

"She wasn't the first woman I've had sex with, but she is the only one that I actually cared about. I'm sorry."

"It's okay."

"Sight is what most people use to avoid bumping into the furniture, but Alex, she sees things, you know?"

Hayley didn't speak again until we were passing through Wayzata. "She's not the one, though, is she? Alex. She's not the one."

"What do you mean?" I asked.

"If you really cared about her, you'd be angrier than you are."

I didn't know what to say to that, so I didn't say anything. The truth is, I wasn't even thinking about Alexandra Campbell. I was thinking about Claire Wedemeyer and the fact that I had put her and her daughter in danger simply by knowing them. It made me feel gloomy. Possibly Hayley could see the gloom in my face.

"I wish you'd say something," she said.

"The devil is inside all of us. With some he resides very near the surface and can be easily released by alcohol, drugs, politics, even bad traffic. With others it requires more powerful motivations like fear, hate, loneliness, ambition, greed. Love."

"The devil made me do it. Isn't that a seventies thing?"

"Are you calling me old again?"

Eventually we reached Orono and turned south toward the City of Mound.

"Taylor," Hayley said, "I like you, too."

The first time I had driven to Axis Mundi I had followed Melissa and Fisk. We had paused at an iron gate that they opened and closed with a remote control. This time there were armed guards outside the gate with the patch of a private security firm stitched to their shoulders. One of the guards approached my car while two others watched, their automatic weapons held with the muzzles pointing downward. I opened my window.

"What's your business here?" he asked.

"Holland Taylor and Hayley O'Brien. We're expected."

The guard looked at both of us and then into the backseat. Hayley leaned forward to look at him.

"What's going on?" she asked.

"Pop the trunk," the guard said.

I did, using the latch on the floor between my seat and the door. He looked inside and slammed it shut again. He returned to the window.

"Don't move," he said. "Keep your hands where I can see them."

I did. He pulled a cell phone from his pocket and made a call. I don't know who he spoke to, but the conversation lasted less than ten seconds. He returned to the window.

"Drive directly to the house," he told me. "Do not stop. Do not leave the road. Do not step out of your vehicle until you're told."

The guard waved at his two companions. They opened the gate. I drove through it. It was shut tight behind me. The private road ran straight as a ruler through the forest that surrounded Axis Mundi. I followed it to the driveway, passing at least two armed guards as I went.

There were several other cars in the driveway, including one with the emblem of the City of Orono Police Department and another with the blue, yellow, and red stripe of the Hennepin County Sherriff's Department. I parked the Camry. Several more guards approached. Hayley didn't wait for permission, though. She released her seat belt, hopped out of the car, and started running toward the huge house, not even bothering to close the door behind her. The guards seemed peeved yet kept their weapons pointed down just the same.

Hayley's mother must have been watching for us. Maura came out of the house and started sprinting toward her daughter. They met in a splendid collision, and I thought, whatever their problems, mother and daughter should be fine. Melissa and Kurtis Guernsey followed close behind. Additional hugs were exchanged and I thought some more. From a distance it looked like a loving family greeting a favorite child home from a faraway land.

"Looks can be deceiving," I said aloud.

A guard had approached the Camry and was standing close to my window.

"Huh?" he said.

"Just thinking out loud. What the hell's going on, anyway?"

"There's been a threat against Mr. Guernsey's life."

"By whom?"

"Man named Fisk."

For a moment I didn't know what to do. My first thought was that I should get Hayley out of there. Take her back to Alex's house where she would be safe. But was it really necessary to do that? Besides, the job was finished. We kept the hacked computer files from reaching NIMN, which is what the lawyers had hired Freddie and me to do. I told the hacker that the mayor of Minneapolis was willing to be her pal, for which we were paid five thousand dollars with the promise of five thousand more. Plus, we had delivered Hayley to her mother, fulfilling the contract we made with her. It was time to go home. Yet I couldn't bring myself to start the Camry and drive away. The guard helped me out.

"Are you Taylor?" he asked.

"Yeah."

"Cops are running a command post out of the garage. They want to talk to you."

He opened my car door as a way to stifle any argument. I slipped out of the car and followed him to the huge garage off the driveway, telling myself that there was probably a practical reason they had gathered there instead of inside the house besides the danger of bruising the carpets. A Hennepin County sheriff's deputy with sergeant's stripes was looking over a map. Orono Police Officer Arthur Cerise was standing at his shoulder. That was the extent of any official presence. One deputy and one cop. Everyone else was wearing the insignia of the private security firm.

The deputy watched as I approached. When I was near enough that he could speak to me without raising his voice, he said, "Taylor?"

"Yes."

"Private investigator from Minneapolis?"

"That's right."

"As you can see, we have a situation. A disgruntled employee named Fisk has threatened to kill his employer, Robert Paul Guernsey. We're trying to prevent that from happening."

"Just the two of you and an army of hired guns?"

"What's that supposed to mean?"

"A man of Guernsey's resources, I'd expect a greater official presence."

"Mr. Guernsey insists that we maintain a low profile for publicity's sake. He said you were present when Fisk made terroristic threats against him and his family."

"No."

"Are you calling Mr. Guernsey a liar?" Cerise asked.

"I'm saying I wasn't present when Fisk made terroristic threats against him or his family."

"What's that supposed to mean?"

"What I saw, Fisk was upset. He didn't like being fired. There were no threats, though, not by him or Guernsey. Guernsey said he'd take care of Fisk financially, and Fisk left."

"That's not the way we heard it," the deputy said.

"That's the way I heard it, what I'll tell the Hennepin County attorney should I be asked to make a statement. I might even be persuaded to tell him everything else I heard, too, if it comes to that."

Cerise was clearly angered by my stance. The deputy seemed confused.

"Is there a warrant for Fisk's arrest?" I asked him.

"I...I don't know."

"This isn't the way things are supposed to work, is it? It goes against all protocols and procedures."

"The bosses want it kept quiet," he said.

"Are you supposed to cooperate with Guernsey, or is he supposed to cooperate with you?"

"I was told—"

"Yes?"

The deputy didn't finish his thought.

"The security guards are well armed," I said.

"We put no faith in slingshots." Officer Cerise grinned broadly because he thought he'd said something clever.

"What are their orders?"

"To protect—"

"They were told to shoot on sight, weren't they? Shoot to kill."

"If that's what it takes."

"Is it possible, do you think, that Guernsey doesn't want the county attorney to hear Fisk's side of the story?"

The deputy gave it a moment's thought before he answered. "If he's innocent, Fisk won't come anywhere near the place."

He had me there, except Fisk wasn't innocent, was he? What's more, from what I was told, Guernsey rarely strayed from Axis Mundi. If Fisk really did want to kill the old man, he'd have to come here.

None of us could think of any reason for me to keep hanging around. I left the garage and headed for my Camry. My job was done. The problems of the Guernsey family no longer meant anything to me. I was just a bystander now. The Guernseys were still engaged in their love fest, although the old man was nowhere to be seen. Maura waved at me, and I waved back. She beckoned for me to join them. I didn't want to, yet I did anyway.

"Thank you, Taylor," she told me. "Thank you for bringing my daughter home."

"You're welcome."

"I can't believe the change in her. Is that your doing?"

"No."

"She looks so pretty," Kurtis said.

"She was pretty before. You just didn't notice."

Hayley smiled at me yet said nothing. Her face was flushed, and her eyes were bright. She seemed happy, the only time I'd seen her happy since we met. Well, except for when she was playing tongue hockey with Alex. I was still unsure what to think about that.

"I couldn't help but notice all the security," I said.

Melissa took my arm, led me two feet away, and spoke softly. "We don't wish to frighten Hayley," she said.

"I'm standing right here," Hayley said.

Melissa looked at her as if she was surprised.

"Yes, of course," she said. "My father, your stepfather—"

"Where is he?"

"In the maze," Kurtis said. "He went there just a few minutes ago."

"Is he hiding from me?"

"Hayley," Maura said. She draped her arm over her daughter's shoulders, and for a moment she was Claire Wedemeyer shielding Amanda. "He loves you."

"We'll find out in a little bit."

"What do you mean?"

Hayley looked me in the eye and smiled, and I knew that she was going to go all in. She was going to tell the old man everything she had done and why and see what became of it. I wanted to watch. Besides, I told myself, the girl might need a ride back to the Cities.

"You say he's in the maze," I said.

"Taylor, terrible things happened after you left yesterday," Kurtis said. "Father contacted the Orono Police Department and spoke to an acquaintance of Maura's. He said that Fisk had become irrational and violent. He said that Fisk had threatened the family. Fisk heard this. He hadn't left the house, yet. They argued. Fisk told Father that all he had to do was write a check and this—he didn't say what 'this' was, but he said that it would have gone away. Father said he doesn't pay losers. Fisk left, but he said that he would be back. Father said if he was smart, he'd start running. You know what kind of man my father is, what kind of man Fisk is. We're all very upset."

"Did you tell this to the police?"

Kurtis answered sheepishly. "Some of it, but not all. Father was...he was standing there. Later—what happened—this morning the security system crashed. For ninety minutes, all of our cameras and alarms were off-line. Father called the security company, of course, and their people searched the house and grounds thoroughly and found nothing. No one. Still, we're all on edge."

"I bet Fisk knows everything there is to know about your security system," I said.

"That's why we have so many armed guards now. We're sorry, Hayley, to bother you with all of this."

"It's all right," she said. "I'm probably to blame, anyway."

"How could you be?"

"I want to talk to Stepfather. Taylor, will you come with me?"

"I wouldn't miss it."

"I'm coming, too," Maura said.

Inside the maze, the silence was almost absolute. Shadows lay softly from one hedgerow to the next. We moved casually while in my head I chanted right-left, right-left, right-left and then left-right, left-right, left-right. Hayley led the way, with Maura close behind her, and me behind Maura. I heard Maura say, "I never come in here by myself. I'm always afraid I'll never get out again."

"That's why people take wrong turns," Hayley said. "They become afraid."

We didn't hear them until we reached the opening. Hayley halted. Maura and I were jammed together behind her. I watched the scene unfold over her head.

"I said you'd be well compensated," old man Guernsey said.

"You put the cops on me," Fisk replied.

"I was protecting myself."

"Like you were protecting yourself when you had me kill Cowgill and all the others?"

"You know who I am. You know how I do things."

They were standing near the fountain. Fisk was pointing a handgun at Guernsey. The old man was standing off to the side with his back to us. He looked like he didn't care about the gun.

In that moment I knew what had happened. Fisk cut the camera feeds just long enough to hide himself in the maze, knowing that none of the security guards would have dared to patrol it, knowing that it was where the old man enjoyed hiding from the world for which he had such contempt. A single gunshot from a small-caliber weapon might go unnoticed, and then Fisk would hide inside the maze, which he probably knew very well after all those years working at Axis Mundi, until escape was possible.

Except now we were there.

Neither Fisk nor Guernsey saw us.

"Yes, I know how you do things," Fisk said.

He brought his gun up.

"You've always been a loser," Guernsey said.

Hayley dashed forward. I reached for her, but Maura was in the way.

"You've lived too long, old man," Fisk said.

He took aim.

Hayley shouted, "No," and leapt in front of her stepfather.

Fisk squeezed the trigger.

The bullet caught Hayley in the center of her chest.

She fell backward against the old man. Blood quickly spread, creating a giant stain on her pink pullover.

Guernsey grabbed Hayley's shoulders to keep her upright. He released her, though, when he saw the blood, as if he were afraid he'd catch her disease.

Hayley wavered yet did not fall.

The old man stood by her side. He whispered, "Hayley? Honey?"

She clutched the wound, a surprised expression on her face.

I watched helplessly as the life drained from her eyes.

"Mama?" she said.

Hayley pitched forward and fell, sightless, onto the grass.

Her mother screamed and kept screaming until her voice could no longer express her grief.

Fisk turned and dashed into the maze. I shoved Maura out of the way and went after him.

I paused at the opening and pulled my Beretta. I could only stand by uselessly while Hayley was killed, surprised that she had leapt in front of Fisk's gun, unable to prevent it. It had happened so fast, I told myself. My helplessness festered a rage deep inside me that I could barely contain. I wanted to scream the way Maura had screamed.

At moments like this, your senses become heightened. Sight, sound, touch—it all becomes magnified. The muscles tense, the heart beats faster, breathing and perspiration increase, eyes dilate, and the stomach clenches. The world becomes much smaller, consisting solely of what's directly in front of you. It's called perceptual narrowing. At the same time, problem-solving capabilities are reduced, along with your ability to concentrate. For example, it became obvious I wasn't thinking clearly when I rounded the first turn of the maze too quickly and the bullet clipped the hedge an inch from my right ear, raining splinters and leaves on my head as I ducked down.

The condition is labeled "body alarm reaction" by some psychologists. It's an automatic and instantaneous response that increases the body's ability to cope with an emergency. I learned all about it at the police academy. It lasts until the cause of the alarm is removed or the body becomes exhausted. Or until your training and experience kick in.

Soon everything became clear to me. My anger became a weapon instead of a detriment.

I continued to follow Fisk through the maze, advancing slowly, deliberately. I could hear him moving just steps in front of me, yet he remained out of sight.

I took more turns right and left before it occurred to me that we had taken one of the dead-end exits. All we were doing was making ourselves lost. I could imagine old man Guernsey laughing at us.

I crouched low to the ground in case Fisk decided to start spraying bullets through the hedge and spoke loudly.

"Hey, Fisk," I said. "Fisk."

There was no answer.

"C'mon, man. Talk to me."

"Taylor?"

"There's no way out, Fisk. I'm not trying to be theatrical. There really isn't any way out of the maze except the way you came in."

"I know. I panicked and took the wrong exit. Bad judgment."

"Drop your gun and come out. Things will go badly for you, we both know that, but at least you'll be able to take Guernsey down with you. Let the world know who he is and what he did."

"Is Hayley all right?"

"Yes."

"Don't lie to me, Taylor. I shot her in the heart. I was trying to shoot the old man and she came out of nowhere. Do you believe she did that? After the way he treated everybody?"

"Drop your gun and come out."

"I loved that girl. She was so damned fierce. Stood up to the old man, stood up to them all every day of her life. It was fun to watch."

"Fisk."

"Why would she sacrifice herself like that, Taylor? After everything that happened. Can you tell me why?"

"I don't know, Fisk. Maybe in that split second Hayley decided the old man was family after all."

"Oh, hell."

Fisk appeared in the narrow path fifteen steps in front of me.
He shot high and missed, but he meant to.
I fired low and didn't miss, but that's the way he wanted it.

CHAPTER TWENTY-FIVE

By the time I left Axis Mundi, the shooting was already big news on TV and the radio. Apparently old man Guernsey had shrugged off his grief long enough to control the story. My name wasn't mentioned, which was fine with me. Instead, it was reported that a disgruntled employee murdered Hayley O'Brien, the stepdaughter of prominent Minnesota financier Robert Paul Guernsey Sr., at his Lake Minnetonka estate, before the assailant was shot dead by private security guards. Fisk, according to authorities, had been fired the day before over allegations of substance abuse. The Hennepin County Sheriff's Department was investigating the incident.

There was a lot more, but I lost interest by the time I drove to Edina. I found a parking space near the Galleria. A few minutes later, Brooke St. Vincent opened her apartment door to me.

"Taylor," she said. She wrapped her arms around my shoulders and held me tight. "Were you there? Did you see it?"

"Yes."

"I was in my office when I heard. I tried to call Axis Mundi, but I couldn't get through. What a terrible thing. I don't know what to do with myself. I couldn't work, so I came home."

Eventually she released me and made her way to her sofa. She was dressed in pajamas, an opened robe, and fluffy slippers. Her eyes were puffy from crying. There was a box of tissues on the coffee table. Brooke took one and blew her nose. She sat on the sofa and wrapped herself in a quilt.

"I feel so cold," she said.

"You're being unnecessarily dramatic, aren't you, grieving for your friend with no one to see? Or were you expecting visitors?"

"What do you mean?"

I pointed at the photographs on the wall above the sofa, the ones with Brooke holding all those rifles.

"Tell me about it," I said.

Brooke's eyes went from the photos to me. "How long have you known?" she asked.

"The pieces started falling together when I met Fisk at Axis Mundi. He said he never would have hurt Hayley, and I believed him."

"He killed her."

"He didn't mean to. He meant to kill the old man and she jumped in the way. You, on the other hand..."

"Me?"

"You knew Hayley would be at the Minneapolis Institute of Art; you're the one who told me. Later, you conveniently slipped away so we could talk. You knew she would be at the Library, too, because I told you. Brooke, where did you get the rifle and suppressor? Where did you get the subsonic rounds? You know what? Don't tell me. It doesn't matter, anyway. I know a guy who'd be happy to sell you an M-60 machine gun."

"You're wrong, Taylor. I loved Hayley. I wouldn't have done anything to harm her. Just the opposite."

"Explain it to me, then."

"Sean and Chad were trying to blackmail me over the pre-nuptial agreement thing. 'Course, I didn't know who they were at the time. I didn't know who was responsible for the computer hacks until you told me. It broke my heart when I found out it was Hayley. At the same time, I was frightened because you said that two men were after her. That's why I brought my rifle to the MIA. I spoke to Hayley, remember. I said so when we were in David Helin's office. She told me she would never have uploaded the email David sent me. I had no reason to harm her."

"Why did you shoot at her in the park, then?"

"I didn't shoot *at* her. Those were warning shots."

"Who were you warning?"

"You grabbed her, Taylor. You grabbed her by the arms and shook her. You were working for the lawyers, after all. I knew you wanted the files, and I thought you were threatening her."

"And at the Library?"

"When you pulled your gun I thought you were in trouble."

"Did you know that the two men were Sean and Chad?"

"I guessed."

"Putting them away saved you a lot of money, didn't it? How lucky for you."

"Taylor, I shot them to save Hayley and you."

"It wasn't necessary."

"I didn't know that at the time."

"Yes, you did."

"Are you going to call the police?"

"What would I tell them?"

"What I just told you."

"Are you going to confess if they knock on your door?"

"Probably not."

"Do you still have the rifle?"

"I kept the laser sight, but the rifle and the subsonics are gone. I watch TV, Taylor. I know the first rule is you never keep the gun."

I thought about Chad's automatic that I dropped at the scene of Clark Peterson's murder.

"Actually, that's the second rule," I said. "The first rule is never talk to the police with or without a lawyer present."

"I'll remember."

"In any case, I can't prove anything, can I?"

"No."

"A good lawyer could sue me for slander and probably win. Do you know any good lawyers?"

"One or two."

"Good-bye, Brooke."

"We're not going to get together, are we, Taylor?"

"I don't think so."

"I'm sorry to hear that. I think you're attractive."

"I used to think the same of you."

It was a lousy thing to say, and I told myself so while I made my way back to my car. Did Brooke do anything that I hadn't done? No, except she did it for money, I told myself. She did it for three-point-seven million dollars. What did I do it for? I did it to protect my friends. I did it for love. Did it make any difference? I liked to think so.

CHAPTER TWENTY-SIX

"I'm sorry about the girl," Freddie said.

"There were so many things I should have done for her that I didn't."

"It wasn't your fault."

"Feels like my fault."

Freddie didn't have anything to say to that. Instead, he went to the bulletin board and removed the index cards and red yarn until all that remained was the card labeled NIMN. I stared at the card while I absently fingered the flash drive Hayley had given me.

"Why did Hayley do it?" Freddie asked.

"Fisk asked the same question."

"It just doesn't make sense after everything else she did."

"Would you ever take a bullet for someone?"

"Echo. My son. Probably my mom."

"Why?"

"Love, man. You do it for love."

"As good an explanation as any, I guess."

Freddie gestured at the flash drive I was playing with.

"I know where we can get a good cup of coffee," he said. "If that's what you're thinking."

"What are you talking about?"

"It's a cryin' shame that we didn't anticipate that Hayley had established a dead man's switch, you know, just in case. That she gave a copy of the hacked files to a friend with instructions that if anything happened to her, the information should be sent directly to NIMN. The lawyers can't fault us for that, can they?"

"You wouldn't think so, especially after how things worked out."

"It's not enough that Fisk went down, Taylor. For what happened to Siegle and O'Neill, even Sean, Chad, and that kid Cowgill—for what happened to Hayley—they should all go down. Every one of them damn Guernseys, including the rapist hiding out in Texas. The lawyers, to hell with them, too. They should all pay. Don't you think? And"—Freddie waved a single finger in the air—"and we'd be helping out the cops in St. Paul and Minneapolis without looking like we did, get 'em off our backs. It'd be a win-win, is what I'm sayin'."

"We'd be crossing the line," I said.

"Fuck the line. Just this once, fuck it."

Hours later I was sitting in my apartment with a bottle of bourbon and a glass that I never seemed to keep empty, no matter how hard I tried, when my cell phone rang. The call was from Dr. Alexandra Campbell, and I was tempted to swipe left. I answered instead.

"Hey," I said.

"Taylor, I heard the news..."

Alex began to weep. She didn't speak another word while she wept, and neither did I. Eventually, the phone went dead.

There was a knock on my door. It was after ten, and I thought it was too late for Amanda to visit, yet I hid the bourbon anyway. I opened the door and Claire stepped across the threshold. She closed the door and leaned her back against it.

"I waited until Mandy was asleep," she said.

"Claire…"

"I heard on the news Clark Peterson was shot near Linwood Park."

"Yeah, I did, too. That was crazy, so near the field where you and Amanda were."

"Taylor, I need to know. Did you kill him?"

"God, no. Why would you ask a thing like that?"

"He was at Linwood, and I called you."

"I know, and I'm so sorry I wasn't able to get there in time. Claire, what you heard—did it say what Peterson was accused of?"

"It talked about how he had been acquitted at trial for murdering his wife."

"I'm going to tell you something, but you need to promise not to tell anyone else. Not Mandy, not anyone. Okay?"

"All right."

"If it gets out that I violated attorney-client privilege, it could cost me my license as a private investigator."

"I promise."

"I was working for Peterson's lawyer. The computers in his law firm were hacked. The information that was stolen included facts about Peterson that hadn't been revealed at trial."

"Are you saying he really did kill his wife?"

"He killed his wife and at least three other women as well. We don't know how many for sure."

"Oh my God, Taylor. Why was he hanging around Mandy and me?"

"Like I said, I was working for his lawyer. Peterson wanted me to tell him who hacked the law firm. He was afraid that the information would get out and the cops would come looking for him. It's going to get out anyway. In a day or two you'll be able to read all about it. Claire, I don't have the words to tell you how sorry I am about all of this. He was bothering you and Mandy because he knew that I cared for you both. He figured that if he threatened you, I'd tell him what he wanted to know.

Claire, I didn't kill Peterson. We think that he was shot by someone close to one of his victims. We might never learn who. If he had tried to hurt you or your daughter, though—I don't know what I would have done. I'm sorry."

"I don't know what to say, Taylor. Half of me is absolutely appalled by all of this. The other half, knowing that you're looking out for us…"

She finished her thought by giving me a gentle hug, kissing my cheek, and resting her head against my chest. We stood like that for a long time, my arms wrapped around her waist. Or maybe it was for only a second or two. It was hard for me to judge.

"Mandy and I are going all out making dinner tomorrow night," Claire said. "Roasted chicken. Corn on the cob. Mashed potatoes. Gravy. Mandy is trying her hand at making buttermilk biscuits. Please dine with us. There'll be plenty of food, I promise."

"I'd like that very much."

"You won't mention any of this to Amanda, though, will you? What we talked about? I don't want her to be frightened."

"I wouldn't do that to save the world."

ACKNOWLEDGMENTS

Specials thanks from the author to Jeff Blossom, India Cooper, Tammi Fredrickson, Keith Kahla, Alice Pfeifer, Alison J. Picard, and Renée Valois for all their help in writing this book.

A past president of the Private Eye Writers of America, **DAVID HOUSEWRIGHT** has published 23 crime novels and counting. His first novel *Penance* earned an Edgar Award from the Mystery Writers of America as well as a Shamus nomination from the PWA. He has also won three Minnesota Books Awards for *Practice to Deceive, Jelly's Gold*, and *Curse of the Jade Lily*. Housewright is best known for the Rushmore McKenzie and Holland Taylor novels set mostly in Minnesota, books that have been favorably compared to Raymond Chandler, Ross MacDonald and Robert B. Parker. A reformed newspaper reporter and ad man, he has also taught novel-writing courses at the University of Minnesota and Loft Literary Center in Minneapolis. His name and face were recently added to *Minnesota Writers on the Map* by the Minnesota Historical Society and Friends of the St. Paul Public Library.